THE BERLITZ

"The strength of the [Berlitz Travellers Guides] lies in remarks and recommendations by writers with a depth of knowledge about their subject."
—*Washington Times*

"The most readable of the current paperback lot."
—*New York Post*

"Highly recommended."
—*Library Journal*

"Very strong on atmosphere and insights into local culture for curious travellers."
—*Boston Herald*

"The [Berlitz Travellers Guides] eliminate cumbersome lists and provide reliable information about what is truly exciting and significant about a destination. . . . [They] also emphasize the spirit and underlying 'vibrations' of a region—historical, cultural, and social—that enhance a trip."
—*Retirement Life*

"Information without boredom. . . . Good clear maps and index."
—*The Sunday Sun* (Toronto)

CONTRIBUTORS

JOHN DORNBERG has reported on Germany for more than 30 years and has been based in Munich since 1971. The author of several books, he is also a frequent contributor to *Travel & Leisure, Bon Appetit, National Geographic Traveler,* and the travel sections of the *New York Times* and the *Washington Post.* He is the editorial consultant for this guidebook.

JENNIFER BECKER began travel writing after many years of teaching German and French language and literature at the Munich International School. British born, she has lived and worked in Germany for more than 20 years and is a frequent visitor to Berlin.

JUNE CAROLYN ERLICK, a correspondent for Fairchild News Service, arrived in Berlin shortly before the fall of the Berlin Wall. She has written on travel and other subjects for many publications, including the *New York Times, Newsday,* the *Wall Street Journal,* and the *Miami Herald,* from both Latin America and Europe. She is a contributing editor to *World Press Review.*

PHYLLIS MÉRAS, travel editor of the *Providence* (Rhode Island) *Journal,* contributes travel articles to *Newsday,* the *Chicago Tribune,* and the *San Francisco Examiner.* She travels frequently in eastern Germany and is the author of a guidebook to Eastern Europe.

DONALD S. OLSON, a freelance writer and editor, has written a guidebook to Berlin and contributed travel articles to many American magazines. The author of three novels, he has also had plays produced in New York and Europe.

THE BERLITZ
TRAVELLERS GUIDES

THE BERLITZ TRAVELLERS GUIDE TO BERLIN 1993

ALAN TUCKER
General Editor

BERLITZ PUBLISHING COMPANY, INC.
New York, New York

BERLITZ PUBLISHING COMPANY LTD.
Oxford, England

THE BERLITZ TRAVELLERS GUIDE
TO BERLIN 1993

Berlitz Trademark Reg U.S. Patent and Trademark Office
and other countries—Marca Registrada

Published by Berlitz Publishing Company, Inc.
257 Park Avenue South, New York, New York 10010, U.S.A.

Distributed in the United States by
the Macmillan Publishing Group

Distributed elsewhere by Berlitz Publishing Company Ltd.
Berlitz House, Peterley Road, Horspath, Oxford OX4 2TX, England

ISBN 2-8315-1788-5
ISSN 1065-6294

Designed by Beth Tondreau Design
Cover design by Dan Miller Design
Cover photograph by Alon Reininger/Woodfin Camp
Maps by Mark Stein Studios
Illustrations by Bill Russell
Copyedited by Norma Frankel
Fact-checked in Germany by Ortrud Otto
Edited by Debra Bernardi

Printed in the United States of America
1 3 5 7 9 10 8 6 4 2

THIS GUIDEBOOK

The Berlitz Travellers Guides are designed for experienced travellers in search of exceptional information that will enhance the enjoyment of the trips they take.

Where, for example, are the interesting, out-of-the-way, fun, charming, or romantic places to stay? The hotels described by our expert writers are some of the special places, in all price ranges except for the very lowest—not just the run-of-the-mill, heavily marketed places in advertised airline and travel-wholesaler packages.

We indicate the approximate price level of each accommodation in our description of it (no indication means it is moderate in local, relative terms), and at the end of every hotel entry we supply more hotel rate information as well as contact information so that you can get precise, up-to-the-minute rates and make reservations.

The Berlitz Travellers Guide to Berlin 1993 highlights the more rewarding parts of the city and the surrounding area so that you can quickly and efficiently home in on a good itinerary.

Of course, this guidebook does far more than just help you choose a hotel and plan your trip. *The Berlitz Travellers Guide to Berlin 1993* is designed for use *in* Berlin. Our writers, each of whom is an experienced travel journalist who either lives in Berlin or Germany or regularly visits the city and tours the surrounding area, tell you what you really need to know, what you can't find out so easily on your own. They identify and describe the truly out-of-the-ordinary restaurants, bars, cabarets, shops, museums, activities, and sights, and tell you the best way to "do" Berlin.

Our writers are highly selective. They bring out the significance of the places they *do* cover, capturing the personality and the underlying cultural and historical resonances of the city's neighborhoods and of the Berlin region—making clear their special appeal.

Some sections of this book are based on parts of *The Berlitz Travellers Guide to Germany*—but are greatly revised and expanded. Others, including the Berlin Museums and Day Trips from Berlin section, are found only in this guide to Berlin.

The Berlitz Travellers Guide to Berlin is full of reliable and timely information, revised and updated each year. We would like to know if you think we've left out some very special place. Although we make every effort to provide the most current information available about every destination described in this book, it is possible too that changes have occurred before you arrive. If you do have an experience that is contrary to what you were led to expect by our description, we would like to hear from you about it.

A guidebook is no substitute for common sense when you are travelling. Always pack the clothing, footwear, and other items appropriate for the destination, and make the necessary accommodation for such variables as weather and local rules and customs. Of course, once on the scene you should avoid situations that are in your own judgment potentially hazardous, even if they have to do with something mentioned in a guidebook. Half the fun of travelling is exploring, but explore with care.

ALAN TUCKER
General Editor
Berlitz Travellers Guides

Root Publishing Company
330 West 58th Street
Suite 504
New York, New York 10019

CONTENTS

MAPS

THE
BERLITZ
TRAVELLERS
GUIDE
TO
BERLIN
1993

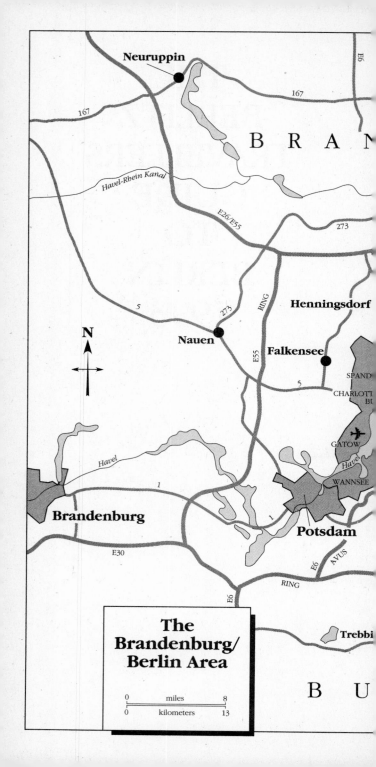

The
Brandenburg/
Berlin Area

0 miles 8
0 kilometers 13

OVERVIEW

By John Dornberg

John Dornberg has reported on Germany for more than 30 years and has been based in Munich since 1971. The author of several books, he is also a frequent contributor to Travel & Leisure, Bon Appetit, National Geographic Traveler, *and the travel sections of the* New York Times *and the* Washington Post. *He is the editorial consultant for this guidebook.*

During the Cold War, when the city was the setting for countless spy novels, the scene of recurring international crises, and divided by the Wall, municipal tourism promoters in West Berlin—then a self-contained, democratic, prosperous, glittering consumer-oriented island in a grimly egalitarian, repressive Communist sea, 110 miles from the nearest West German "shore"—coined two slogans: *Berlin Bleibt Berlin!* ("Berlin will always be Berlin!") and *Berlin ist eine Reise Wert!* ("Berlin is worth a journey!").

In those days Berlin was the *Frontstadt*—the "front-line city"—where two sociopolitical systems, two ideologies, indeed two worlds met, occasionally collided, but most of the time coexisted with more or less apathetic indifference toward each other, somewhat like an estranged couple that is compelled by circumstances to continue living in the same house or apartment. And those slogans were far more than the usual catchy phrases of a local convention-and-visitors bureau. They spelled defiance and resistance, grit and determination, and implied swimming doggedly against what then seemed to be the current of world affairs.

After all, in those years going to Berlin from West Germany or Western Europe was more than just a journey. You could fly, but only on an airline of the three Allied powers—American, British, and French—and have the eerie experience of suddenly dropping from a comfortable cruising altitude of 30,000 feet to the choppy one of 10,000 as the plane crossed the East German border and entered the invisible tunnel of one of the three Soviet-controlled air corridors leading to the city. If you went by train it was an arduously long and uncomfortable trip over neglected tracks, and your car was sealed as it passed through the sovereign territory of the German Democratic Republic (GDR). Or you could drive: an ordeal of queues and surly, machine-gun toting border guards at the frontier between the two Germanys; a DM 5 fee for a transit visa; a jarringly bumpy ride on an Autobahn highway, which had seen virtually no repair since Hitler built it in the 1930s, with strict rules on where and where not to pull off for a rest stop; and, when you finally reached Checkpoint Bravo at the Dreilinden exit, the crossover point from the GDR to West Berlin, the humiliating experience of having your vehicle completely searched for any possible East German refugee you might have taken aboard.

To go from West Berlin to East Berlin, the official capital of the GDR, in order to see the city's greatest architectural and historical sights on and around Unter den Linden boulevard, was equally tortuous for travellers. If you drove through the Wall at Checkpoint Charlie on Friedrichstrasse you were subjected to the same arrogant treatment as at the frontier, replete with customs and currency declarations and the surrender of all books, magazines, and recordings banned by East German ideological censorship, and you went through an even more exhausting search of the car upon leaving. If you went by public transit—subway (U-Bahn) or elevated train (S-Bahn)—you experienced the same denigrating formalities at the only gateway, the Friedrichstrasse S-Bahn station, plus the discomfort of queueing at various control booths and windows in a dimly lighted, poorly ventilated maze reminiscent of scenes in George Orwell's *1984*. In both cases you also paid dearly: DM 5 for a visa, DM 25 in mandatory daily exchange at an unrealistic rate of one-to-one for 25 east marks, which you either spent or gave away because there would be no refund. And you had to leave again by midnight. Looking back on what seems like only yesterday—the reality of Berlin only a split second ago in the city's history—one wonders whether there was ever a place as disdainful of visitors and as difficult to visit.

For West Berliners themselves, it was in many respects even more restrictive. The Wall, with its death strip, grim watchtowers, armed guards, fierce dogs, blinding spotlights, and self-triggering shrapnel guns, not only cut West Berliners off from East Berlin and sliced the city in half, but it *enclosed* them, sealing them off from the rural areas and villages that had traditionally been the suburban hinterland as well as the weekend and vacation turf of Berliners. It was forbidden territory. And to leave for West Germany, Western Europe, or anywhere else, on business or pleasure, Berliners had to endure the same strictures as visiting travellers.

The nightmare lasted 40 years. It ended suddenly, unexpectedly, and rather miraculously in November 1989 when the Wall opened and began disappearing as the GDR imploded, and the two Germanys started moving toward their formal October 1990 reunification as one country, with reunified Berlin now its designated capital.

Yet those slogans coined during the Cold War still apply. Berlin will always be Berlin, and it is definitely worth a special journey.

To be sure, that spine-tingling excitement of being on the front line and entering another world, no matter how grim, inhospitable, and difficult, is gone. The Glienicker Brücke, the bridge in the southwest corner of the vast city, where real-life spies in trench coats and slouch hats actually did come in from the cold for secret, nocturnal exchanges, is now just the bridge to Potsdam and Frederick the Great's splendid Baroque palaces, with the consequence that it is choked with traffic on weekends. And although the Wall is gone, with only a few short segments preserved under "monuments protection" to remind people of what was, its scar in the form of a weed-grown no-man's-land through the center of town remains. In many ways Berlin is still two cities: the pulsating, affluent west, and the long neglected, run-down east whose economy is in paralysis if not actually free fall. Now a new wall, *die Mauer in den Köpfen,* "the wall in people's heads," divides Berliners in attitudes and lifestyles, and it is likely to do so for at least another generation. Enterprising souvenir merchants at what used to be Checkpoint Charlie even hawk it in the form of graffiti-covered chips and fragments of the real Wall cemented into head shapes.

Twelve years of Nazi dictatorship, wartime devastation, postwar occupation, Cold War division, and isolation from the European mainstream have, of course, left their mark on Berlin. It also helps to remember that, at age just over 750, Berlin is somewhat of an upstart, a newcomer by German and other European standards, so that there is a paucity of medieval, let alone Roman, marvels. After all, the ancestors of today's Berliners were barely doffing their bearskins at a time when lesser and much smaller German cities such as Augsburg, Cologne, Erfurt, Hamburg, and Münster (not to mention London, Paris, Rome, or Vienna) were already venerable metropolises and the capitals of powerful states and kingdoms.

Berlin was the capital of a united Germany—that of the kaisers, then the democratic Weimar Republic, and finally Hitler's Third Reich—for a mere 75 years, and of the rump Communist one-third of the country for 40. It will be the late 1990s, more likely well after the year 2000, before it again becomes more than just Germany's capital in name, as it is today, and resumes its role as the actual seat of government. Those facts raise some questions and doubts about the city's real future, and about its position in the Germany and Europe of the 21st century.

Certainly it will not again become the innovative cultural hub of Germany and Europe it was during the Golden Twenties of the short-lived Weimar era. Not only was that spirit stifled by the Nazis, but too much has changed in Berlin and the rest of the world to revive it. There were attempts to resuscitate it synthetically in the 1970s and '80s, but they foundered on the reefs of Berlin's and Germany's division, the cultural and economic atomization of West Germany, and the attempt to keep West Berlin afloat artificially with billions of marks in subsidies during the Cold War.

Prospects that it can again become the economic, media, and financial nerve center of the country, as it was before the 1945 Götterdämmerung, are equally slim. Frankfurt will remain the German "Wall Street" and "City" because the banks and brokerages are ensconced in the skyscrapers that make it a "Manhattan on the Main." The big German corporations and publishing enterprises that abandoned their Berlin headquarters during the Cold War are now entrenched in Düsseldorf, Frankfurt, Hamburg, Munich, and Stuttgart.

Much will depend on what happens a mere 60 miles east of Berlin—in Poland, the Czech Republic, Russia, and the other new countries that once were the Soviet Union or part of the Communist bloc. Berlin has always looked eastward in terms of commerce and culture and is doing so again. But until its eastern hinterland emerges from the economic morass and reintegrates into Europe, decades will pass.

Berlin today, with its 3.5 million inhabitants, is the largest city in Europe between Paris and Moscow, but it is in a state of limbo, uncertain of its identity and of its future. It is trying to make up for lost time, and for the next few years will be a vast construction site as investors from not only Germany and Europe but also the rest of the world stake out claims on the barren turf in the heart of the city, the wasteland left by World War II, the Cold War, and the Berlin Wall. A huge new American Business Center on Friedrichstrasse and a vast Sony complex on Potsdamer Platz are but two of the projects.

Berliners, in the face of adversity, or because of it, are unique among the peoples of today's so-called world cities—in their can-do spirit, indomitable optimism, sense of humor, love of art and culture, and sheer zest for life. The city's carefree and innovative atmosphere is infectious. And although it is in a holding pattern, with more talk about the future than present action, it offers travellers more than they could possibly take in on a first or even second visit. Few other capitals have as many truly first-rate museums, art collections, symphony orchestras, opera houses, and theaters and cabarets, or as vibrant a café life and nightlife.

Berlin for Travellers

Visiting Berlin does require a strategy, though. It cannot be explored fully or enjoyed to its maximum in a couple of days. Even a week, if you allow time for suddenly being distracted by this museum, spellbound by that art gallery, or amused longer than you had planned people-watching at some sidewalk café, may be insufficient. Besides its large size—it covers an area in which all of New York's boroughs would fit with some room to spare—Berlin has an amazing array of neighborhoods, each with its own character and important sights. Approach the city by selected districts, preferably with a cultural, historical, or artistic theme, and if that whets your appetite plan to return for a different view some other year.

Our book is therefore arranged to introduce you to the

neighborhoods and show the way not only to the most popular whistlestops and well-trodden tourist areas, such as Unter den Linden, Kurfürstendamm, and Charlottenburg Palace, but also out-of-the-way places far from the center.

CENTRAL BERLIN

By Central Berlin we mean first of all **Berlin Mitte**, the borough in the former East Berlin where the city originated as two rival trading towns on opposite banks of the Spree river in the 13th century. This is the area not only on but around Unter den Linden, the grand boulevard of 18th- and 19th-century palaces and the Brandenburger Tor (Brandenburg Gate), which were the expression of Prussia's and then Imperial Germany's ascendency, and symbolize Berlin's role as a European and world capital. Here are found some of the city's greatest museums and finest examples of Baroque, Rococo, and Neoclassical architecture.

But Central Berlin also means the **Tiergarten** borough, west of Berlin Mitte, with its beautiful park; the Kulturforum with its complex of museums, libraries, and concert halls; and the zoo, which is the world's largest.

Not least, it also means the grand avenue **Kurfürstendamm** and the areas around it, the district that has become, since World War II and the Cold War, the commercial, shopping, entertainment, dining, and hotel heart of the city. Here, southwest of the Tiergarten, there is less to see than to do, and in all likelihood it is where you will probably choose to stay.

AROUND THE CENTER

Around the Center is what we mean by the boroughs of Kreuzberg, Schöneberg, and Prenzlauer Berg. Just south of Berlin Mitte, **Kreuzberg**, a mixture of artists' colony, Turkish enclaves, several important art and historical museums, ethnic restaurants, and gentrified areas, is just four square miles in size but could keep you occupied for days. Its eastern Berlin counterpart is **Prenzlauer Berg**, the area, northeast of Berlin Mitte, in which East Germany's anti-regime peace movement originated and where the peaceful revolution began that opened the Wall and sent the GDR to the dustbin of history. West of Kreuzberg, **Schöneberg** is best known for its city hall, from which President John F. Kennedy proclaimed, *"Ich bin ein Berliner."*

AWAY FROM THE CENTER

In Away from the Center we will take you first of all southwest of the central city to the **Dahlem** area museums, among them the Gemäldegalerie (Picture Gallery), with its huge store of Old Masters, including 25 Rembrandts and 19 Rubenses, and the Brücke Museum of German Expressionists. Then it's a half-hour walk north of Kurfürstendamm to **Schloss Charlottenburg** (Charlottenburg Palace), the largest and finest of Berlin's surviving Baroque palaces, and the museums in and around it, including the Ägyptisches (Egyptian) Museum, with its bust of Queen Nefertiti.

OUTLYING AREAS

In Outlying Areas we include **Spandau**, at the western edge of the city, a formerly independent town, half a century older than Berlin itself. A visitor to Spandau will find an old quarter of medieval streets, houses, and churches, and a fortress, the Zitadelle, which goes back to the days of German conquest and colonization of the March of Brandenburg in the 12th century.

There are also districts in eastern Berlin's outskirts that were virtually inaccessible to, or ignored by, foreign visitors until the Wall came down. **Köpenick**, the largest and most pastoral of Berlin's boroughs, also includes the Grosser Müggelsee and the Köpenicker Forst, the largest of the lakes and forests within the city limits, and Berlin's oldest surviving palace, Schloss Köpenick, where Frederick the Great, then merely the crown prince, was court-martialed for trying to flee Prussia with his lover in 1730. It is now a museum of applied art. Northwest of Köpenick, **Lichtenberg** is the borough of Berlin's other zoo, started as East German competition to the one in the west in the 1950s. Farther north and west, **Pankow** is where East Germany's first president had his official residence—in Schloss Niederschönhausen, where Frederick the Great put his wife, whom he had been forced to marry.

Travellers who need a break from city sightseeing should keep in mind that more than one-third of the city's area is covered by large **forests**, such as the Grunewald, Spandau, Tegel, and Köpenicker Forst, and one-seventh is **lakes**, such as the Wannsee, Tegeler See, and Müggelsee. Besides the châteaux and museums that should be seen in the forests, you could also spend days here on hiking or biking tours, oblivious to the fact that you are still within the city limits. While the lakes provide many opportunities for water sports, from surfing to water-skiing, the **rivers and canals** are arteries for entire fleets of excursion steamers that will take you not only to every corner of Berlin itself but beyond, into the March of Brandenburg, the region of most of our proposed day trips.

In addition to the above-mentioned sights of interest to travellers, visiting Berlin also means seeing some of its 55 **village churches** and the **industrial and technological architecture** of the late 19th and early 20th century, which expressed Berlin's rise and preeminence as Germany and Central Europe's biggest manufacturing center.

Day Trips from Berlin

Though Berlin is no longer a political island, it is geographically insular, a scant 60 miles from Germany's eastern border with Poland, and 120 to 160 miles from even *eastern* Germany's other great urban centers and major travel destinations, such as Dresden, Leipzig, Halle, Weimar, and Erfurt. Moreover, with road and rail conditions in the former GDR being what they are currently—and, despite much work and improvement, what they are likely to be for the next few years—those distances in travel time are actually twice as long as the mileage indicated. These are not really places you can visit in a day from Berlin, with the aim of returning to the city in the evening. At least not if you also want to see something.

This is one reason we have cast the day-trip net close to Berlin itself, including Potsdam, which is reachable by Berlin's S-Bahn (the elevated train), even though it is an independent city and capital of the state of Brandenburg. Every destination is within an hour's or at most one and a half hours' driving distance from central Berlin (except at rush hour), to give you ample opportunity to explore in a relaxed manner, enjoy yourself, take a lunch and a couple of coffee breaks, and return to your Berlin hotel—and maybe even have dinner in the city—without feeling pressured. But another reason behind our day-trip choices is that these are fascinating destinations in their own right, with castles, churches, monasteries, villages, and unusual landscapes that for decades were inaccessible to Western visitors, West Berliners and West Germans included. They provide an insight to life in the March of Brandenburg and provincial East Germany.

Though there are train connections to a number of the places (we give practical travel information at the end of each section), and in some cases even excursion steamer voyages on the Havel, the Spree, and canals from Berlin, the itineraries are outlined for driving yourself, an especially enjoyable experience on Brandenburg's country roads and federal highways, which are still lined by decades-old linden, chestnut, oak, and sycamore trees that will give you the feeling of driving through leafy green tunnels.

Besides **Potsdam**, which, with Schloss Cecilienhof and Frederick the Great's Sanssouci, certainly requires a day by itself, our chosen points include the old, medieval city of **Brandenburg**, northwest of Potsdam; a drive farther north to **Neuruppin**, where both the architect Karl Friedrich Schinkel and the novelist Theodor Fontane were born, and beyond that to **Rheinsberg**, with the castle in which Frederick the Great spent many years; a tour northeast of Berlin to **Eberswalde**, the Chorin monastery (once one of the largest in Europe), Niederfinow and the largest ship elevator in Europe, the resort town of Bad Freienwalde, and the eastern banks of the Oder river; a leisurely journey east of the city through the **Märkische Schweiz**, the "Switzerland of the March of Brandenburg," with a stop at the château of Neuhardenberg; a trip southeast into the unique **Spreewald**, the land of the Slavic-speaking Sorbs, and a ride on one of the colorful punts along the many side arms and canals of the upper Spree; and, southwest to **Wittenberg**, the charming medieval capital of Saxony where Martin Luther lived, taught, preached, and started the Protestant Reformation.

Whichever trips you choose, you will find a choice of museums, castles, churches, picturesque villages, and rustic inns to fill your day.

USEFUL FACTS

When to Go
The best months to visit Berlin are May through October. The weather in March and April can be fickle, and from November through February it can get grim. Berlin usually has a bracing, temperate climate, with low humidity. But in July and August expect some real scorchers, and in January and February you can count on some arctic days.

Whatever the season, be sure to reserve hotel accommodations *well* in advance. Berlin's calendar is crammed with trade fairs, festivals, conventions, and congresses. There have been occasions in recent years when hoteliers have put cots and folding beds in lobbies and hallways to accommodate overflow guests. The busiest times are the Green Week agricultural show in late January to early February, the International Film Festival in the second half of February, the International Tourism Bourse (ITB) in early March, the Berlin Festival (a music and theater festival) in September, and the biannual International Radio-TV-Electronics Exhibition during the last week of August and the first week of September (there will be one in 1993).

Entry Documents

Only a valid passport is needed for citizens of the United States, Australia, Canada, or New Zealand wishing to visit Berlin and the rest of Germany for stays of three months or less. Identity cards are sufficient for British citizens.

Getting There

The best way to get to Berlin is by plane or by car. Rail connections from cities in western Germany are few (about 40 trains a day from a dozen different cities, most with one or two transfers) and the journey is arduously long. Bahnhof Zoo, five minutes' walk from the Europa-Center, is the main terminal in the west and center; Bahnhof Lichtenberg and Hauptbahnhof are the main terminals in the eastern part of the city.

Airlines flying to Berlin from the United States, in addition to Lufthansa, are American, Delta, TWA, and United. Major European airlines offer connecting service through their countries. Canadian service from Montreal, Toronto, and Vancouver is via Frankfurt and Munich, where you must change carriers.

The traveller from Britain has a choice of eight daily nonstop flights from London and one daily, except Saturdays, from Birmingham. In addition to Lufthansa, the carrier is British Airways. British Airways also flies to Berlin from Cologne, Düsseldorf, Munich, and Stuttgart, and has a number of daily flights to those cities from London, Birmingham, and Manchester. From Singapore there is a twice-weekly Singapore Airlines flight to Berlin.

Tegel airport, northwest of the city center, is serviced by Delta, American, TWA, United, British Airways, Air France, Alitalia, KLM, SAS, Swissair, Austrian Airlines, and Lufthansa. Aeroflot, Austrian Airlines, El Al, Japan Airlines, and Singapore Airlines fly into Schönefeld airport at the southern edge of the city. Various regional and feeder carriers, as well as Lufthansa, service Tempelhof airport, located in the borough of Neukölln, south of the city center.

Getting in from the Airports

City bus number 109 runs between Tegel and central Berlin, stopping along Kurfürstendamm, Bahnhof Zoo, and the hotel area on Budapester Strasse. Departures are every 10 minutes and the ride is 40 minutes. A cab to the center from Tegel will cost about DM 35. S-Bahn elevated train number 9 operates from near Schönefeld airport in the southeastern part of the city with stops at Alexanderplatz, Friedrichstrasse, and Bahnhof Zoo. The cab ride from Schönefeld will cost about DM 50 to the center. From Tempelhof there is a subway connection (U-6) to the center, as well as buses 119, 184, and 341. The cab ride will be about DM 15.

Renting a Car and Driving

A car is more a curse than a convenience in Berlin, despite the city's enormous size. It *is* almost indispensable for day trips out of Berlin because of poor and sporadic rail service to those destinations. If you want a car for day trips, you'd probably do best to keep it parked at your hotel while in the city. If your hotel does not have a garage, ask at the desk where you can park for an extended period.

There are four Autobahn routes from western Germany, three from the east to Berlin. Driving time from Frankfurt or Munich to Berlin is six to eight hours, depending on traffic conditions.

When you are buying your airline ticket you can arrange at the same time to rent a car at the airport where you will be landing. Autohansa, Avis, Budget-Sixt, Europa Service, Hertz, Severin and Company, and Inter-rent-Europcar are among the car-rental companies. Arrangements for car leasing for short and long stays can also be made in North America through Auto-Europe at Box 1097 in Camden, Maine 04843 (Tel: 800-223-5555). Most major credit cards are accepted for car rental in Germany. Liability insurance is required, but is usually included in the rental fee. Either a national or an international driver's license is required.

Though Germany as a whole has an outstanding road system with many superhighways (the Autobahnen) where service stations are open 24 hours a day, 40 years of Communist neglect left the highways and Autobahnen in eastern Germany and the area around Berlin a shambles of potholes and washboard surfaces. Repairing and improving this has been the government's top priority since reunification. Progress on many roads to the daytrip destinations has been remarkably fast, and massive improvements may be being made on the Autobahn sections that you want to use, albeit with the disadvantage that these cause numerous, long traffic jams. In parts of eastern Berlin and in many smaller towns and villages streets and roads are still paved with cobblestones, and sometimes just with large stones.

Speed limits within Berlin and the city limits of surrounding towns are 50 km/p/h (31 mph) unless marked otherwise (there are marked 30 km/p/h—18½ mph—zones in many residential areas). On numbered federal highways (*Bundesstrassen*) and unnumbered country roads, unless otherwise marked, the speed limit in eastern Germany is 80 km/p/h (50 mph). On the eastern German Autobahnen, unless posted otherwise, a 100 km/p/h (62 mph) limit is in force. The traffic signs are international.

Road assistance is provided free of charge (except for the cost of the materials) by the Allgemeiner Deutscher Automobil Club (ADAC), which has emergency patrols on frequently travelled roads and motorways. There are orange-colored emergency phone boxes along all Autobahn routes at frequent intervals.

Telephoning

The international telephone code for Germany is 49; for Berlin, 30. When calling from within Germany, dial zero before the city code.

Both local and long-distance calls can be made from all post offices and coin-operated street booths. Thirty pfennigs is the base charge for a local call from a booth—but from a hotel it is considerably—up to three times—higher. Though internationally known phone credit cards do not work, there are public card phones (*Kartentelefon*) which accept *Telefonkarten* (phone cards) of the German postal service's Telekom. They are sold in denominations of DM 12 and DM 50 at all post offices. A DM 12 card is valid for 40 local calls or 40 message units on long-distance calls. An LED on the phone tells you how much credit is left on the card.

Addresses

Street names in Berlin are correct in this book as of press time, but keep in mind that some streets still bearing the names of heroes of the former Communist regime could change in the coming months.

The international postal code for Germany and Berlin begins with a D (Deutschland); we follow this with (W) if the district is in western Berlin, or (O) if it is in the eastern part of the city.

Local Time

Berlin is nine hours ahead of Pacific Standard Time, six hours ahead of Eastern Standard Time, and one hour ahead of Greenwich Mean Time, and during the change-over to daylight savings time there is a brief period when Berlin is another hour behind or ahead. Sydney is ten hours ahead of Berlin.

Electric Current

The electric current is 220 volts; North American appliances will require an adapter and adapter plugs.

Currency

The monetary unit of Germany is the deutsche mark—DM or D-mark— made up of 100 pfennigs. Coins come in denominations of 5, 2, and 1 mark and in 50-, 10-, 5-, 2-, and 1-pfennig pieces; bills in denominations of DM 1,000, 500, 200, 100, 50, 20, 10, and 5. Credit cards are not as widely accepted here as in the U.S. and the U.K.

Tipping

In restaurants and cafés the service charge and value-added tax are included in the bill, but rounding out the total bill with an extra amount is expected. Tipping is also expected by taxi drivers (just round up the tab) and porters and in beauty parlors. Be sure to carry small change for tipping attendants in some WCs; the amount is often posted—otherwise about 20 pfennigs will do.

Business Hours

There are mandatory closing hours for all stores and shops throughout Germany: 6:30 P.M. Monday through Wednesday and Fridays; 8:30 P.M. Thursday; 2:00 P.M. Saturdays except the first Saturday of each month when shops may remain open until 6:00 P.M. October through April, until 4:00 P.M. May through September. Except at major railway stations and airports no stores are permitted to be open after these hours or on Sundays and holidays. Most stores and shops open at 9:00 A.M. A daily lunchtime closing from 12:00 to 3:00 P.M. is common in shops in residential neighborhoods, smaller towns, and villages.

Bank hours are normally from 9:00 A.M. to 12:30 P.M. and from 2:30 to 3:45 P.M. weekdays (Thursdays until 5:30 P.M.).

Museums in western Berlin are almost always closed on Mondays; in eastern Berlin museum days vary widely. Hours otherwise tend to be from 10:00 A.M. to 5:00 P.M. year round, slightly longer in summer. Churches—even some of those of historic and architectural importance—are certain to be open only for Sunday services; for other hours of opening it is wise to check with the local *Verkehrsamt* (tourist office).

Offices and shops in Berlin and the state of Brandenburg are closed on New Year's Day, Good Friday, Easter Sunday and Monday, Labor Day (May 1), Ascension Day (May or June), Whit Monday (May or June), Corpus Christi Day (June), German Unification Day (October 3), All Saints Day (November 1), the Day of Prayer and Remembrance (November), and Christmas Eve, Christmas Day, and the day after Christmas.

Safety

By the standards of most other large international cities, Berlin is remarkably safe. There is very little street crime, though do take precautions with handbags when sitting at a sidewalk café and against pickpockets at crowded outdoor markets. By all means avoid the sidewalk shell games (called *Hütschenspiele* in German) that have become an epidemic on the Kurfürstendamm in recent years. They're run by teams of con artists: you'll never win, your losses can be astronomical, and the sharpsters will be gone before you can shout for the police.

Prostitution is legal and streetwalkers are out in force by about 10 P.M. on the Ku'damm and northern Friedrichstrasse. Many hookers are even unionized. Police maintain surveillance to make sure they stick to permitted streets and areas, at least in theory.

Bahnhof Zoo and the area around it became the focal point of Berlin's hard drugs scene in the 1970s, tragically immortalized in the semi-documentary film *Marianne F.: The Girl from Bahnhof Zoo*. What has changed is that the crowd has gotten younger—teenagers like "Marianne F." now predominate. The action is exacerbated by the drunks who hang out. It's an area to avoid after 11 P.M. or midnight.

Women travelling alone are safe on the subways (U-Bahn) and buses, even late at night, but are advised to avoid using the elevated train system (S-Bahn) after 11:00 P.M. or midnight, especially in eastern boroughs of the city, where there have been several incidents since early 1992. Those troubles were all of a xenophobic-racist nature, with nonwhite foreigners the victims: Turks, Vietnamese and other Asians, Africans, Arabs. The perpetrators were invariably radical rightists, neo-Nazis, and skinheads. As we went to press, the German government and Berlin authorities had finally started to crack down hard, so that by spring or early summer tougher law enforcement and harsher penalties may well have put this ugly postreunification phenomenon back into the bottle.

For Further Information

The Verkehrsamt Berlin (Berlin tourist information) has offices in the Europa-Center, Tel: 262-60-31; Fax: 21232520, open Monday through Saturday 8:00 A.M. to 10:30 P.M., Sundays 9:00 A.M. to 9:00 P.M.; at the Brandenburg Gate, Tel: 242-46-75 or 242-45-12, open daily 8:00 A.M. to 8:00 P.M.; Tegel Airport in the central hallway, Tel: 41-01-31-45, open daily from 8:00 A.M. to 11:00 P.M.; and at Bahnhof Zoo, Tel: 313-90-63, open Monday through Saturday from 8:00 A.M. to 11:00 P.M.

German National Tourist Offices are maintained at 122 East 42nd Street, New York, New York 10168 (Tel: 212-661-7200); 444 South Flower Street, Suite 2230, Los Angeles, California 90071 (Tel: 213-668-7332); 175 Bloor Street East, North Tower, Toronto, Ontario M4W 3R8, Canada (Tel: 416-968-1570); Nightingale House, 65 Curzon Street, London W1Y 7PE, England (Tel: 071-495-3990); Lufthansa House, 12th Floor, 143 Macquarie Street, Sydney 2000, Australia; (Tel: 02-221-1008).

—*John Dornberg and Phyllis Méras*

BIBLIOGRAPHY

PETER ADAM, *Art of the Third Reich* (1992). Few other powerful and dictatorial rulers used art and architecture as extensively and ruthlessly as Hitler to mold their subjects and forge people's minds into subordination to an ideology. This engrossing book, crammed with photographs and illustrations, is the most illuminating and authoritative to date. The author, a native Berliner who fled the Nazis, is an expert on design and photography and has spent many years as a prize-winning documentary-film producer for the British Broadcasting Corporation in London.

JOHN ARDAUGH, *Germany and the New Germans* (1987). A British Francophile's view of Germany before the fall of the Berlin Wall, with the emphasis on West Germany: how people think, lifestyles, social attitudes, and opinions.

BABEL TRANSLATIONS, EDS., *Germany, A Phaidon Cultural Guide* (1985). An English translation of a German hardcover guide, indispensable for the traveller who wants additional background on the artistic, architectural, and cultural sights of the country.

ROLAND BAINTON, *Here I Stand: A Life of Martin Luther* (1950). A fascinating and meticulously researched account, regarded by many as the best one-volume Luther biography in any language. Illustrated with many woodcuts and engravings.

DENNIS L. BARK AND DAVID R. GRESS, *A History of West Germany* (1989). This brilliant and provocative two-volume study covers the period from 1945 to 1988, bringing postwar German history alive in vivid detail with an all-star cast of diplomats and politicians including Adenauer, Brandt, Strauss, Erhard, Heuss, Reuter, and many others.

GEOFFREY BARRACLOUGH, *The Origins of Modern Germany* (1946; frequently revised). This short and comprehensive survey by a leading British scholar of Germany begins with the formation of medieval Germany around A.D. 800 and traces the nation's history to 1939.

VICKI BAUM, *Grand Hotel* (1930). A novel about Weimar-era Berlin that is set against a backdrop of the legendary Adlon Hotel. It became a bestseller and a popular movie.

HERBERT BAYER, WALTER GROPIUS, ILSE GROPIUS, EDS., *Bauhaus 1919–1928* (1938; many times reprinted). This small book is required reading for anyone who is interested in modern art.

IRENE BLUMENFELD, *Berlin Arts Guide* (1986). Although out of print and somewhat dated because of the city's reunification, it remains the only English-language guide to the Berlin art scene, chock-full of information about the programs of commercial galleries and popular artists' hangouts.

THOMAS CARLYLE, *History of Frederick II of Prussia* (1858–1865). Until the Prussian state archives were opened in the early 20th century, historians and biographers of Frederick the Great had to rely largely on the king's own thirty volumes of his written works, including six volumes of verse, seven of history, two philosophical, three military, and twelve of correspondence. Carlyle's six-volume biography and history of Frederick's reign is based on these works.

GEORGE CLARE, *Before the Wall* (1990). This highly personal and anecdotal book, by the author of the best-selling *Last Waltz in Vienna,* deals with the postwar occupation and the beginnings of the Cold War in Berlin.

GORDON CRAIG, *Germany 1866–1945* (1978). Beautifully written and indispensable for readers interested in Germany's recent past, this book by the Sterling Professor of Humanities emeritus at Stanford University remains the best single account of the turbulent political, cultural, and economic life of Germany during the years 1866–1945.

———, *The Germans* (1982). A highly readable and knowledgeable portrait of postwar Germany—a tour rooted in the past but with a contemporary view of religion, business and finance, literature, the role of women, academic life, the German-Jewish relationship, and the changing German language.

EDWARD CRANKSHAW, *Bismarck* (1981). An objective and highly readable life of Prince Otto Eduard Leopold von Bismarck, the first chancellor of the German Empire (1871–1890) and a seminal figure in Germany's Prussian past.

ROBERT DARNTON, *Berlin Journal 1989–1990* (1991). The first eyewitness account, by a noted historian, of the events of late 1989 and early 1990 that led to the opening of the Berlin Wall and the collapse of East Germany's Communist regime.

SEFTON DELMER, *Trail Sinister* (1961). In this autobiography Delmer, Germany correspondent for London's *Daily Express* from 1928 to 1933, gives his colorful first-hand observations of the Berlin scene in the crucial years of Hitler's rise to and grab for power.

————, *Weimar Germany* (1972). Here Delmer, a witness to many of the events he describes, relates the tortuous course of the Weimar Republic's existence, examines the forces on both Left and Right that always threatened it, and outlines his thesis that, at the moment of its birth in 1919, the Republic contained within itself the contradictions and tensions that drove Germany inexorably from a tentative democracy to the dictatorship of Hitler's Third Reich.

ALFRED DÖBLIN, *Berlin Alexanderplatz* (1931). This major novel by the German writer and physician, who fled in 1933 and died in France in 1957, is not only a masterpiece of realistic description and probing insight into the psychological torment of an ex-convict attempting to reintegrate his life with "normal" society in the 1920s, but a vivid description of life in Prenzlauer Berg, Wedding, Kreuzberg, and other working-class boroughs of Berlin during the Weimar era. It was made into a 13-part TV series by the late Rainer Werner Fassbinder, then into a six-hour feature film in the late 1970s.

JOHN DORNBERG, *The Other Germany* (1968). The first full-scale study by a foreign corrrespondent of the German Democratic Republic depicts how the Communists gained power in East Germany and describes the life, inner workings, and ruling figures in Berlin and the GDR during the 1950s and 1960s.

LOTTE EISNER, *The Haunted Screen* (1973). An intriguing survey of the great Expressionist films (*Nosferatu, The Cabinet of Dr. Caligari,* and *Metropolis* among them) produced during the Golden Age of German cinema, which began at the end of World War I and ended with the advent of sound. Translated from the French.

BERNT ENGELMANN, *In Hitler's Germany: Everyday Life in the Third Reich* (1985). A gripping and haunting account of the war years in Berlin and elsewhere.

ERIK ERIKSON, *Young Man Luther* (1962). Psychobiography at its best investigates the origins of a rebel.

MARTIN ESSLIN, *Brecht: The Man and His Work* (1960). An acute and penetrating analysis of Bertolt Brecht, one of the most influential playwrights of the 20th century.

JOACHIM C. FEST, *Hitler* (1973). There are several good biographies of Adolf Hitler to choose from, including works by Robert Payne and John Toland, but Fest's is one of the best researched and most objective.

LION FEUCHTWANGER, *Success* (1930), *The Oppermanns* (1934), and *Paris Gazette* (1940). This compelling trilogy deals with the rise of the Nazis in the author's native Munich, Hitler's takeover in Berlin, and the exile of German intellectuals—Feuchtwanger and his friend Bertolt Brecht included—in France until their escape to the United States.

THEODOR FONTANE, *Effi Briest* (1894). Considered a masterpiece of social realism, this novel by the 19th-century Neuruppin-born pharmacist, journalist, essayist, and poet deals with the decline of the Prussian nobility and the rise of the bourgeoisie in Brandenburg and Prussia, as do most of the 15 other novels he wrote during the last 20 years of his life. Rainer Werner Fassbinder made it into a highly successful television series and feature film in 1974.

————, *Wanderungen durch die Mark Brandenburg* (1862–1882). Though unfortunately never translated into English (despite the fact that Fontane had spent five years as a newspaper correspondent in London and was a frequent visitor to Britain), this four-volume collection of his travel stories and essays about the region surrounding Berlin offers a delightful and insightful description of the life and nature of Brandenburg.

OTTO FRIEDRICH, *Before the Deluge: A Portrait of Berlin in the 1920's* (1972). A comprehensive, fascinating historical portrait by a noted American journalist of the political, cultural, and social life of Berlin between the wars and the people who created and destroyed it.

BELLA FROMM, *Blood & Banquets* (1990). The secret diary of "Frau Bella," a social columnist for an influential German daily from the 1920s to the mid-1930s, who moved in the top political, business, diplomatic, and social circles of the day. Smuggled out of Germany when she escaped to America, the diary bursts with names and information about the small and big events of the time.

MARY FULBROOK, *A Concise History of Germany* (1990). An unusually clear and informative guide to the twists and turns of German history from the early Middle Ages to the present day, and the only single-volume history of Germany in English that offers a broad, general coverage of the main themes and topics.

H. F. GARTEN, *Modern German Drama* (1959). A lively and readable analysis of dramatists from Hauptmann to Brecht to the Swiss Dürrenmatt, exploring the art form that has served as Germany's main vehicle for spiritual, social, and political thought.

PETER GAY, *Weimar Culture: The Outsider as Insider* (1968). A brief historical introduction by a prominent scholar to the seminal between-the-wars epoch.

FELIX GILBERT, *A European Past: Memoirs 1905–1945* (1988). A well-known historian who was born and raised in Berlin reminisces about life in pre-Nazi Germany, with illuminating reflections on German culture, history, and politics—and what might have been.

GÜNTER GRASS, *The Tin Drum* (1959). Probably the most famous novel about life in immediate post-World War II Germany as it struggled to come out from under the devastation of war and defeat. Translated from the German.

LEONARD GROSS, *The Last Jews in Berlin* (1982). Gripping true stories of a handful of Jews who remained in Berlin during World War II and managed to escape the Gestapo and SS by hiding out in the homes of non-Jewish German friends.

CHARLES W. HAXTHAUSEN AND HEIDRUN SUHR, EDS., *Berlin Culture & Metropolis* (1990). Scholars in art history, film studies, literature, history, and sociology cover diverse aspects of Berlin from the turn of the century to the present day, writing on topics such as 20th-century cabaret, the celebration of Berlin's 750th anniversary, and the cultural contributions of Ernst Ludwig Kirchner, George Grosz, Alfred Döblin, and Christa Wolf.

FRIEDRICH HEER, *The Holy Roman Empire* (1968). In this excellent survey, a noted Austrian historian traces the Holy Roman Empire from the time of Charlemagne through the rise and decline of the Hapsburgs and the attendant political, religious, and social turmoil.

HEINRICH HEINE, *The Poetry and Prose of Heinrich Heine.* Edited by Frederic Ewen. These writings, by one of Germany's all-time literary greats who lived at the end of the Enlightenment in the Napoleonic era, are full of wonderful evocations of the Germany of his day.

HAJO HOLBORN, *A History of Modern Germany* (in three volumes: 1959, 1964, 1969). A massive study covering modern German history from the Reformation to the fall of Hitler by an expatriate German scholar who, forbidden to teach by the Nazis, continued his distinguished career at Yale University.

WALTER HUBATSCH, *Frederick the Great: Absolutism and Administration* (1965). This more recent biography and study of Frederick II by a German historian and expert on Prussia examines the king's style of rule and government.

CHRISTOPHER ISHERWOOD, *Berlin Stories* (1946). The Anglo-American novelist, short-story writer, and playwright was a member of the talented group of young leftist writers of the 1930s, including W. H. Auden and Stephen Spender, who lived in Berlin during the Depression and the early years of the Third Reich. This volume, including his stories *Sally Bowles* (1937) and *Goodbye to Berlin* (1939), became the basis for John van Druten's 1952 play *I Am a Camera* that subsequently was turned into the musical *Cabaret.*

MICHAEL JACKSON, *The New World Guide to Beer* (1977). This comprehensive volume, recognized as the standard in its field, lives up to its name by covering the world, with Germany coming in for a lion's share of the *prosits.*

CHRISTOS M. JOACHIMIDES, NORMAN ROSENTHAL, AND WIELAND SCHMIED, EDS., *German Art of the 20th Century* (1985). Filled with illuminating essays and breathtaking reproductions of work from the pre-World War I era through the "Golden Twenties," the Nazi period, and West German painting and sculpture of recent years, the book includes a chronology that links the major political/artistic/cultural events in 20th-century Germany.

FLETCHER KNEBEL, *Crossing in Berlin* (1981). In this novel the author of *Seven Days in May* spins an intriguing Cold War tale of suspense, romance, and human drama, set against the backdrop of the Berlin Wall. His descriptions of life in the divided city and the two Germanys are based on prolonged on-scene research and are remarkable for their insightful accuracy.

HILDEGARD KNEF, *The Gift Horse* (1970). Berlin-born Hildegard Knef, one of Germany's most popular postwar stars, reveals her considerable gifts as a writer in this best-selling account of her childhood in a working-class neighborhood in the thirties, her involvement with a Nazi officer, and the subsequent twists and turns of her long career in theater and films.

KÄTHE KOLLWITZ, *The Diary and Letters of Käthe Kollwitz* (1988). This diary of one of the great German Expressionist artists explains much of the spirit, wisdom, and internal struggle that was eventually transmuted into her art.

CLAUDIA KOONZ, *Mothers in the Fatherland: Women, The Family, and Nazi Politics* (1987). An eye-opening, groundbreaking study, compulsively readable and never less than fascinating, this is the first major comprehensive history of the experience of women in the Third Reich.

BARBARA MILLER LANE, *Architecture and Politics in Germany 1918–1945* (1968). The author shows that Nazi cultural policy was largely the product of conflicting ideas about art held by Nazi leaders.

VICTOR LANGE, *The Classical Age of German Literature* (1982). A survey of the central, or "classical," period of German literature, with special attention to, of course, Goethe and Schiller, as well as Herder, Lessing, Richter, Wieland, and others.

————, ED., *Great German Short Novels and Stories* (1952). A Modern Library edition that provides a rich sampling of classic German short fiction, from Goethe's romantic novella *The Sorrows of Young Werther* to Thomas Mann's *Death in Venice*. Works by Schiller, von Kleist, Heine, Annette von Droste-Hülshoff, Schnitzler, and Rilke are included. Translated from the German.

JOHN LE CARRÉ, *The Spy Who Came in from the Cold* (1963). This classic thriller of Cold War espionage evokes vivid pictures of what Berlin was like during the days of the Wall.

GEORGE LICHTHEIM, *Europe in the Twentieth Century* (1972). A survey of thought and culture in relation to political events, much of it focused on developments in Germany.

GOTTFRIED LINDEMANN, *History of German Art* (1971). A well-rounded survey in which the author discusses the special characteristics of German architecture, sculpture, painting, and the graphic arts, and describes the features that German art shares with the art of other European countries.

CHARLES S. MAIER, *The Unmasterable Past: History, Holocaust, and German National Identity* (1988). A study of West German attempts to come to terms with the Holocaust and the recent controversy surrounding conservative attempts to downplay the historical uniqueness of the German genocide against Jews and other minorities.

GOLO MANN, *The History of Germany Since 1789* (1968). The author, the son of Thomas Mann and one of the foremost German historians of our time, traces the sweep of intellectual developments in Germany since the French Revolution and chronicles political events as well. Translated from the German.

DAVID MARSH, *The Germans* (1990). A masterful and up-to-date account of the new, united Germany by the former chief Germany correspondent for London's *Financial Times,* especially interesting for its speculations on Germany's new superpower future.

GERHARD MASUR, *Imperial Berlin* (1970). No other book describes more colorfully, graphically, and readably the cultural and political life of the city from the advent of Prussia's kings as Germany's kaisers to the end of World War I and the November 1918 revolution. The author is a native Berliner who fled to the United States when Hitler came to power, then taught modern history at Sweet Briar College in Virginia and was also a guest professor at West Berlin's Free University.

KYNASTON MCSHINE, ED., *Berlin Art 1961–1987* (1987). If you're bored by Baroque and repulsed by Rococo, this highly browsable catalogue published in conjunction with a show at the Museum of Modern Art in New York offers essays on recent developments in art in Berlin as well as an overview of the arts in Berlin in this century.

NANCY MITFORD, *Frederick the Great* (1970). Frederick, brilliant military strategist and statesman, scholar, musician, and patron of the arts, is sketched with wit and humor by the author, who draws almost all of her material from contemporary sources. With lavish illustrations.

HELMUTH JAMES VON MOLTKE, *Letters to Freya, 1939–1945* (1990). Lucid, compelling, often heartbreaking, this collection of letters from a young German aristocrat to his wife reveal how a man of great moral integrity responded to desperate times. The leader of the Kreisau circle of resisters, Moltke was eventually executed by the Nazis. Translated from the German.

JAMES P. O'DONNELL, *The Bunker* (1978). This is the riveting, meticulously researched, nearly incredible (but true) story of Hitler's last days in his underground headquarters bunker in Berlin in April 1945, based on interviews with a large number of eyewitnesses and the available documents. The author, a student in Berlin in the 1930s and a U.S. Army Signal Corps captain during the war, was one of the first Americans to enter the Führer's bunker, under the Reich Chancellory, after the fall of Berlin. He subsequently became *Newsweek*'s first Germany bureau chief and when the Wall was erected in 1961 joined the state department as special assistant to General Lucius D. Clay in Berlin.

DIETHER RAFF, *A History of Germany from the Medieval Empire to the Present* (1985). The concentration here is on the post-Bismark era and on relationships between Germany and the other nations of Europe (and the United States), with numerous chapters about the post-World War II era. Translated from the German.

BERNARD RIVKIN, *The Gourmet's Companion: German Menu Guide & Translator* (1991). If you break out into a sweat when you see words like *Büchsenstangenspargel* on a menu, this handy, alphabetized German/English food/menu/wine dictionary will relieve your dietary angst.

WILLIAM RUSSELL, *Berlin Embassy* (1941). The author, later a journalist and foreign correspondent, worked as a consular officer in the American Embassy during the crucial years beginning with the start of World War II in 1939 until late 1940. In this book he presents the day-to-day reports of what Berlin's people were thinking, saying, and doing in that period when the embassy was besieged by hordes of tormented, hounded people begging for an escape route out of the city and the country.

JEFFREY L. SAMMONS, *Heinrich Heine: A Modern Biography* (1979). The author shows how Heine distilled a pattern of poetic insight and humanistic responsibility in the face of obstacles not unlike those affecting dissident writers throughout the world in our own day.

HORST SCHARFENBERG, *The Cuisines of Germany: Regional Specialties and Traditional Home Cooking* (1989). The book has some cookbook elements, but is also useful for reading about the food itself, as the title indicates. Translated from the German.

KARL FRIEDRICH SCHINKEL, *Collection of Architectural Designs* (1989). A pricey but superbly produced volume dedicated to the works of Schinkel, an exponent of Romantic Classicism and the most influential of all 19th-century architects.

HUBERT SCHRADE, *German Romantic Painting* (1977). The early- and mid-18th-century German Romantics were the first to exploit landscape as a theme in itself. The author, a leading German art historian, focuses on individual painters such as Caspar David Friedrich, Phillip Otto Runge, and Joseph Anton Koch.

PETER SELZ, *German Expressionist Painting* (1974). The first comprehensive study of one of the most pivotal movements in 20th-century art, this book examines the work of the *Brücke* and *Blaue Reiter* artists working in Dresden and Munich between 1905 and 1914. Beautiful reproductions of paintings by Kirchner, Kokoschka, Schmidt-Rottluff, Max Pechstein, Max Beckmann, and others.

WILLIAM SHIRER, *Berlin Diary* (1941). In this, his first book, the author of *The Rise and Fall of the Third Reich* relates his day-to-day experiences and observations from the time of his arrival in Berlin as an American correspondent in 1934 until his departure in December 1941, just a few days before Pearl Harbor. It is the classic of observers' memoirs and records for the period, and describes life in the city three-dimensionally.

————, *End of a Berlin Diary* (1947). Shirer arrived for a second, albeit far briefer, stint as CBS correspondent in October 1945, when the smoke of war was still drifting over the ruined city and the broken country. He uses the same diary technique in this volume to relate his experiences and report his observations.

————, *The Nightmare Years* (1984). In this second of his three-volume memoirs, *20th-Century Journey,* Shirer again covers the period when he was an American correspondent in Nazi Berlin, but does so with the benefit of the hindsight of nearly 50 years. He also has the freedom to identify some of the friends and sources who had provided him with inside information in the 1930s.

————, *The Rise and Fall of the Third Reich: A History of Nazi Germany* (1959, 1960). A three-volume account of the Hitler years in fast-paced, gripping, and exhaustively researched detail by this distinguished American foreign correspondent, news commentator, and historian of the contemporary world.

MICHAEL SNODIN, ED., *Karl Friedrich Schinkel: A Universal Man* (1991). No artist and architect left a more lasting impression on Berlin, Brandenburg, and Prussia than Schinkel, born in 1781—like Theodor Fontane—in Neuruppin. This book is the catalogue of the Schinkel exhibition held at London's Victoria and Albert Museum August through October 1991.

ALBERT SPEER, *Inside the Third Reich* (1970). These memoirs by Hitler's favorite architect and the Third Reich's minister of armaments provide an inside view of official Berlin and the Nazi administration from the early 1930s until the 1945 Götterdämmerung. Speer spells out in detail some of the bombastically zany architectural and urban renewal plans he had for the city.

————, *Spandau* (1976). Speer, one of the most powerful men in Nazi Germany at the end of the war, was tried for war crimes at the Nürnberg tribunal in 1946 and sentenced to 20 years in prison, which he served together with six other top Nazi officials, including Rudolf Hess, at the Allied prison in Berlin's Spandau borough. These are the secret diaries he kept during his incarceration.

DONALD SPOTO, *The Blue Angel: The Life of Marlene Dietrich* (1992). The life of the great German film star, who began her career in the theaters and cabarets of Berlin in the 1920s and went on to become a glamorous Hollywood icon, is juicily detailed in this well-researched biography.

WOLFGANG STECHOW, *Northern Renaissance Art 1400–1600: Sources and Documents* (1966). An intriguing assortment of documents, contracts, and letters of the period, the German portion relating particularly to the work of Tilman Riemenschneider, Dürer, Grünewald, and Hans Holbein the Younger.

JOHN TOLAND, *Adolf Hitler* (1976). This biography of Hitler by the author of *The Last 100 Days* and *Battle: The Story of the Bulge* is the best and most comprehensive by an American writer, based on countless interviews and correspondence with contemporaries and eyewitnesses.

MARK TWAIN, *A Tramp Abroad* (1899). Twain's account of his travels in Germany are must reading for any visitor today, especially the hilarious chapter titled "That Awful German Language," in which he relates his attempts to cope with the grammar, syntax, and pronunciation of German.

MARIE VASSILTCHIKOV, *Berlin Diaries 1940–1945* (1987). Days in the wartime life of a young aristocrat; extraordinary reading.

C. V. WEDGWOOD, *Thirty Years' War* (1962). The classic historical account of the religious wars that tore Germany asunder.

FRANK WHITFORD, *Bauhaus* (1986). Setting the school's philosophy and teaching methods firmly against the backdrop of the time, the author traces the ideas behind the conception of the influential Bauhaus movement founded in Germany in 1919 and closed down by the Nazis in 1933.

JOHN WILLET, *Art & Politics in the Weimar Period: The New Sobriety 1917–1933* (1978). Germany as a post–World War I center of a new cultural movement. Illustrated.

CHRISTA WOLF, *A Model Childhood* (1980). Christa Wolf, one of the former GDR's best-known writers, examines her past as a youthful member of the Nazi Youth Organization in this fictionalized account of a childhood spent under Nazism. Translated from the German.
                                        —*John Dornberg and Donald S. Olson*

BERLIN

By John Dornberg

It used to be claimed that you could get by with less sleep in Berlin than anywhere else in the world because of *Berliner Luft*—Berlin air. Souvenir merchants even sold it in cans to the gullible. Unfortunately, the air that Berliners breathe is no longer as bracingly pure as it once was, due to pollution. But one thing about it has not changed: its electrifying quality. And you have to go to Berlin to experience that.

Few cities have made so much news and history. Berlin has usually been associated with something startling, stimulating, and significant, not just in politics but also in business, science, technology, art, theater, music, literature, cinema, fashion, and architecture.

Politically, the city has played many roles. It was the capital of the duchy of Brandenburg, which became the kingdom of Prussia in 1701 when Frederick I crowned himself king. By 1871, Berlin was the capital of the Second German Reich, that of the kaisers; later it was the capital of the short-lived democratic Weimar Republic; and eventually it became the headquarters of Hitler's Third Reich. After the war Berlin was on the front line of the Cold War, the place where two ideologies, two political systems, and, indeed, two different worlds, met and occasionally collided. The city's people were physically divided for 28 years by the grim Berlin Wall that separated West from East.

The Wall opened and began crumbling in November 1989. That ugly symbol of a dark era is gone, except for four small segments until now preserved as monuments, two of which will soon be gone, and broken fragments of the Wall, mostly fake, being hawked near the Brandenburg

Gate and at the former Checkpoint Charlie by souvenir vendors. The city is whole again, one immense metropolis, and by resolution of the *Bundestag,* Germany's parliament, on the road to becoming reunited Germany's capital not just in name but in fact by the late 1990s or early next century. Yet, in many ways the Wall remains—"in people's heads," as Berliners say when speaking of the social, economic, and cultural differences between the city's western and eastern boroughs, and in the physical scars of wasteland real estate, such as Potsdamer Platz, once Europe's busiest square and now a huge, empty lot, deliberately carved by the Wall and its adjacent "death strip." Most of the physical scars will undoubtedly have disappeared by the year 2000.

The mental and emotional wounds of Germany's and Berlin's division, however, will take at least a generation to heal. And in a strange way those wounds are taking their toll. No longer is it the city of the chilling thrills of the Cold War that gave visitors the feeling of being on the front line between two ideologies. Today it is just Central Europe's largest city, with a fascinating past but an uncertain future, and a very troubling present of urban problems facing every huge metropolis anywhere in the world, including racism and political polarization that, occasionally, lead to violence.

Its current difficulties notwithstanding, however, Berlin is special. It is delightfully kaleidoscopic, a vibrant city supercharged with high-voltage vitality and imbued with an optimism that seems to underscore its citizens' ability to survive all crises with humor and wit.

Berlin is not a city that can be mastered in three or four hours. To "see" Berlin may take three or four days; to figure out what makes it tick could take a lifetime.

Sheer size has something to do with this. In population—3.5 million—Berlin is the largest city between Paris and Moscow. In area, 341 square miles, it is one of the biggest in the world. Parts of Berlin are still so bucolic that the city hosts the annual *Grüne Woche,* Germany's biggest agricultural fair. There are 113 miles of rivers and canals and about 1,000 bridges—more than in Venice. Before World War II it was Germany's second-largest inland port, and both commercial shipping and pleasure boating are still practiced.

Life in Berlin is as diverse as its geography. You'll find not just one Berlin, nor even the two once divided by the Wall, but dozens: a jigsaw puzzle of neighborhoods, communities, impressions, moods, and scenes. Within the city limits there are still four 18th-century windmills, one of which was grinding grain as recently as 1980; 55 village churches dating from the 13th century; and 70 weekly outdoor produce markets. The city is also the site of more than 160 major and minor museums; ten palaces, castles, and châteaux; three opera houses; six symphony orchestras; six dozen theaters; and 8,000 restaurants, cafés, pubs, and night spots—all working together to create a continually fascinating city.

To understand this diversity it helps to know that it was only in 1920 that Berlin became the huge metropolis it is today. That year nearly a dozen independent cities and 59 small towns were incorporated.

If anything here approximates a common denominator, it is the distinctive Berlin dialect, plus a kind of braggadocio that other Germans call *Berliner Schnauze,* which, loosely translated, means "Berlin lippiness."

MAJOR INTEREST

Central Berlin: Eastern
The Brandenburg Gate and historic buildings along Unter den Linden
The Dom, St. Hedwigs-Kathedrale, and the Marienkirche
Museumsinsel and the Pergamon Museum
Alexanderplatz, the Nikolaiviertel, and the Gendarmenmarkt

Central Berlin: Western
The Tiergarten, the Reichstag, Schloss Bellevue, the Zoologischer Garten
Museums in the Kulturforum complex
Kurfürstendamm, the Kaiser-Wilhelm-Gedächtnis-Kirche, and the Käthe Kollwitz Museum

Around the Center
Kreuzberg and the Luftbrückendenkmal (Airlift Monument)
Dahlem and its museums
Schloss Charlottenburg and its museums

Outlying Areas
Spandau and the Zitadelle Spandau
Treptow and the Soviet War Memorial

Köpenicker Forst, Grosser Müggelsee, and Schloss
  Köpenick
Grunewald and Wannsee

The City's History

The Wall that divided West from East Berlin from August
13, 1961, to November 9, 1989, did not mark the first
separation of this city. Indeed, Berlin started off as two
small rival trading settlements on opposite banks of the
Spree river in what was then the easternmost region of
the Holy Roman Empire, the March of Brandenburg.

This remote area had been settled by barbarian Germanic tribes in the early part of the first century. By A.D.
500 they had moved westward and southward, leaving the
land to the Wends, a Slavic people whose modern descendants, now called Sorbs, still inhabit the Lausitz district
southeast of Berlin. Throughout the Dark Ages the Wends
and Germans battled frequently. In the eighth century
Charlemagne conquered the Wendish lands; by the tenth
century a coalition of Wendish tribes had regained the
territory.

In 1147 Emperor Conrad III, Duke Henry the Lion of
Saxony, and Count Albrecht (Albert) the Bear joined
forces against the Wends and defeated them for good.
Albrecht settled the newly won land and, forging alliances
through marriage, became margrave of Brandenburg. His
margraviate, or "march," meaning frontier zone, was the
cradle of what would become the kingdom of Prussia and
the German Reich.

Germans soon began settling and reinforcing the forts
the Wends had built, one of which was the Zitadelle
Spandau. Around 1230 they founded two towns: Cölln on
an island in the Spree river, and Berlin on the river's
northeastern bank. Popular legend holds that the name
Berlin may derive somehow from Albrecht the Bear, and
is is true that the bear has been the city's symbol for many
centuries. However, most city historians scoff at the idea
and say that no one knows the origin of the name or what
it once meant. Although they profited from commerce on
the east-west trade route between Poznan in Poland and
Magdeburg, the two towns were bitter rivals. Each had its
own *Rathaus* (City Hall) and was surrounded by its own
protective wall. Although only a few yards of water divided them, the towns steadfastly rebuffed attempts at
amalgamation. It wasn't until 1307, when robber barons

were ravaging the March of Brandenburg, that Cölln and Berlin agreed on a confederated union. A third city hall, where the combined towns' councillors could meet, was built on the Lange Brücke (Long Bridge), now called Rathausbrücke.

Shortly after their union, Berlin-Cölln, which then had a population of some 5,000, joined the Hanseatic League, an alliance of trading and shipping cities along the Baltic and the North Sea. Along with the land route that carried business to the town, the Spree gave Berlin-Cölln access to the Havel river, a tributary of the Elbe which in turn empties into the North Sea, and an overland link was established with the Oder river, which flows into the Baltic Sea.

Berlin's history during most of the 14th and early 15th centuries was tumultuous. In 1323 the last of Albrecht's descendants died without heirs, and ownership of the Brandenburg margraviate reverted to the Holy Roman Emperor, Ludwig IV. He gave it to his son, but 50 years later Emperor Charles IV conferred the margraviate on his own son, Wenceslaus, who, in turn, gave Brandenburg to his brother Sigismund, who then transferred ownership to one of his most loyal supporters and lieutenants, Burgrave Frederick von Hohenzollern. On several occasions during this period Brandenburg was also pawned to various moneylenders to finance the wars of its various owners.

Much changed with the advent of Frederick and the Hohenzollerns, who were to rule Berlin, Brandenburg, and all of Germany (not to mention a good chunk of Europe) for the next 400 years. They were a South German clan with vision and a lust for power. They not only routed the robber barons and subjugated the gentry, but they also crushed the independent cities, including Berlin itself. Frederick dissolved the merger of the two towns, disbanded their assembly of councillors, and forbade Berlin and Cölln to enter into alliances. He also confiscated substantial plots of land.

On one of those confiscated plots he laid the cornerstone for a grand palace, thus turning Cölln into his residence, seat of government, and capital of Brandenburg.

The Hohenzollerns, who also acquired Prussia to the east (though the name Prussia did not come into use until Frederick I crowned himself its king) and territories as far west as Kleve on the Rhine, were among the first German rulers to adopt the views of Martin Luther and make Protestantism their state's official religion. To this day less than 15 percent of Berlin's population is Catholic.

Although epidemics and starvation during the Thirty Years' War cut Berlin's population from 12,000 to 6,000, its political prospects continued to improve. Duke Frederick William, *der Grosse Kurfürst* (the Great Elector), who took office in 1640, consolidated and expanded the Hohenzollern lands and encouraged immigration. By 1677 religiously motivated French refugees had already settled in Berlin, and when Louis XIV decided he could no longer tolerate the Calvinist Huguenots in Catholic France, the Great Elector offered them refuge in Protestant Brandenburg.

Of the 15,000 Huguenot immigrants who eventually came to Brandenburg 6,000 settled in Berlin itself. By the time of the Great Elector's death in 1688 nearly one third of the city's population was French. They were granted the right of self-government and the right to found their own schools and churches. The Französischer Dom (French Cathedral) on Gendarmenmarkt, built in 1764 and now restored after more than 40 years as a World War II ruin, is one of their greatest legacies.

The French influence on the city's economic life, administration, armed forces, arts, sciences, language, educational system, and fashions was immense. To this day Berlin's curious dialect contains some French contributions. For example, Berliners still refer disparagingly to weak coffee as *Muckefuck,* which comes from the French expression *moka faux,* meaning a false mocha, or coffee substitute.

Yet when Frederick William died in 1688, Berlin was still a provincial town of fewer than 20,000, a backwater compared to London, Paris, Vienna, Prague, or Moscow.

His son, Frederick I, changed all that. In 1701, after 13 years as duke and elector, he decided that the duchy should become a kingdom. He ordered royal insignia from a jeweler and, standing before a mirror, crowned himself king of Prussia. As a kingdom needs a proper capital, he then set out to create one. He merged Berlin and Cölln into a single city and hired some of the greatest German architects to expand and complete the Royal Palace (which was badly damaged during World War II and then demolished by East Germany's Communist regime in 1951). He also built the Zeughaus, or armory (now the Museum of German History) on Unter den Linden, as well as a number of summer palaces, including

Schloss Charlottenburg, which has been restored following its devastation during World War II.

Although the city's territory was still limited to what is today the borough of Berlin Mitte (about 4.1 square miles), by the time Frederick I died, in 1713, the capital's population had grown to 60,000. Under his son, Frederick William I, known as the "Soldier King," and his grandson, Frederick the Great, Berlin became grander by the year. Stunning public buildings, including the Brandenburg Gate, were erected along or near Unter den Linden. By 1790 Berlin had a population of 147,000.

The 19th century brought the Industrial Revolution and Prussia's transformation into the German Reich, with the kings of Prussia being also the German kaisers, or emperors. This was an epoch of explosive growth for Berlin: Between Napoléon's defeat in 1815 and the start of World War I in 1914, the population grew tenfold, from 193,000 to 1.9 million. Yet despite incorporation of some surrounding towns and villages, the city's area was still only one-thirteenth of its present size. Some of Germany's largest industrial concerns—Siemens and AEG, electrical engineering companies; Borsig, the locomotive and steam engine manufacturer; Schering, the pharmaceuticals producer—were launched during this period. As many as 50 new factories started up each year. And to work in them, under grueling sweatshop conditions, hundreds of thousands of people streamed into the city.

The barons of industry built their factories to resemble medieval castles and cathedrals, with crenellated walls and spires. The industrialists also built villas and mansions that rivaled the royal palaces, prompting the kings and kaisers to build even grander edifices in an ornate style that critics dubbed "Reich braggadocio."

There was nothing ornate about the mass housing for the growing labor force: endless rows of five- or six-story buildings of dingy flats, most without plumbing, built around shaftlike inner courtyards as small as 18 by 18 feet. While Berlin was becoming Germany's biggest industrial center, it was also becoming Europe's largest tenement city. This aspect of life in Berlin was eloquently portrayed by the art of Heinrich Zille and Käthe Kollwitz and in the writings of Alfred Döblin, Joachim Ringelnatz, and Kurt Tucholsky.

Although the destruction of World War II, postwar reconstruction, and the urban renewal and renovation projects of the 1970s and 1980s have erased much of this housing, you can get a vivid idea of what it was like in the boroughs of Neukölln (southeast of Berlin Mitte), Kreuzberg (just south of Berlin Mitte), Wedding (northwest of Berlin Mitte), and Prenzlauer Berg (northeast of Berlin Mitte). These areas are home to the typical *Kneipe,* a tavern that is the focus of a real neighborhood, or *Kiez,* as a neighborhood is called in Berlin dialect. A good Kiez is an intersection with four corners and four taverns where wheat beer with a shot of corn schnapps flows like water.

There was a brighter side to life in the city. Impressionist painters Max Liebermann, Lovis Corinth, and Max Slevogt were at work; the Expressionist art of Max Pechstein, George Grosz, and Karl Schmidt-Rottluff was winning acclaim; and *Jugendstil,* or Art Nouveau design, was at its height. With two major opera houses, the Philharmonic orchestra, and the Deutsches Theater, the latter under the direction of Max Reinhardt, Berlin won international stature as a music and drama center. Leading scientists, including Albert Einstein, Max Planck, Fritz Haber, Walther Nernst, Adolf von Bayer, Robert Koch, and Emil Fischer, worked at various times in Berlin. And Berlin became one of the world's greatest museum cities, thanks to its matchless collections of painting, sculpture, and ancient art.

After World War I and the 1918 revolution, which toppled the kaiser and made Germany a republic, Berlin became a center of the Golden Twenties, indeed *the* cosmopolitan crossroads of that decade. Movie stars Marlene Dietrich, Greta Garbo, Peter Lorre, and Pola Negri and directors Fritz Lang, Ernst Lubitsch, F. W. Murnau, and Josef von Sternberg, working at the huge studios in suburban Potsdam Babelsberg, made the city a cinema capital. Berlin was the home of Dadaist art; of artists Hans Arp, Max Beckmann, Max Ernst, Grosz, Paul Klee, and Schmidt-Rottluff; of the Bauhaus architects and designers, notably Walter Gropius and Ludwig Mies van der Rohe; of essayists, poets, and writers W. H. Auden, Arthur Koestler, Christopher Isherwood (whose *Berlin Stories* was the basis of the later play *I Am a Camera* and the play and film *Cabaret*), Heinrich Mann, Vladimir Nabokov, Carl von Ossietzky, and Kurt Tucholsky. Berlin was the stage for Bertolt Brecht, Kurt Weill, Erwin Piscator, Carl Zuckmayer, and Lotte Lenya. Wilhelm Furtwängler presided over the Philharmonic. The city had yet another opera house, and the local conductors were Bruno Walter, Otto Klemperer, and Erich

Kleiber. It was also in 1920 that Berlin became the sprawl-ing metropolis that it is today. In October of that year eight independent surrounding cities, among them Charlotten-burg, Schöneberg, Spandau, and Köpenick, plus dozens of smaller towns were incorporated to create Greater Berlin.

Today that period seems like a lost paradise. It was lost, of course, because of Adolf Hitler and the Third Reich. Berlin, the mecca of culture and tolerance, became the center of anticulture and intolerance. In their racist mega-lomania the Nazis even began restructuring the city. Char-lottenburger Chaussee (today called Strasse des 17. Juni), the extension of Unter den Linden west of the Branden-burg Gate, is twice as wide as it was before the Third Reich: Hitler had it widened to accommodate his military and political parades. Albert Speer, his favorite architect, drafted plans for a bombastic new city center near Tempel-hof airfield. He envisioned, among other things, a railway station plaza 3,300 feet long and 1,000 feet wide, and a new triumphal arch so big that the Brandenburg Gate would have fit into it several times. Those plans were never realized, but other architectural relics of the Third Reich remain: Tempelhof itself, the Olympic Stadium, and grim-looking government office buildings south of Unter den Linden.

Worst of all, Berlin became the cauldron for World War II and the Holocaust, a reign of terror and genocide that culminated in the city's own Götterdämmerung.

Of the 4.4 million prewar inhabitants, only 2.8 million remained in 1945, and the city was a wasteland. Streets and squares, especially in the historic center, were strewn with dead bodies, burned-out tanks, and the debris of artillery attacks. Some 75 million cubic meters of rubble—one seventh of all the rubble in Germany—were in Berlin. Of the city's 245,000 prewar buildings, 50,000 were com-pletely destroyed and as many again were near ruins. Transportation was at a standstill; public utilities were nonexistent. And once again Berlin, as it had been with the Russians during the Seven Years' War and with the French under Napoléon from 1806 to 1808, was under foreign occupation—first by the Russians alone, and from August 1945 on by the Americans, British, and French as well.

The situation was made worse by the conflicts between the wartime victors that led to the Cold War. The 1948 Soviet blockade, which the Western Allies met with the 11-month-long airlift called Operation Vittles, was followed by the tragic June 17, 1953, workers' uprising in East Berlin, and finally by the 1961 construction of the Berlin Wall.

To this day, the scars and wounds of World War II, not to mention those of the Cold War, are more visible in Berlin than in any other German city. Many building façades, especially in the eastern boroughs, are still pock-marked with bullet holes from the 1945 street fighting, large areas are still weed-covered lots on which nothing has been built for nearly 50 years, or they are wastelands created because of the Wall.

Getting Oriented

Berlin's size, the distance between its most important sites, the legacy of postwar division between Communist East and capitalist West with a dramatic shift of cosmopolitan life, business, shopping, hotels, restaurants, theaters, and nightlife from the old center—Alexanderplatz, Unter den Linden, Leipziger Strasse, and Potsdamer Platz—westward to Kurfürstendamm: all make the city difficult to master.

Though Berlin is again one, with a single public transit network and with streets once divided by the Wall that now connect as if that barrier had never existed, Berliners themselves still think in terms of West and East, and the differences between the two halves are—and will long remain—glaringly apparent. Immense investments over a period of many years will be needed to give central east Berlin, once the throbbing heart of the whole city, the urban glitter of the formerly Western area around Kurfürstendamm. And even when the investments bear fruit, much of it may become artificial. A good example is the planning for Potsdamer Platz, south of the Branden-burg Gate, where by the year 2000 large German and Japanese industrial firms (Daimler-Benz and Sony) intend to complete a vast office, residential, shopping, and entertainment center.

The logical way to explore a city is to start with its old quarter. This historic center, traversed by Unter den Linden boulevard and Karl-Liebknecht-Strasse, its east-west axis, is the borough of **Berlin Mitte**. On and around the axis, its western end being the Brandenburg Gate, its eastern one Alexanderplatz, are the most important sites and sights. It is also the logical and most sensible part in which to start your tour. But because of the paucity of hotels and interesting restaurants, it is unlikely that you will be staying here. The real "weight" of Berlin, that which thus far has made and will for the next five to ten years make it the international city it is, is in the west, on and around **Kurfürstendamm**, where most hotels are.

To make sense of western Berlin is also not easy, in part because of its size and the fact that many of its sightseeing highlights are far from its center, the Kurfürstendamm. This avenue runs on a northeast-to-southwest axis for almost 3 km (2 miles) through the heart of west Berlin. Its northeastern terminal, not far from Bahnhof Zoo, Berlin's main railway station, is the **Europa-Center**, more than 3 km (2 miles) southwest of the Brandenburg Gate. This 22-story office, commercial, and shopping complex, topped by the huge revolving emblem of Mercedes-Benz, is in the center of Berlin's "downtown" area at the convergence of Kurfürstendamm, Kantstrasse, Hardenbergstrasse, Budapester Strasse, and Tauentzienstrasse. As it is one of central Berlin's tallest buildings, replete with 70 stores, 20 restaurants, five cinemas, cabarets, nightclubs, a gambling casino, airline offices, and the Berlin tourist bureau, you can hardly miss it. An observation platform on the 20th floor provides a view of most of the city and a sense of its layout.

Even if excursion-bus rubbernecking is not usually your style, Berlin is where you should make an exception, for no other mode will provide such an excellent overview of the city. There are a variety of tours, all covering basically the same routes. Most have their ticket offices and departure points on or just off Kurfürstendamm, within a few minutes' walk of the Europa-Center, or close to and on Alexanderplatz. There are two- to four-hour tours of the entire city in both German and English.

The best, fastest, and cheapest way to get around is by public transit, which is excellent throughout the city. Renting a car may seem inviting because of Berlin's size, but it is also an invitation to headaches. Traffic is always heavy, parking spaces are rare, and gridlock is common. Moreover, the layout of the city is so complex that you are bound to get lost, no matter how detailed your map. On the other hand, except for a few specific, relatively manageable areas—such as Berlin Mitte or Köpenick (the large borough in the southeastern outskirts of the city) or the Kurfürstendamm neighborhood, the Tiergarten district (north of Kurfürstendamm), the museums in Dahlem (south of Kurfürstendamm), and around Schloss Charlottenburg (northwest of Kurfürstendamm), and Span-

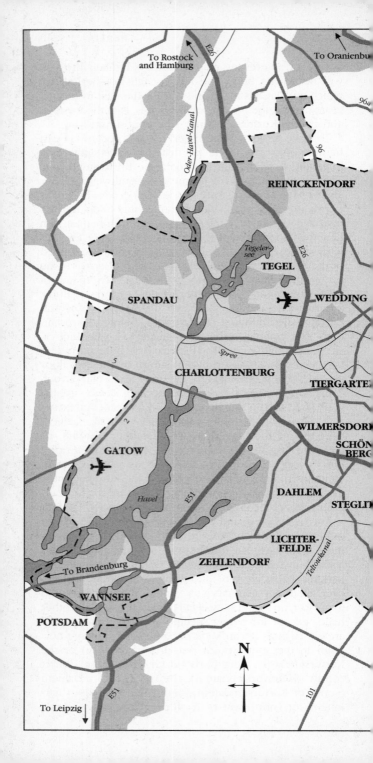

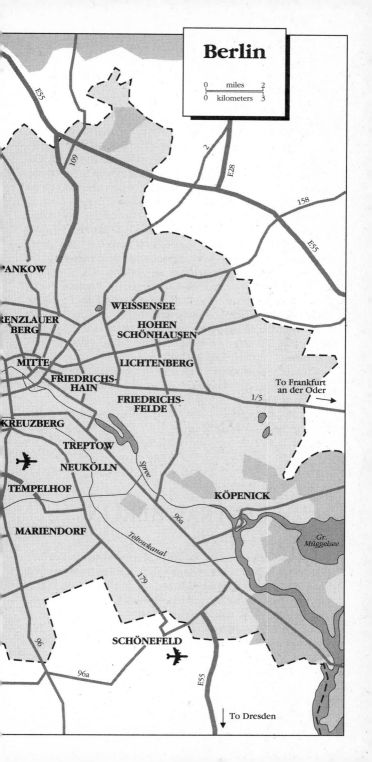

dau's Altstadt (on the city's western edge)—walking tours can become endurance tests.

We begin of course with **Central Berlin:** first, as we have already suggested, with Berlin Mitte, the traditional heart of the city, in what used to be East Berlin, and which includes Unter den Linden, Museumsinsel, and the Alexanderplatz area, and other former East Berlin areas of the center—the Nikolaiviertel, the Märkisches Ufer and Gendarmenmarkt areas, and Friedrichstrasse.

Next comes the former West Berlin center: the Tiergarten area, the Kulturforum, and of course in and around Kurfürstendamm—which remains the "new" Berlin center for hotels, shops, restaurants, and nightlife.

Around the Center are the neighborhoods of Kreuzberg, Schöneberg, and Prenzlauer Berg. Farther, **Away from the Center,** are the Dahlem museums and Schloss Charlottenburg and the museums there.

In the **Outlying Areas** are the citadel at Spandau, Köpenick, Treptow borough, Lichtenberg, Pankow, and the forests and lakes of Berlin.

This is followed by a section on **Special Sightseeing,** which focuses on village churches and interesting industrial attractions.

Finally, we discuss all of the city's museums again, together in a separate section.

CENTRAL BERLIN

The 4.1-square-mile borough of **Berlin Mitte** is Berlin's historic heart, the spot where Cölln and Berlin were first settled in the Middle Ages. It was the font of Prussian and German power, the district from which kings, kaisers, and also Adolf Hitler ruled. During the 40 years of postwar Germany's division, when East Berlin was the capital of the Communist East German Democratic Republic (GDR), this third-smallest of the city's 20 boroughs was East Berlin's political, economic and cultural center. Within it are the entire city's most important sites: the Brandenburg Gate; Unter den Linden; the Deutsche Staatsoper, the city's main opera house; Humboldt Universität; the state's library, Deutsche Staatsbibliothek; the Zeughaus (armory); Museumsinsel, a complex of museums and galleries; and Alexanderplatz, now dominated by the 1,200-foot TV tower, Berlin's tallest structure, nicknamed the "Speared Onion." Berlin Mitte also contains the Dom and St. Hedwig's, St. Mary's, and St. Nicholas churches; the Gendarmenmarkt (known until recently as Platz der Akademie), with the Schauspielhaus theater and the French and German cathedrals; and the Rotes Rathaus, the city hall so called for its Neo-Renaissance red-brick façade.

In other words, when the devastated city was divided into four occupation sectors at the 1945 Potsdam Conference, the Soviets, and by inference East Berliners, got most of the nuggets. Moreover, though it seemed to take ages, most of it was rebuilt, restored, refurbished, renovated, and enriched with luxury hotels and restaurants, cafés, cozy taverns, special shops, department stores, theaters, and cinemas—in order to make East Berlin as much a showcase of Communism as West Berlin became of capitalism.

The price of rebuilding a few streets, squares, museums, palaces, and monuments was the neglect and decay, or the shoddy prefab restoration, of much of the rest of the eastern city. Moreover, for 28 of the more than 40 years that East Berlin was destined to play its role in the Cold War, it was a showcase within a cage, sealed off from West Berlin by the Wall with its bristling array of guard towers and barbed wire. Many would-be visitors wondered whether a visit was worth it, given the bureaucratic formalities, the surliness of the border guards, and the real or imagined restrictions on freedom of movement.

All that changed dramatically on November 9, 1989, when the Wall opened up and the two Berlins as well as the two Germanys began moving toward reunification. Yet at the same time some things have not changed. To be sure, the two Berlins are already being stitched back together. As just one example, the Rotes Rathaus is again, as it was before 1945, the city hall of all of Berlin and seat of the burgomaster and his cabinet, called the Senate. Federal government agencies have moved into a number of ministerial buildings of the former German Democratic Republic. But the scars of division and of the Wall will long remain, as will those of East Berlin having been the far poorer showcase and the capital of a far poorer country. How long? That depends on how fast the Germans and Berliners move ahead with their costly plans—

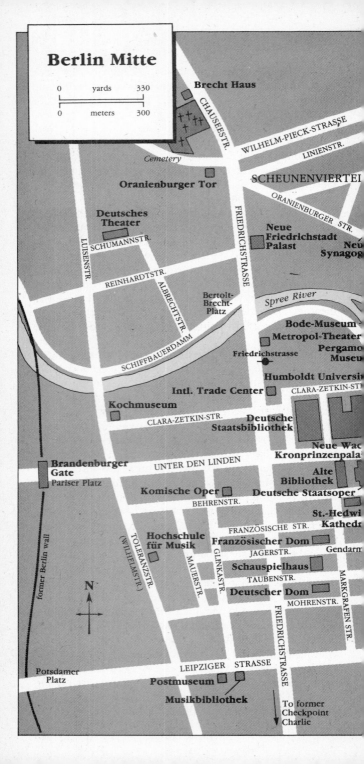

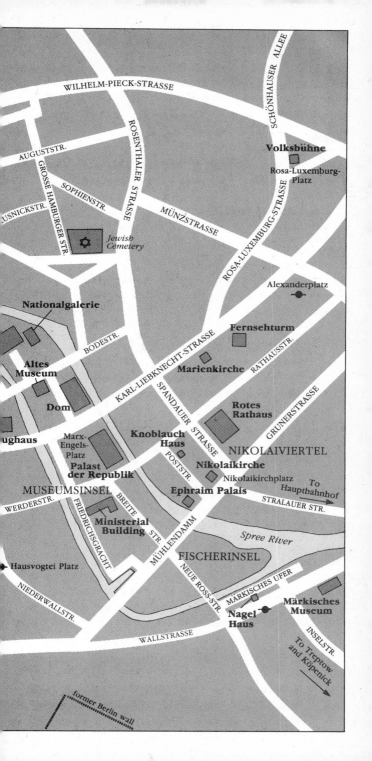

DM 40 billion by the most optimistic estimates, thrice that according to the pessimists—to make Berlin instead of Bonn not just a capital in name but in fact: the seat of government and parliament.

ON AND AROUND
UNTER DEN LINDEN

Unter den Linden is Berlin's most famous avenue. It runs from east to west for about a mile from Marx-Engels-Platz (known until 1951 as the *Lustgarten,* or Pleasure Garden), to Pariser Platz and the Brandenburg Gate.

The boulevard's pedigree goes back to 1573, when Elector Johann Georg laid it out as a bridle path from his palace to his hunting grounds in the Tiergarten. Three quarters of a century later, in 1647, the Great Elector ordered 1,000 nut trees and 1,000 lindens planted along the road. Although these were cut down in 1680 in order to pave the street and make room for residential and public buildings, the name Unter den Linden stuck and became official a century later when Frederick the Great widened the street into a parkway and again planted it with linden trees.

In the late 19th and early 20th centuries it was the unchallenged main street of Berlin, divided at midpoint by its intersection with Friedrichstrasse. Along its eastern end were the great palaces, the university, opera, libraries, and other institutional buildings. The western half was lined by foreign embassies, elegant shops, luxury hotels, cafés, and restaurants. Wilhelmstrasse, (the East Berlin end called Otto-Grotewohl-Strasse during the Communist era, now named Toleranzstrasse), which intersects Unter den Linden close to the Brandenburg Gate, was the street of government, flanked by the presidential residence, the ministry of justice, and the Reich chancellory. To speak of "Wilhelmstrasse" in those days was like speaking of the White House or 10 Downing Street. By contrast, the intersection of Unter den Linden and Friedrichstrasse was the epicenter of Berlin's political, intellectual, cultural, and commercial life, the location of the Café Kranzler and of the Café Bauer, which was reborn in 1987 as part of the Grand Hotel.

In May 1945, when the bombs stopped falling and the guns were silenced, Unter den Linden was a bleak moonscape of craters and mountains of rubble, with only charred, crumbling façades of gutted buildings still standing. The few linden trees that survived were soon cut down for firewood. Yet today Unter den Linden is again one of Berlin's finest boulevards, reconstructed almost as it was. Unfortunately its western half, although again lined with foreign missions, stores, and government offices, was rebuilt in faceless steel, glass, and concrete. But from Friedrichstrasse eastward virtually every building of note was recreated: Frederick the Great would see hardly any changes. Even the 45-foot-high equestrian statue of "Old Fritz" stands in its proper place in the middle of the avenue. Erected in 1851, it was removed for safekeeping during World War II, then hidden for 35 years behind a clump of bushes on the grounds of Sanssouci palace in Potsdam because East Germany's rulers wanted no reminder of the Hohenzollerns and Prussia. In 1980, in an about-face, they allowed this monument to Frederick the Great to return to Unter den Linden.

The **Brandenburger Tor** (Brandenburg Gate), at the avenue's western end, is the very essence of Berlin. The huge gate—66 feet high, 204 feet wide, and 36 feet deep—modeled after the Propylaeum on the Acropolis, was officially opened in 1791. Frederick William II attended the ceremony. Originally called the Friedenstor (Peace Gate), it assumed a more martial appearance two years later when it was crowned by the bronze **Quadriga**, a four-horse war chariot driven by the Goddess of Victory. The goddess was originally nude, but her appearance triggered so much indignation and so many ribald jokes that the sculptor, Johann Gottfried Schadow, clad her in a sheet of copper. She kept her vigil for 13 years, until 1806, when Napoléon marched triumphantly into Berlin. Like many conquerors before and after, he looted art. He had a policy: "Take a nation's symbols, and you have it in your hands." He dismantled the Quadriga and had it shipped to Paris to be mounted on the Arc de Triomphe. Eight years later, however, the Prussians marched into Paris and recaptured the Quadriga. It was taken to Jagdschloss Grunewald for repair, then replaced on the Brandenburg Gate in June 1814, with one small alteration: The Prussian eagle in the center of Victory's oak wreath was replaced with an Iron Cross.

Few structures have witnessed as many of the vicissitudes of German history as the Brandenburg Gate. In 1871 it was the stage of the victory celebration after the war with France and the establishment of the kaiser Reich. In 1919 leftist revolutionaries and government troops had a shoot-out around its Doric columns. Battalions of brown-shirted Nazi troops marched through it on the night of January 31, 1933, in a torchlight parade hailing Hitler's appointment as Reich chancellor. In May 1945, like the rest of Berlin, the gate and monument were in ruins. Reconstruction was not completed until 1958. The gate became the symbol of Berlin's division when the Wall was built in 1961, and of the city's reunification when it was opened to pedestrian traffic in 1989. The subsequent celebrations did so much damage to the Quadriga that in the spring of 1990 the monument was removed for renovation and repair and the gate sheathed in scaffolding. The scaffolding came down, and the totally restored Quadriga went back up in time for the Brandenburg Gate's bicentennial celebration, a gala show with Mozart music and fireworks, August 6, 1991. The only sour note was that the Prussian eagle and Iron Cross were back in place on Victory's wreath in 1814 style, bringing protests from many in Germany who, not surprisingly, consider them symbols of Prussian militarism.

From Brandenburg Gate back to Friedrichstrasse, where the main sights of Unter den Linden begin, is a ten-minute walk. Stay on the north side of the boulevard for a while. The Neo-Baroque structure at number 8 is the **Deutsche Staatsbibliothek** (German State Library), housing a collection of 5.5 million books, manuscripts, musical scores, etchings, and maps. Just past the library, at number 6, is **Humboldt Universität**, which has often been referred to as the University of Berlin. Built in 1753 as a palace for Prince Henry, the brother of Frederick the Great, it was given to Wilhelm von Humboldt in 1809 when he founded the university. Twenty-seven Nobel Prize winners have been members of its faculty, and the philospher Hegel taught here. Statues of both Wilhelm and Alexander von Humboldt flank the elaborate wrought-iron gateway.

Directly across Unter den Linden, at number 11, is the **Alte Bibliothek** (Old Library), built between 1774 and 1788 by the Prussian architect Georg Friedrich Boumann according to plans made by Joseph Fischer von Erlach for the St. Michael wing of Vienna's Hofburg. Today, the building houses various university institutes.

A few paces beyond is the **Deutsche Staatsoper**, Berlin's main opera house, commissioned by Frederick the Great,

designed by his favorite architect, Georg von Knobelsdorff, and opened December 7, 1742, with a performance
of Carl Heinrich Graun's *Caesar and Cleopatra.* One of the
world's oldest opera houses and a gem of Neoclassical
design, it was thrice destroyed and rebuilt: first by a fire in
1843, then by an air raid in 1943, and finally by bombs and
artillery in 1945. The present reconstruction dates from
1955. Erich Kleiber was among its conductors and musical
directors, and Daniel Barenboim has been in that position
since the start of the 1992 season. For all its fame it is just
one of three opera houses in Berlin. Its competitors are
the **Komische Oper** (Comic Opera) on nearby Behrenstrasse and the **Deutsche Oper Berlin**, Bismarckstrasse 35,
which was the opera house of the city of Charlottenburg
and became the Berlin municipal opera after Charlottenburg's 1920 incorporation into Berlin as a borough.

St. Hedwigs-Kathedrale, the squat, domed structure
(modeled on the Pantheon) behind the opera house, is
the Roman Catholic cathedral of Berlin and one of the
few Catholic churches in this predominantly Protestant
city. Construction of it began in 1747. The cast of planners
and architects was stellar: Frederick the Great, Knobelsdorff, Johann Boumann, and the Frenchman Jean Legeay.
The Seven Years' War halted work, and the church, finally
completed in 1772, is named for Hedwig, the beatified
wife of Duke Henry of Silesia. It was destroyed by fire
during World War II and rebuilt in the early 1960s, with its
interior starkly simple and modern and the exterior
much as it used to be.

You might enjoy lunch, coffee and pastries, or even
dinner at the **Opernpalais**, a complex of restaurants and
cafés, Unter den Linden 5, in the former **Prinzessinen-
palais**. This was the Baroque residence of the daughters
of King Frederick William III before their marriages. On a
fair day you can sit on the terrace, which provides a
splendid view of Unter den Linden's historic buildings.

Next to the café, at number 3, is the **Kronprinzenpalais**, a mid–17th-century mansion that was enlarged in
1732 for Frederick the Great when he was the 20-year-
old crown prince and in open rebellion against his
tyrannical father, Frederick William I, known as the "Soldier King." As a teenager, for all his later impact on
world history, Frederick had no interest in government,
in war, or in being a future king. His preferences were
for art, literature, philosophy, and music, being a virtu-
oso flutist as well as a composer of chamber music. For

this he was despised by his father, an extraordinarily coarse man whose main achievement was to make the Prussian army into an instrument of war, or as some have phrased it, "Prussia into an army with a state." Frederick reciprocated: He hated his father. In 1730, then 18, repeatedly abused and humiliated, he planned to escape to England with his friend and lover, Lieutenant Hans Hermann von Katte. They were intercepted by the king's agents and both imprisoned on treason charges. Frederick was forced to watch Katte's beheading, but was ultimately himself released. In 1732, a year before his arranged marriage, he moved into the Kronprinzenpalais. It served as the official residence of Prussia's and Germany's crown princes to the end of the monarchy in 1918. Heavily damaged during the Battle of Berlin, it was finally rebuilt and reopened in 1969 for use as a government guest house. When Berlin takes on its role as the seat of government it will be the official residence of the German president and his staff.

On the other side of Unter den Linden, just east of the university, is the **Neue Wache** (New Guardhouse), at number 4. This is one of Karl Friedrich Schinkel's Neoclassical masterpieces, designed in the style of a Roman temple.

Schinkel, born 1781 in Neuruppin (see our Day Trips from Berlin chapter) was—in addition to being a painter and illustrator and a furniture, china, and stage-set designer—a master builder and architect. Starting around 1800 and until his death in 1841 he virtually changed the face of Berlin and Potsdam and left a legacy of hundreds of innovative, beautiful, and enduring structures all over Prussia and today's state of Brandenburg. As you explore the city, you will encounter his work in many places.

The Neue Wache, which Schinkel designed in 1816 as the royal guardhouse, became the Tomb of the Unknown Soldier, a memorial to the fallen of World War I, after the 1918 revolution that toppled the kaiser and set the stage for the Weimar Republic. The East German regime turned it into a Monument against Fascism and Militarism, which it will remain.

The **Zeughaus** (Armory), just past the Neue Wache at Unter den Linden 2, is the oldest public building on the avenue. It was completed in 1706 as an armory and gave a fairly clear indication of where Prussia was headed. This four-story structure is the largest and best-preserved example of Baroque architecture in all of Berlin. For nearly a century and a half, from 1730 to 1877, it was used to store captured war matériel. It was then converted into a military museum and a hall of fame celebrating victories by Brandenburg's and Prussia's armies. In 1952 the East German government turned it into the **Deutsches Historisches Museum** (German Historical Museum), a purpose it will serve for a number of years until a new German history museum has been built.

Right behind the Zeughaus is the **Palais am Festungsgraben** (Am Festungsgraben 1), a late-Rococo, early Neoclassical mansion, originally built for Frederick the Great's chamberlain and then used for over a century and a half as the official seat of the Prussian minister of finance. During GDR times it was the "House of German-Soviet Friendship," but it is now being used by Sotheby's, the auctioneers; Barclay's Bank; Salomon Brothers, the investment bankers; an avant-garde theater group that performs in the ornate ballroom; and an Italian restaurant, **Ristorante dell' Arte**, where you can have a very pleasant lunch.

THE MUSEUMSINSEL

The Museumsinsel (Museum Island) is a complex of museums and galleries at the east end of Unter den Linden. It was on this island that the town of Cölln was founded in the 1230s. (Berlin took shape on the east bank of the Spree.) It is also where Berlin's incomparable art collections, now shown in more than 50 museums, 28 of them under the administration of the Prussian Cultural Properties Foundation, had their start.

The origins of Berlin's hoard go back to the Brandenburg dukes and Prussian kings, who were lavish patrons and collectors of art. In the early 19th century the royal family sponsored the formation of museums open to the public. The first of these galleries, the Altes Museum, on the Museumsinsel, was built between 1824 and 1828, and opened in 1830. It is one of the world's oldest public art museums. Over the next 100 years the collections were expanded and four more museums were built on the island. Because the collections were state owned, their status remained unchanged during the Weimar Republic and the Nazi Reich.

During World War II the museums were closed and most of their treasures evacuated to safer places: air-raid bunkers in Berlin, warehouses in the suburbs, salt mines in what then became West Germany. Toward the war's end, as the Allied armies advanced through Germany, the Americans and British confiscated the hidden art they found in their occupation zones and sectors of Berlin, and the Russians did the same in the territory under their control.

More than 200 Old Master paintings, for example, were taken to the United States in 1945, exhibited around the country, and kept for many years. The Soviets shipped art to Moscow, where it remained until 1959. Many objects are still missing and presumed to be in Soviet and U.S. hands. By the time the wartime victors were willing to release the treasures, the Cold War was in full swing and both Germany and Berlin were divided. Prussia no longer existed as a legal entity, having been formally abolished in 1947 by the Four Power Allied Military Government. That raised the knotty question of who actually owned the Prussian treasures from Berlin's museums, and to whom they should be repatriated.

For the Russians the answer was easy: They turned over their share to the Communist East German government, which restored most of the buildings on Museumsinsel. In West Germany the matter was finally resolved in 1961 with the creation of the Stiftung Preussisches Kulturgut (Prussian Cultural Properties Foundation), jointly owned by the Bonn government, the states, and Berlin.

That is why Berlin today has two of each kind of museum—one in the west and one in the east. Considering the haste and disorder with which some of the objects were evacuated during the war, it is also understandable why you may find the head of a statue in one part of the city, its torso in the other, the frame of a painting in the east, and the picture itself in the west.

The two collections, now under one administrative hat, are moving toward gradual amalgamation, which will entail shifting entire divisions from one end of the city to the other and also building or completing construction of entirely new museum structures. The process will take many years—at least until 2000–and cost billions of marks. While the moves are going on many museums and divisions may be closed, their treasures in storage. (See the Museums section at the end of this narrative.)

Of the five original museums at the northern tip of the island—the Altes Museum, the Neues Museum, the Nationalgalerie, the Pergamon Museum, and the Bode Museum—all except the Neues Museum have been rebuilt since the war. Reconstruction of the **Neues Mu-**

seum, hampered by difficult soil and foundation conditions, is scheduled to begin in 1995; when completed it will house all of Berlin's Egyptian collections.

The **Altes Museum**, the oldest in the complex, was built between 1824 and 1828 by Schinkel in Greek-temple style. At present it is being used only for rotating exhibitions. It will be closed for renovations and repairs starting in 1994, and after reopening will house the two antiquities collections, one of which is presently in a wing of the Pergamon Museum, the other in a building across the street from Schloss Charlottenburg in western Berlin. East Berlin's *Kupferstichkabinett* (print collection), an assemblage of 200,000 drawings, etchings, engravings, woodcuts, watercolors, and other kinds of graphic art from the 15th century to the present, previously housed in the Altes Museum, is being moved to a new Kupferstichkabinett building in the Kulturforum area of Tiergarten borough, which is scheduled to open in June or July 1993. It will be joined there by the 400,000 pieces from the western Berlin Kupferstichkabinett in the Dahlem complex. For the first time since the war the 120 Botticelli drawings illustrating Dante's *Inferno* (40 of them previously in the Altes Museum, 80 in Dahlem) will again be under one roof.

The **Nationalgalerie**, built between 1866 and 1876 in the style of a Roman temple with Corinthian pillars, is set on a high base and approached by an imposing flight of stairs. Originally it was intended as a kind of festival hall for state receptions and royal ceremonies, but as the city's collection of 19th- and 20th-century art grew it took on its current role. It has a large collection of Neoclassical German sculptures, including works by Schadow, Rauch, and Tieck, and paintings from the 18th, 19th, and early 20th centuries, among them the most important works by Adolf von Menzel, Anselm Feuerbach, Hans von Marées, some fine Goyas, French and German Impressionists, and pictures by Lovis Corinth, Max Slevogt, Oskar Kokoschka, and Karl Schmidt-Rottluff. It will be closed for total renovation and repairs in December 1993, and after reopening will house the entire 19th-century collection, including the works in the Galerie der Romantik, presently in a wing of Schloss Charlottenburg.

The **Bode Museum**, named for Wilhelm von Bode, director of the Berlin museums from 1872 to 1929, is a triangular two-story structure built in Neo-Baroque style. In it are eastern Berlin's Egyptian museum, Museum of

Pre- and Early History, the Late-Ancient Early Christian-Byzantine collection, the numismatic collection, the sculpture collection, and the picture gallery. The Egyptian museum's mummies and its collection of 15,000 papyrus rolls are among the best in the world. The sculpture collection is strong on German, Dutch, and French works from the 12th through the 18th centuries. The Bode's **Gemäldegalerie** (Picture Gallery) features works by German, Flemish, and Dutch artists from the 15th through the 17th centuries, and English and French artists from the 18th. (The best examples of this period, however, are all in western Berlin's Dahlem complex.) The two picture galleries, with a combined lode of nearly 2,900 paintings, from the 13th through the 18th centuries, will move to a new building in Tiergarten's Kulturforum, expected to be ready in 1996.

The largest and newest of the museums is the **Pergamon Museum**, completed in 1930. It takes its name from the huge altar from the ancient city-state of Pergamum, in what is today western Turkey. The vast two-story structure also contains the Antiquities collection, the Islamic museum, the East Asian collection, the Folk Crafts museum, and the Western Asian museum. To see it all will take at least half a day. But most visitors make a beeline for the half-dozen main drawing cards on display: the Neo-Babylonian collections from the time of Nebuchadnezzar II, including the monumental Ishtar Gate, the Processional Way, and portions of Nebuchadnezzar's throne room; the gate of the Roman Market in Miletus; and the Pergamum Altar. The altar, dedicated to Zeus, ranks as one of the best-preserved examples of Hellenistic bas-relief. It was erected as part of a temple on Pergamum's Castle Hill between 180 and 160 B.C., when Pergamum was a powerful, independent city-state. Portions of it were found in 1871 during excavations at the city's Byzantine wall, and by 1880 almost the entire altar and temple had been dug up. The sections were brought to Berlin in 1902. It took curators until 1930 to reconstruct the altar. Enveloped in sandbags and concrete, it survived the World War II air raids. However, the Russians removed it to "protective custody" in Moscow in 1945 and did not return it until 1957. Two more years passed before the altar was reassembled and the museum reopened.

THE MARX-ENGELS-PLATZ AREA

This 1,200-by-600-foot square that extends south from the Altes Museum, called Marx-Engels-Platz since 1951, incorporates much of what used to be the Lustgarten, or Pleasure Garden. The northern section of the square, in front of the Altes Museum, has been renamed Lustgarten. Laid out in 1573 as an herb and vegetable garden for the ducal family, it was transformed into an ornamental garden in the 1640s, and then turned into a military parade ground by Frederick William I in 1715. Trees were planted here in the 1830s, a portion of the park was ceded to the Altes Museum, and in 1895, on the ground and foundations of an earlier church, work began on the Dom, Berlin's Protestant cathedral.

The **Dom** (cathedral) was completed in 1905. It is an example of ostentatious turn-of-the-century Neo-Renaissance style, with heavy overtones of Reich braggadocio. In many ways it resembles St. Peter's in Rome; in fact, it was considered the "Mother Church of Prussian Protestantism" and often called the "St. Peter's of the North." Many of the electors of Brandenburg and kings of Prussia are buried in its crypt.

Like everything else in the neighborhood, it was destroyed during the war, but East Germany's Lutheran Evangelical church authorities, with financial help from their brethren in West Germany, restored most of the exterior, and work on the interior is expected to be completed in 1994.

The square is flanked on the east by the ultramodern steel, marble, and glass **Palast der Republik**, which occupies the site of the former royal palace. Completed in 1976, the new palace became the home of the Volkskammer (People's Chamber), East Germany's parliament, and did double duty as a community center with cafés, restaurants, exhibition halls, and a central auditorium and theater. Shortly before Germany's and Berlin's reunification in October 1990 the entire building was closed for health and safety reasons because of fiber emissions from the spray asbestos used in its construction. Removing the asbestos will cost nearly DM 200 million and will take several years. After that, the building will be used either as a public library or as a convention center.

THE ALEXANDERPLATZ AREA

Once one of Berlin's busiest squares, Alexanderplatz today is the central shopping and commercial district of Berlin Mitte. It bears no resemblance to what it looked like before World War II.

To reach it, go east from the Dom, cross the Spree, and continue along Karl-Liebknecht-Strasse. The left side of the street is lined with shops, the right with a block-wide park whose main features are the Marienkirche, the Fernsehturm, and, on the right side along Rathausstrasse, the Rotes Rathaus. The church and town hall are virtually all that remain of the prewar district.

The **Marienkirche** (St. Mary's Church), at the foot of the TV tower, is one of Berlin's oldest parish churches. Its austere brick and stone exterior belies its rich decorations and furnishings. Begun in 1270 and first mentioned in town records in 1294, it was in the center of Berlin's Neumarkt (Newmarket Square). A fire devastated the church in 1380, but it was rebuilt. The tower was added in the 16th century.

Among the art treasures inside is the *Totentanz* (Dance of Death) mural—28 depictions of Death painted in 1485 during an epidemic of the plague in Berlin. The paintings were uncovered in the course of restoration work 130 years ago. There is also a beautifully crafted 15th-century bronze baptismal font, a Baroque pulpit from 1703, many elaborately carved stone epitaphs, and a fine Neo-Baroque organ, on which recitals are frequently given.

The **Fernsehturn** (TV tower), completed in 1969, presents a mind-boggling accumulation of statistics. If you include the antenna, the "Speared Onion" is 1,204 feet high. The concrete shaft is 825 feet high and 105 feet in diameter, and weighs 26,000 tons. The sphere weighs 4,800 tons. There is room for 200 people on the bulb's observation platform and for another 200 in the revolving **Tele-Café** above it, which makes one complete circle each hour. Two high-speed elevators, with altimeters for the amusement of passengers, take you up into the "onion," and on a clear day you'll have a view extending 25 miles. The observation platform and café are open daily from 9:00 A.M. to midnight. (Every second and fourth Tuesday they open at 1:00 P.M.) On weekends, holidays, and in the tourist season, crowds can be large here.

Named for its red-brick color, the Renaissance-revival

Rotes Rathaus was opened for its first town council session in 1865, replacing several older town halls in central Berlin, including the one that Cölln and Berlin built on the Lange Brücke when they formed their confederation in the 14th century. Since Berlin's enlargement in 1920 the Rotes Rathaus has served as both the borough and city town hall and is now again the seat of Berlin's mayor, senate, and city-state administration. The city-state legislature, still meeting in the Schöneberg Rathaus in western Berlin, will move to the Prussian Parliament building, now being reconstructed, after its completion in 1994.

THE NIKOLAIVIERTEL

The St. Nicholas quarter, tucked between the southwest façade of the Rathaus and the Spree river, is the oldest part of Berlin, the heart of the frontier settlement of the early 13th century. It certainly looks old, with its narrow cobblestone streets and gabled medieval-style houses. But don't let appearances fool you. It's all almost brand new, as artificial as a movie set. A scant decade ago the little four-block neighborhood was still a wasteland, with only the gutted shell of the **Nikolaikirche** (St. Nicholas Church), Berlin's oldest church, still standing. To prepare for the city's 750th anniversary, East German officialdom launched a crash program to create something "historic," with modern methods. All those "ancient" houses were built with prefab concrete slabs, then covered with cement and stucco, upon which craftsmen and artisans were free to indulge themselves with oriel windows, bartizans, Gothic arches, loggias, gargoyles, front stoops, helix ornaments—you name it.

The new "old" buildings added color and atmosphere to a city very short on both. Moreover, the reconstruction and restoration of the church of St. Nicholas is a remarkable achievement. It is now a division of the **Märkisches Museum** of Berlin history, showing Slavic and early German ceramics, terra-cottas from medieval burgher houses, architectural fragments of the Hohenzollern palace, Berlin's municipal seal from 1280, and some fine objects of ecclesiastical art.

Even more remarkable was the re-creation of the **Ephraim Palais**, at the corner of Poststrasse and Mühlendamm. This richly ornamented Baroque mansion was built in 1765 for Veitel Heine Ephraim, a Jewish banker and financial adviser to the royal court. In 1935, during the Nazi era, the elegant town house was razed, supposedly to provide space for the widening of the Mühlendamm. Somewhat mysteriously, hundreds of decorative elements of the façade and interior were stored in various depots and warehouses, most in what became West Berlin. When East German authorities decided to rebuild the mansion, West Berlin provided some 2,000 sections of the house. They were melded with new pieces of stone masonry and stuccowork crafted on the basis of old photographs and illustrations of the house. Today, the Ephraim Palais is also a division of the Märkisches Museum, showing 17th- through 19th-century portraits and busts by Berlin artists.

Directly across the street from the Ephraim Palais is one of the few buildings in the quarter that is virtually original, the **Knoblauchhaus** at Poststrasse 23. Built in 1760 for the Knoblauchs, a family of silk merchants, it is the only Neoclassical burgher house that survived the air raids relatively unscathed. In the late 19th century it was turned into a wine tavern, which it is again, and among the imbibers who immortalized themselves by scratching their names in tables were the playwrights Henrik Ibsen, August Strindberg, Gerhart Hauptmann, and the Norwegian Nobel Prize winner Björnstjerne Björnson. Ten rooms in the building are a division of the Märkisches Museum and document the history of the Knoblauch family through original furnishings and artifacts that will give you an idea of upperclass life in the 19th century. The pub on the ground floor, the **Historische Weinstube**, serves light meals and snacks to accompany the wines on the prodigious list, and is open daily from noon until 2:00 A.M.

When it was completed in 1987 the Nikolaiviertel had become East Berlin's favorite residential and shopping district. Most of the new-old buildings are actually apartment houses, and specialty stores line the narrow cobblestone streets. There are numerous cafés, restaurants, and taverns, such as **Zur Rippe**, at Poststrasse 17, which specializes in traditional Berlin dishes like pea soup and sauerbraten.

AROUND THE MÄRKISCHES UFER

The **Märkisches Ufer** is the left embankment of the Spree's left arm as it starts to encircle the island on which

Museumsinsel is located. The neighborhood, started as a bucolic suburb of Cölln in the 17th century, is less than a kilometer (about half a mile) south of the Nikolaiviertel, though to reach it you must first cross the river by way of the Mühlendamm bridge to the Fischerinsel, now a complex of faceless high-rise apartment buildings, and double back along Neue Rossstrasse.

This is one of the few areas of central Berlin that suffered comparatively little war damage. That fact, combined with decades of neglect during GDR times, gives it an appearance of what such neighborhoods once looked like: cobblestone streets, rows of turn-of-the-century apartment houses, Art-Nouveau–style subway stations, little shops. No doubt, if the GDR hadn't gone out of business the neighborhood would eventually have been subjected to Communist-style "urban renewal," with the loss or adulteration of much of its historic architecture. Now, instead, it is being preserved and gentrified. Art galleries are starting up on Wallstrasse and Inselstrasse. Smaller hotels have opened. Here and there you'll find a cozy café or pub.

The Märkisches Ufer itself is a lovely, cobblestoned riverside street lined with restored burgher mansions and town houses, some of which actually stood a couple of blocks away and were meticulously reconstructed along the embankment. One of these is the Ermeler-Haus.

The **Ermeler-Haus**, Märkisches Ufer 10–12, now an expensive restaurant, draws its name from Wilhelm Ferdinand Ermeler, a rich tobacco merchant who bought it in 1824 and whose family owned it until falling upon hard times during the runaway inflation of the 1920s. But its origins go back to the 18th century, when one Friedrich Damm, a wealthy purveyor of supplies to the Prussian army, had it built in Rococo style by the architect Friedrich Wilhelm Diterichs (around 1760). Neoclassical alterations were made on the façade shortly before Ermeler acquired it, but he left the gaudy interior decorations much as they are today in the restaurant.

A couple of elaborate façades up the street is the **Otto-Nagel-Haus** (Märkisches Ufer 16–18), two adjoining 18th-century mansions that now serve as a branch of the National Gallery, showing paintings and sculptures with a proletarian-revolutionary and anti-Nazi message. Nagel, who died in 1967 at age 73 and for whom the museum is named, was one of the leading painters of Socialist Realism. In 1924 he organized the first exhibition of German art in the Soviet Union. When Hitler came to power the Nazis forbade him to work professionally as an artist; most of his paintings, depicting blue-collar life, were confiscated and destroyed as "degenerate art," and Nagel himself was incarcerated in a concentration camp. After the war and the establishment of the GDR he became one of East Germany's and East Berlin's leading art officials, and during his six-year term as president of the Academy of the Arts laid down the rules for what could and could not be painted. But the museum is more than just a repository of Nagel's work, which includes some fine 1940s Berlin street scenes. The collection on the second floor features small sculptures by Käthe Kollwitz and Ernst Barlach, as well as paintings by Conrad Felixmüller, Hans Grundig, and Franz Radziwill.

A stroll up Wallstrasse, which parallels the Märkisches Ufer and the river, will lead you to the little **Köllnischer Park**, a tree-shaded oasis resembling a village square, with a statue of the Berlin satirist and caricaturist Heinrich Zille, and to the Märkisches Museum.

The **Märkisches Museum** (March of Brandenburg Museum), Am Köllnischen Park 5, was built between 1899 and 1908 to look like a Gothic-and-Renaissance brick church, and is an eclectic replica of various monasteries and cathedrals that dot the countryside surrounding Berlin. The massive, square, gabled tower is a copy of the keep in the bishop's castle at Wittstock, the step-gabled "nave" resembling that of St. Catherine's church in the city of Brandenburg. The figure of Roland (the sword-bearing knight who symbolizes municipal freedom in many northern German cities) that stands at the museum entrance is a cement imitation of the 14th-century original in front of the Brandenburg Rathaus.

From its official opening 85 years ago the museum's aim was to document and exhibit the social, economic, and cultural history of Berlin and the March. Eighty percent of the building and 20 percent of its objects were destroyed during the war, but reconstruction began almost immediately, and in July 1946 it became the first museum in Berlin to reopen. Meanwhile it has acquired various branches with specialized divisions around the eastern part of the city, such as the Nikolaikirche, the Ephraim Palais, and the Knoblauchhaus in the Nikolaiviertel, and others, not to mention a competitor in the western part of the city, the Berlin Museum in Kreuzberg. But as a kind of "attic" of Old

Berlin lore and artifacts the Märkisches itself is hard to beat.

Its 38 rooms are crammed with the city's legacy. Be sure to see the third-floor applied art section showing Berlin and Brandenburg porcelain, including some price-less pieces from KPM, the royal Prussian manufactory; faïences; mock-ruby glasses; and embossed cast-iron ob-jects. The sculptures division has some 300 objects, in-cluding works by Schadow, Tieck, Rauch, and Kollwitz. The graphics department of 42,000 drawings, sketches, engravings, and prints includes works by Max Beckmann, Otto Dix, and George Grosz and nearly 1,000 sketches and first prints by Heinrich Zille that are on permanent loan from his estate. There is also a delightful collection of mechanical musical instruments, and a division for Berlin theater history, with original manuscripts of E. T. A. Hoffmann's *The Sandman* and his opera *Undine,* and a collection of letters and correspondence by the literati of the Weimar Republic era, such as Thomas Mann, Rainer Maria Rilke, Roda Roda, Kurt Tucholsky, Frank Wedekind, and Arnold Zweig. To see it all you'd need a couple of days.

To get to the next destination, the Gendarmenmarkt, you can either hop the U-2 subway at the Märkisches Museum station and ride two stops to the Hausvogtei-Platz station, or walk back up Neue Rossstrasse and Breite Strasse toward Marx-Engels-Platz and there turn left onto Werderstrasse.

THE GENDARMENMARKT AREA

A walk west on Werderstrasse, the Nikolaiviertel's north-ern boundary, will take you back across the island on which Museumsinsel is located, the Spree canal, past the **Schinkelmuseum** in the Friedrichswerderische kirche, an exhibition of Neoclassical sculpture, and onto Franzö-sische Strasse. At the corner of Französische Strasse and Markgrafenstrasse (formerly Külzstrasse), turn south and go another block to the Gendarmenmarkt. All told, it should take you ten minutes.

The **Gendarmenmarkt** is named for the 18th-century gendarmes who had their barracks and stables here. The name was changed to Platz der Akademie in 1950 on the occasion of the 250th anniversary of the Academy of

Sciences, whose main building is on the plaza's eastern side, and was changed back to the original in 1992. One of Berlin's finest squares, it was the heart of the French quarter at the end of the 17th century, when Huguenot refugees accounted for one third of the city's population.

Two magnificent churches, the Französischer Dom (French Cathedral) and the Deutscher Dom (German Cathedral), mark its northern and southern boundaries. The Schauspielhaus, another of Karl-Friedrich Schinkel's masterpieces, fronts the square to the west.

The **Französischer Dom**, a majestic example of late Renaissance-early Baroque style, was designed by two emigré French architects, Louis Cayard and Abraham Quesnay, and built between 1701 and 1705. It is the main church of the Huguenot congregation. In the church tower you can visit the **Hugenottenmuseum**, a small collection of artifacts, applied art, and documents pertaining to the life of the French in Berlin at the turn of the 18th century. There is a carillon in the tower that chimes at noon, 3:00, and 7:00 P.M.

The **Deutscher Dom**, a virtual twin of the French cathedral (and not to be confused with the Protestant Dom at Marx-Engels-Platz), was built between 1701 and 1708 according to plans of an Italian architect, Giovanni Simonetti. External reconstruction work was not completed until early autumn 1990, and it will be 1994 or 1995 before the interior will be ready for use as an art gallery for rotating exhibitions.

The **Schauspielhaus**, a jewel of Greco-Roman-revival style, was one of Schinkel's most notable structures. From the time it opened in 1821 until its destruction during the war, it served first as the Royal Court, then as the Prussian state theater. Since its restoration was completed in 1987 it has been used as eastern Berlin's main concert hall.

The **Restaurant Französischer Hof**, Jägerstrasse (formerly Otto-Nuschke-Strasse) 56, offers French and international cuisine in an Art Nouveau ambience. For lunch or dinner it's a delightful spot from which to view the square's architecture.

From the Gendarmenmarkt it is one block west to Friedrichstrasse.

ON AND AROUND
FRIEDRICHSTRASSE

Whatever the prewar fame of central Berlin's showy boulevards—Unter den Linden and Kurfürstendamm—there was one other street, narrow but two miles long, that ranked almost with them in glitter and importance: **Friedrichstrasse**. It was the city's shopping, entertainment, dining, and nightlife center, lined and flanked by elegant stores and leading theaters but also—at its northern tip, where it ends at Oranienburger Tor—by tawdry bars and cheap dance halls.

Most of Friedrichstrasse, from Oranienburger Tor to its southern end at Mehringplatz in Kreuzberg, was reduced to heaps of rubble during World War II. The Cold War gave it the coup de grâce before there was hope of its rising again. The Wall intersected it at Checkpoint Charlie, with the result that the eleven-block section south of Unter den Linden turned into a street to nowhere, a gradually crumbling no-man's land. And in the American Sector of Berlin, the stretch between Mehringplatz and Checkpoint Charlie seemed like a road to the end of the Western world.

All this was starting to change in the waning years of the GDR as the Communist regime set out to rebuild its part of Friedrichstrasse into a kind of showcase of socialism, albeit with the help of Swedish, Finnish, Japanese, and a few West German architects and developers. First there was the functionally modern skyscraper of the International Trade Center, across the street from the equally functional Metropol Hotel, followed in 1987 by the luxurious Grand Hotel. There were to be office and apartment buildings, fancy stores, restaurants, and cafés. No less than the ruler of G.D.R. himself, Erich Honecker, announced the plans for the Friedrichstadt-Passagen, a seven-story shopping-mall complex with 1.2 million square feet of floor space. The reinforced concrete construction shell had just been topped out, with appropriate ceremony, when the Wall came down and the GDR started its hurried plunge into the dustbin of history.

Since then Friedrichstrasse has turned into a crazy-quilt of vast architectural ruins, new construction sites, and a battlefield of property claims. Across from and adjacent to gleaming marble-and-brass storefronts you

will find empty, weed-grown lots and gaping holes. Specu-
lative real estate prices have rocketed to DM 20,000 per
square meter, and more than 30 investment groups from
around the world are fighting each other for pieces of the
asphalt.

There are plans to rebuild the famous Wintergarten
Theater where La Belle Otero and Mata Hari once performed, and on nearby Wilhelmplatz another developer
intends to resurrect the Kaiserhof Hotel, which Kaiser
Wilhelm I claimed was more opulent and elegant than
the Imperial Palace, and where Hitler and Goebbels often
dined. Just north of where the Wall used to run and
Checkpoint Charlie stood, a DM 800 million "American
Business Center" with one million square feet of office,
apartment, and shopping space will line both sides of the
street. Construction is scheduled to start in the summer
of 1993; completion is expected in late 1994 or early
1995.

The carcass of Honecker's grandiosely planned Friedrichstadt-Passagen complex has been razed, because developers didn't like the architectural design. But an
almost identical building will rise from the huge hole in
the ground to accommodate a branch of the Paris department store Galeries Lafayette.

Because most of these projects are unlikely to be finished before the year 2000, Friedrichstrasse may not
seem like much of a tourist attraction. Yet the northern
end of the street and the neighborhoods leading off from
it are rewarding, especially to those interested in German
theater. The U-6 subway line runs along it, and there are
several stops, so that it need not all be walked.

Just as it was in the late 19th and early 20th century,
Friedrichstrasse north of the S-Bahn (elevated train) station is still *the* theater district of eastern Berlin. The
Metropol-Theater, initially built as an ice-skating arena in
1910 and then known as the Admiralspalast-Theater in the
1920s, is at Friedrichstrasse 101 and serves now, as it did
in the 1920s, as an operetta and musical theater. East
Berlin's most biting political-satirical cabaret, Die Distel
(The Thistle), is in the same building complex.

The **Berliner Ensemble Theater**, which Bertolt Brecht
and his wife Helene Weigel managed and directed after
returning to Berlin from exile in 1949, is just across the
Spree at Bertolt-Brecht-Platz. This was originally the
Theater am Schiffbauerdamm, built in the 1890s and as
famous for its revolving stage as the fact that it is where

Brecht premiered his *Three Penny Opera* in 1928. It was also the scene of the first German performance of *Mother Courage,* with Helene Weigel in the title role. A revolving stage like this, on which she seemed to be pulling her market wagon throughout the play, became a prerequisite for any theater putting on the play.

A walk three blocks north along Albrechtstrasse to Schumannstrasse will take you to the **Deutschestheater und Kammerspiele** (Schumannstrasse 13a). Built in 1850 and meticulously restored a decade ago, it was first an operetta and light-opera house in which Albert Lortzing, Jacques Offenbach, and Johann Strauss had the German premieres of some of their works, but then reached global fame as a drama theater in 1905 when Max Reinhardt became its general manager and permanent director, a position he held, with a four-year interruption, until forced to emigrate to the United States in 1933.

Back on Friedrichstrasse itself: the **Neue Friedrichstadtpalast** (no. 107), a Postmodern-style building housing a revue and musical theater, stands on the site of the early-20th-century theater, the Friedrichstadtpalast.

Friedrichstrasse ends at Oranienburger Tor, but continue for a block along Chausseestrasse to the **Brecht Haus**, Chausseestrasse 125, officially called the Brecht-Weigel Gedenkstätte. This is the apartment building into which Bertolt Brecht and Helene Weigel moved in 1953, four years after their return from exile; they lived and worked here until his death in 1956, hers in 1972. The rooms, with their library and furnishings, remain unchanged and can be visited on guided tours. There is a Brecht Archive in the building, a bookshop specializing in Brecht and theater literature, and down in the basement the **Brecht Keller** restaurant and café, which serves Viennese and Austrian food (Weigel was Austrian, Brecht a Bavarian).

Directly adjacent to the Brecht House, at Chausseestrasse 126, is the entrance to two of Berlin's most important cemeteries, the **Dorotheenstädtischer Friedhof** and the **Friedhof der Französischen Reformierten Gemeinde** (French Reform Congregation), both dating from the late 18th century. Among the famous who are buried there are Karl Friedrich Schinkel, who before his death in 1841 designed some of the earlier tombstones; the philosophers Johann Georg Fichte and Georg Wilhelm Hegel; the sculptors Christian Daniel Rauch and Johann Gottfried Schadow; the Shakespearian actor Ludwig Devrient;

the artist Daniel Chodowiecki; a grandson of Bach; and, from more recent times, Heinrich Mann, Brecht, Weigel, the composer Hans Eisler, collage artist John Heartfield, and writers Anna Seghers and Arnold Zweig.

Walking back to Friedrichstrasse and the Oranienburger Tor will take you to the northwestern tip of a triangular area known as the **Scheunenviertel**, bordered by Linienstrasse and Oranienburger Strasse, and widening as it reaches eastward to the area just beyond Alexanderplatz. This was the Jewish ghetto and the neighborhood of left-wing Jewish doctor-essayist-writer Alfred Döblin's 1929 novel *Alexanderplatz* (made into a television series and six-hour feature film by Rainer Werner Fassbinder in 1980). East European and Russian Jews, many of them fundamentalist and extreme Orthodox (in contrast to the largely assimilated German Jews) started moving into this predominantly working-class district in the early 20th century and began coming in droves as refugees, largely illegal, during World War I and the postrevolutionary upheavals in Russia. By the early 1920s it was one of Berlin's most densely populated areas, an almost self-enclosed district crowded with illegal immigrants living in slum conditions, rife with vice, crime, black marketeering, and leftist uprisings, and the target of anti-Semitic terror, incessant police raids, and, as the Nazis rose and came to power, of the most vicious persecution.

Berlin's Jewish population today is only 7,000—a fraction of its pre-Holocaust numbers—and only 1,000 live in eastern Berlin. Yet there is a revival of Jewish life in the Scheunenviertel, with a couple of small Orthodox synagogues as well as trendy cafés, such as the **Oren** and **Silberstein**, serving kosher and Israeli food on Oranienburger Strasse, both frequented more by "Wessies" (western Berliners) than by "Ossies" (eastern Berliners). Berlin's grandest temple, the **Neue Synagoge** (Oranienburger Strasse 28–30)—completed in Moorish style in 1866, burned and desecrated during the November 1938 Crystal Night pogrom, heavily damaged in a 1943 air raid—is being rebuilt, with the official reopening scheduled for 1995.

A walk eastward through the district, along Kraunsnickstrasse, then north along Grosse Hamburger Strasse, will take you to **Sophienstrasse**, a street of artisans' shops and galleries, whose Baroque and Neoclassical façades were restored as a showpiece under the Communist regime. The **Jewish Cemetery** on Grosse Hamburger Strasse, now a park, dates from the 17th century and is where the 18th-century philosopher Moses Mendelssohn is buried. The tombstones were all leveled and destroyed during the Third Reich, but there is a poignant bronze memorial near the park entrance calling attention to the Jewish old-age home that stood here, whose residents were transported to Theresienstadt concentration camp in 1943.

It is about a 15-minute walk from this part of the Scheunenviertel southeast to Alexanderplatz, where, unless you want to walk again along Unter den Linden west to the Brandenburg Gate, you can catch the number 100 bus, which will take you into the Tiergarten.

THE TIERGARTEN AREA

Tiergarten (literally, "animal garden") is the name of one of the largest of Berlin's nearly 50 public parks and of an entire borough. The eight-square-mile district is bordered by Berlin Mitte, the Brandenburg Gate and Potsdamer Platz on the east, and the Europa-Center and Bahnhof Zoo on the west.

Although one of the smallest and least populated of western Berlin's boroughs, it is one of the richest in culture and in historic sights. Within its southern half are the Tiergarten itself; the zoo; Germany's former parliament building, the Reichstag; Schloss Bellevue; the Siegessäule (Victory Column); the Soviet War Memorial; Kongresshalle, a gift to Berlin from the United States; the Hansaviertel district of modern architecture; the Kulturforum, including the Philharmonie, the Neue National-galerie, the Kunstgewerbemuseum (Museum of Applied Arts), the Bauhaus-Archiv, and the Staatsbibliothek (National Library); and the former German army headquarters building.

The Landwehr canal and the Spree river cross the borough. Its main thoroughfare, east to west, is the Strasse des 17. Juni.

To explore the Tiergarten you'll have to do quite a bit of walking, because public transit through it is not the best. The U-9 subway runs along the western periphery of the Tiergarten and stops at the Hansaplatz station, close to the Hansaviertel and Bellevue Palace. The S-3 elevated train runs to the Tiergarten station near the Strasse des 17. Juni and to the Bellevue station, close to Bellevue Palace. A number of bus lines provide access; the most

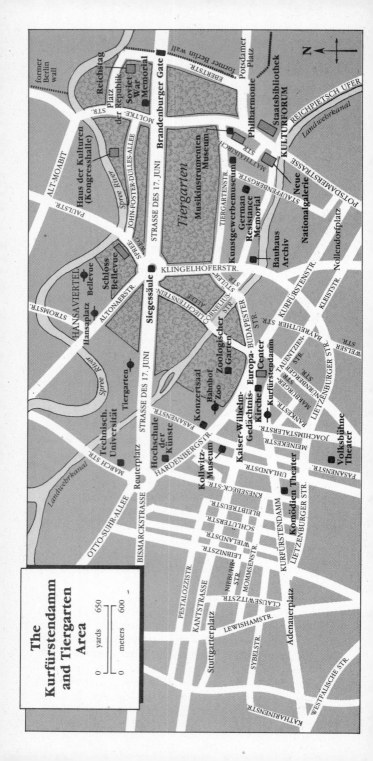

convenient is number 100, which you can board either on Unter den Linden going west or near the Kurfürsten-damm U-Bahn (subway) station going east. The shortest walk into the park and district is west from the Branden-burg Gate or northeast from the Europa-Center along Budapester Strasse, past the entrance to the zoo and the Inter-Continental Hotel.

The Tiergarten

The Tiergarten was originally a hunting preserve of the dukes and electors of Brandenburg. In 1717 it was trans-formed into a geometric, manicured Baroque-style park, which between 1833 and 1839 was relandscaped in the style of a freely growing, unstructured English garden by Prussia's greatest landscape architect, Peter Joseph Lenné. It soon became Berlin's favorite recreation area, dotted with numerous cafés and restaurants.

The park was also a residential area popular with the rich, famous, and powerful, who built their residences and embassies in its southern sector along Lichtenstein-allee, Corneliusstrasse, and Tiergartenstrasse.

The Tiergarten was one of the most embattled areas of the city during the final month of World War II, and was shelled into a virtual moonscape. What survived the fight-ing was ravaged in the first postwar winter by desperate citizens who felled the remaining trees for firewood and planted cabbage and potatoes on the open spaces. Most of the foreign embassies were in ruins, and their bricks and stones were carted off to rebuild the rest of the city. Only the Japanese embassy, recently turned into a German-Japanese cultural center, and the Italian embassy, built in the fascist "Duce Style," survived.

Use of the Tiergarten as a source for produce contin-ued throughout the Berlin blockade and airlift. It was not until the spring of 1949, when the division of Germany was already a certainty, that replanting and relandscaping of the park began. Today the Tiergarten is again full of trees, shrubs, lawns, flower beds, ponds, idyllic little lakes with rowboats, cafés, restaurants, and a staggering 25 km (15.5 miles) of paths and trails.

You might wish to get a bird's-eye view by climbing 285 steps to the observation platform of the **Siegessäule**, the victory column in the middle of the park on the traffic rotary called Der Grosse Stern (Big Star). The 224-foot-high Greco-Roman-style column, topped by a gilded bronze Winged Victory, was built between 1869 and 1873 to commemorate Prussia's triumphs in the wars against Denmark, Austria and Bavaria, and France. Originally it was erected in front of the Reichstag, where it stood until 1938. That year, Albert Speer, Hitler's architect and future minister of armaments, had the column moved to the Grosser Stern on Charlottenburger Chaussee (now the Strasse des 17. Juni).

When originally laid out in the late 17th century, **Strasse des 17. Juni** (the name commemorates the June 17, 1953, workers' uprising in East Berlin) was intended to be a coach road between the royal palace in Berlin Mitte and Schloss Charlottenburg, the new summer palace that Elector Frederick III (later King Frederick I) was building for his second wife, Sophie-Charlotte. In effect an extension of Unter den Linden, it cuts a 4-km (2.5-mile) swath through the Tiergarten in an east–west direction, then changes its name to Otto-Suhr-Allee and continues to Schloss Charlottenburg. It bisects the park, the northern half of which is the more rewarding.

Just north of the Brandenburg Gate, and easily visible from there, is the **Reichstag**, Germany's former parliament building. Whether it will become that again when, as is planned, the Bundestag (Germany's parliament) moves from Bonn to Berlin, supposedly by 1998, depends in part on what it will cost to restructure the interior to meet the needs of a modern legislature. Meanwhile it will be used for occasional celebratory sessions of the Bundestag. A colossus measuring more than 450 feet wide, the Reichstag was built in Neo-Renaissance and "Reich braggadocio" style between 1884 and 1894. Kaiser Wilhelm I personally laid the cornerstone. The Reichstag became the symbol of Hitler's destruction of democracy when the building went up in flames on February 27, 1933.

The Reichstag fire remains one of the unsolved mysteries of the Nazi era. Capitalizing on popular indignation over the blaze, Hitler persuaded aging President Paul von Hindenburg, a World War I hero, to suspend all constitutional liberties and hand him full emergency powers. Thousands of Nazi opponents all over Germany were arrested and put in prisons or hastily created concentration camps. Later that week Hitler and the Nazis handily won their first real majority in national elections. As the embers in the gutted Reichstag building stopped smoldering, democracy disappeared in Germany.

Marinus van der Lubbe, a young Dutchman captured near the fire, was tried with three alleged co-conspirators—Bulgarian agents of the Communist International (Comintern), among them Georgi Dimitrov, who became the first prime minister of Bulgaria after World War II. The Bulgarians were acquitted, but van der Lubbe was sentenced to death and guillotined. Throughout his trial, van der Lubbe insisted that he had acted alone and on his own initiative. The official Nazi version was that the fire had been a Communist plot. However, many suspected that van der Lubbe was a stooge and that the Nazis themselves had set the fire, using an underground passageway into the building to gain access, giving Hitler a pretext for obtaining dictatorial power.

Although the building was partly repaired and restored in the 1930s, Hitler's puppet Reichstag never convened in it again. The "world's highest-paid men's chorus," as the Third Reich's parliament was called, met in the nearby Kroll opera house to rubber-stamp the regime's decisions. The Reichstag was severely damaged during World War II air raids. When the last German defenders of Berlin turned it into a fortress in April 1945, the Soviet army bombarded it with an estimated one million artillery shells. After the Russians captured the city, one of their first acts was to raise the Soviet flag over the building.

For years the Reichstag stood as a ruin. Reconstruction began in 1954 and was completed, after many delays, in 1972. Since then, along with serving as an exhibition hall, the Reichstag has been the occasional site of caucuses of the Bundestag. What will happen to the building now remains to be seen; no final decision has been reached.

There is probably no other spot in Berlin as weighted with politics and history as this easternmost edge of the Tiergarten. During the 28 years that the Wall divided Berlin, the Reichstag, one corner of which was a couple of feet from the Wall itself, represented a kind of outpost against Communism. The Brandenburg Gate was East Berlin's bastion against capitalism. These two symbols of Berlin and of Germany, flying the similar but dissimilar black-red-gold flags of the two Germanys, seemed to be facing each other like two huge warships. Now people move freely between the two.

Just 200 yards west of the Brandenburg Gate, on the Strasse des 17. Juni, is the **Soviet War Memorial**. Constructed in 1946 of marble from the ruins of the Reich chancellery, it bears the bronze figure of a Soviet soldier with fixed bayonet, flanked by the two Red Army tanks that are supposed to be the first to have reached Berlin in 1945. The monument, once guarded by two Soviet troopers, is now under the surveillance of Berlin police.

A 20-minute walk northwest from the Soviet memorial will take you to the Spree river embankment, John-Foster-Dulles-Allee, and the Kongresshalle, now called the **Haus der Kulturen der Welt**. Designed by U.S. architect Hugh Stubbins for the 1957 Interbau architectural exposition, it was a gift of the U.S. Congress to the people of Berlin. Local wagsters dubbed it the "Pregnant Oyster" because of the shape of its roof. In 1980 the roof came crashing down, killing one person and injuring a dozen others. After repairs and reconstruction it reopened as the "House of World Cultures," an exhibition hall for rotating shows of non-European art and as a conference and concert center.

A 10-minute stroll along the Spree embankment or John-Foster-Dulles-Allee will take you to **Schloss Bellevue**, a Neoclassical château built in the 1780s for Prince Ferdinand, the younger brother of Frederick the Great. Although severely damaged during World War II, it was completely restored in 1959. Since then it has served as the Berlin residence of Germany's federal president. When the government moves to Berlin and the president moves into the Crown Prince's Palace on Unter den Linden, Bellevue will be turned into a guest house for visiting foreign dignitaries. It is not open to the public.

Another 10-minute walk northwestward leads to the **Hansaviertel**, a residential and shopping district that is a prime example of 1950s architecture and urban planning. In fact, the district's mixture of high-rise apartment houses, boxlike single-family dwellings, churches, and stores was built as an exhibit for the 1957 Interbau exposition. Leading modern architects including Egon Eiermann, Walter Gropius, Oscar Niemeyer, Alvar Aalto, and Arne Jacobsen are represented here.

The biggest attraction in the southern half of the Tiergarten is the **Zoologischer Garten**, the western Berlin zoo (there is also a zoo in eastern Berlin). Entry, however, is not from the Tiergarten itself: The main gate is at Hardenbergplatz, just east of Bahnhof Zoo, and the side gate, called the Elefantentor, is on Budapester Strasse, virtually across the street from the Europa-Center. There is no way to miss the Elefantentor—it resembles a Chinese temple portal with its columns supported by two stone elephants.

Berlin's Zoologischer Garten is not only the largest zoo in the world, with more than 11,000 animals representing 1,575 species, but one of the oldest, begun in 1841, when Prussia's King Frederick William IV consigned his collection of animals to the city. The **Aquarium**, just inside the Elephant Gate, houses another 10,000 animals: fish, amphibians, reptiles, and insects. It's best to get a combined ticket for both. Zoo and aquarium both open at 9:00 A.M. daily; the aquarium closes at 6:00 P.M., the zoo itself at dusk or 7:00 P.M., whichever is earlier.

The Kulturforum Complex

From the zoo it is a one-mile walk back east along Budapester Strasse, northeast along Stülerstrasse to Tiergartenstrasse, then east again to Berlin's **Kulturforum**. Virtually everything in this area was destroyed during the war. Now the Philharmonie, the Staatsbibliothek, the Neue Nationalgalerie, the Kunstgewerbemuseum, the Musikinstrumenten Museum, and the Kupferstichkabinett are clustered here.

The **Philharmonie**, on Kemperplatz, home of the Berlin Philharmonic Orchestra, is one of the city's most daring pieces of contemporary architecture. Designed by Bremen architect Hans Scharoun and completed in 1963, it is an asymmetrical structure with a tentlike roof. The hall itself, with seating for 2,000, is pentagonal in shape, and the stage is in the center, so that half the audience looks at the backs of the musicians. That arrangement caused a furor at first, but was soon accepted because of the excellent acoustics.

Scharoun also designed the nearby **Staatsbibliothek** (State Library), at Potsdamer Strasse 33, which houses the remnants of the Prussian National Library along with newer acquisitions—some 3.5 million books at present, with space for another 4.5 million, as well as a huge periodicals department.

The **Neue Nationalgalerie**, at Potsdamer Strasse 50, just across from the library, is a stunning steel-and-glass pavilionlike structure, the last major work of Ludwig Mies van der Rohe, completed in 1968, a year before his death. Until about 1994 or 1995 the art collection will consist of paintings, sculptures, and graphics of the late 19th and 20th centuries. Then the 19th-century works will move to the Nationalgalerie on Museumsinsel and the Neue Nationalgalerie will show only 20th-century art and special rotating exhibitions. Contemporary art will be shown in the **Hamburger Bahnhof**, on Invalidenstrasse, north of the Tiergarten. That oldest Berlin railway station (built in 1847) has been a museum and exhibition hall since 1906. It has been under reconstruction, renovation, and expansion for a number of years and is expected to open as a division of the Nationalgalerie in 1994. The new **Kupferstichkabinett**, entrance on Matthäikirchplatz, housing both the western and eastern print collections, will open in the summer of 1993.

The architecture of the **Kunstgewerbemuseum** (Museum of Applied Arts), at Matthäikirchstrasse 10, was thoroughly panned when it opened in 1987: People complained that it looked like a cross between a fortress and a power plant. Be that as it may, its collection is superb— with examples of every kind of European applied art from the Middle Ages through the 20th century.

At the **Musikinstrumenten Museum**, at Tiergartenstrasse 1, you will find a collection of musical instruments from around the world, made from the early 16th to the 19th century.

The Kulturforum also includes the **Bauhaus-Archiv**, Klingelhöferstrasse 14, a building completed in 1978 on the basis of designs by Walter Gropius. It exhibits architectural models, designs, drawings, paintings, furnishings, ceramics, textiles, and numerous other objects by the leading architects, artists, and designers of the Bauhaus school at Dessau, including Wassily Kandinsky, Paul Klee, Oskar Schlemmer, Lyonel Feininger, Walter Gropius, and Ludwig Mies van der Rohe.

A one-block walk back west on Tiergartenstrasse will take you to Stauffenbergstrasse, named for Claus Graf Schenck von Stauffenberg, the Wehrmacht colonel who planted a bomb in Hitler's headquarters on the Eastern Front on July 20, 1944. The street used to be called Bendlerstrasse and the grim, gray building at number 14 was the **German War Office**, where Stauffenberg and three of his co-conspirators were executed when the plot failed. A memorial to the four men stands in the courtyard where they were shot. On the third floor of the building, which now houses various municipal offices, the **Gedenkstätte Deutscher Widerstand** is devoted to a permanent exhibition of documents and artifacts dealing with the resistance movement.

ON AND AROUND THE KURFÜRSTENDAMM

The Kurfürstendamm—Ku'damm for short—runs south-west from the zoo and the southwestern tip of the Tiergarten. It is Berlin's grandest commercial avenue: two miles of conspicuous consumption, round-the-clock enter-tainment, pleasant strolling, and fascinating people-watching. In many ways it symbolizes what West Berlin was during the dark years of the Cold War when it was a *Frontstadt* (front-line city) and a showcase of capitalism. The boulevard is lined with the city's most expensive shops; dozens of restaurants, cafés, and nightspots; numer-ous cinemas and theaters; and some of Berlin's best hotels, including its most luxurious, the Bristol-Kempinski, at Kurfürstendamm 27.

The avenue's name derives from *Kurfürst,* meaning elector, and *Damm,* meaning causeway. Brandenburg's Elector Joachim II had it laid out in the 1540s as a car-riageway between the ducal palace in Berlin-Cölln and his hunting château in the Grunewald. Not until nearly 350 years later, in 1881, at the instigation of Prussia's and the German Reich's prime minister, Otto von Bismarck, was it turned into a 175-foot-wide parkway, divided along its length by a broad strip of grass and trees. Although far from what was then Berlin's governmental, financial, and cultural center, Berlin Mitte, it soon became one of the city's most sought-after strips of real estate, lined by upper-class apartment houses, fancy shops, theaters, ho-tels, and restaurants. There were so many cafés that Ameri-can novelist Thomas Wolfe described the Ku'damm as "the biggest coffeehouse in Europe."

One of the most famous cafés is the **Café Möhring** at Kurfürstendamm 213, a favorite hangout of politicians and intellectuals in the early 20th century. Among its habitués were Reich chancellor Theobald von Bethmann-Hollweg, Russian playwright Maxim Gorky, German writ-ers Gottfried Benn and Frank Wedekind, and the painter-poet Else Lasker-Schüler. The Ku'damm was and is to Berlin what the Champs-Elysées was and is to Paris.

Unfortunately, half of its *Jugendstil* (German Art Nou-veau) buildings were destroyed during World War II and replaced by nondescript steel-glass-concrete structures; so if you're looking for interesting turn-of-the-century architecture, the supply here is a bit skimpy. The rewards are greater on the streets that intersect the Ku'damm, especially Fasanenstrasse, Uhlandstrasse, Knesebeckstrasse, Bleibtreustrasse, Schlüterstrasse, and Wielandstrasse.

If you want a respite from the commerce and consumption, visit the **Käthe Kollwitz Museum** in a late-19th-century villa at Fasanenstrasse 24, just off the Ku'damm. It houses a collection of 100 lithographs, 70 drawings, and 15 bronze sculptures by this Berlin artist who in the late 19th and early 20th century depicted the misery of poverty, hunger, and war more movingly and hauntingly than any other of her generation.

In the adjacent villa at Fasanenstrasse 23, the **Wintergarten Cafe im Literaturhaus** is a delightfully calm and dignified refuge from the avenue, if you want a coffee break, light lunch, or even dinner. They serve breakfast until 1:00 P.M. and stay open until 1:00 A.M.

The best way to see the Ku'damm is to start at the Europa-Center, at its northeastern end, stroll up one side southwest to where it ends at the intersection of Katharinenstrasse and Westfälischestrasse, then cross over and amble back on the other side. You can explore the cross streets according to your mood and fancy. If the mileage seems a bit daunting, don't worry: The myriad eateries and watering places along the route provide ample opportunities to recharge your batteries. Moreover, the buses that run along it—numbers 109, 119, and 129—have a special "Ku'damm" rate of DM 1 one-way.

The only "must see" monument on the boulevard, a virtual landmark of west Berlin, is the **Kaiser-Wilhelm-Gedächtnis-Kirche**, or Kaiser Wilhelm Memorial Church, just west of the Europa-Center. Begun in 1891 to mark the 20th anniversary of the Second German Reich, and completed in 1895, it was originally a Neo-Romanesque structure. Wartime raids leveled all of the church except the western spire and portal, which have been preserved as a memorial to peace. (Berliners, who find humorously cynical names for nearly all their public edifices, call it the "Hollow Tooth.")

For more than a decade after the war there was endless debate about what to do with the ruin. In 1959 Egon Eiermann, one of Germany's leading modern architects, was commissioned to build a new church around it. His complex consists of a hexagonal flat-topped belfry tower, an octagonal central church building, a sacristy, and a chapel. The walls of all these are a concrete honeycomb with 20,000 spaces filled by glass mosaics created by the French glass artist Gabriel Loire of Chartres. The bronze crucifix in the main church building is based on a pencil sketch by the early 20th-century German sculptor Ernst Barlach.

AROUND THE CENTER

KREUZBERG

While the 19th-century entrepreneurs built their cathedral-like factories and ostentatious mansions, Berlin became Europe's largest tenement city. You can still get a vivid idea of what living conditions were like in the boroughs of Wedding, Neukölln, and especially Kreuzberg.

Southeast of Tiergarten, and bordered on the north and northeast by Berlin Mitte, Kreuzberg is just four square miles in area. However, with a population of 130,000 it is the borough that most closely resembles the original scene: run-down, neglected, and crowded. But it is also where Berlin's cultural, subcultural, and countercultural renaissance began in the 1970s. Here is where the *Neue Wilden* (New Wild) artists had, and in some cases still have, their studios. This is also the borough of punks and skinheads, of squatters and revolutionaries, of the old and impoverished, of people seeking alternative lifestyles, and of Turkish "guest workers," who account for one third of the district's population.

To be sure, opinions about Kreuzberg vary. Some call it a "zoo," others liken it to New York City's East Village, and some consider it "an intellectual prison." The common denominator here is variety. Some streets look as if they had been lifted right out of Istanbul. Art galleries, bookshops, second-hand emporiums, health-food stores, boutiques, hole-in-the-wall theaters, kebab stands, and countless dives line the shabby streets that run through canyons of 19th-century houses. From the Möckernbrücke subway stop in the west to the Schlesisches Tor station in the east, from the Kochstrasse stop at the northern periphery to the one at the Platz der Luftbrücke and Tempelhof airfield on

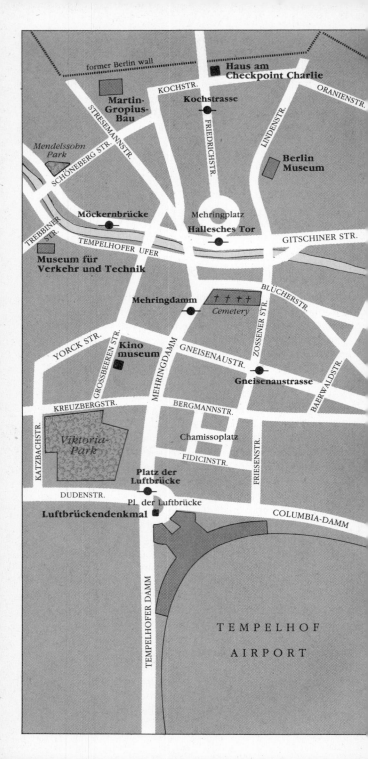

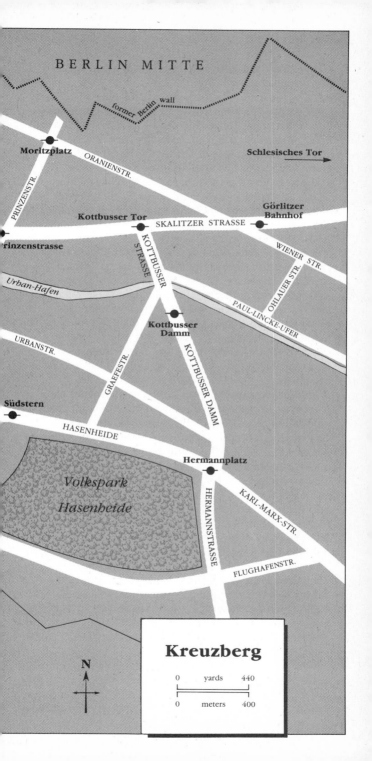

the southern edge, Kreuzberg is Berlin at its wildest and most confusing.

The easiest and fastest way to get into Kreuzberg is by subway. The U-1 goes west–east through the borough to the Schlesisches Tor station. The U-6 line runs through Kreuzberg on a north-south axis. The U-8 subway's northern stop in Kreuzberg is Moritzplatz; it then runs southeast through the borough and intersects with the U-1 at Kottbusser Tor. The U-7 line runs generally southeast.

The off-off art scene in Kreuzberg is represented by a string of commercial galleries on Oranienstrasse, and on and around Chamissoplatz, near the Platz der Luftbrücke. Two of the most interesting cafés in the district are **Café Jedermann**, Dieffenbachstrasse 18, near the Kottbusser Damm subway stop, open from 9:00 A.M. to 2:00 A.M., and the **Café**, Muskauer Strasse 23, open from 11:00 A.M. to 3:00 A.M., with breakfast served as late as 4:00 P.M. The latter is near the Gorlitzer Bahnhof subway stop. The borough is also going upmarket with a profusion of medium- to high-priced restaurants and bistros, not to mention skyrocketing rents. The most established spot, frequented by all the artists, is the **Exil**, at 44a Paul-Lincke-Ufer, near the Kottbusser Tor station.

Kreuzberg is also home to five unusual museums and to what in many respects is the city's most important postwar monument. The first of the museums, the **Berlinische Galerie**, located in the **Martin-Gropius-Bau**, Stresemannstrasse 110, at the northwest tip of the borough, is devoted entirely to late 19th- and early 20th-century Berlin visual arts: painting, sculpture, graphics, design, architecture, and applied art. Only the Brücke group of Expressionists is not included here, as the Expressionists have their own museum: the Brücke, near the Dahlem complex (see below). The collection of more than 12,000 art works, including 3,000 paintings, is especially strong on Dada art, Berlin Realism of the 1920s, and late 19th-century Impressionists who lived and worked in Berlin. The building itself is almost as interesting as the exhibits. It was designed in the early 1880s by Walter Gropius's uncle, Martin Gropius, also an architect, as Berlin's museum of applied art, and reconstructed after its near-total destruction during World War II.

Next to the Martin-Gropius-Bau, adjacent to a remnant of the Wall, is what at first appears to be just a vast empty lot. But it is a space of horror, the **Topographie des Terrors** (Topography of Terror), also known as the

Prince-Albrecht-Site. The Prinz-Albrecht Palais and other buildings that stood here, bounded by what was then Prinz-Albrecht-Strasse (now Niederkirchner Strasse), Wilhelmstrasse, and Anhalter Strasse, as well as the Gropius Bau, is where the offices of the Gestapo, SS, and Reich were located and where Heinrich Himmler, Reinhard Heydrich, and Ernst Kaltenbrunner had their headquarters. It was the Third Reich's most feared address, the focal point of Nazi terror. Subterranean bunkers, prison and interrogation cells, and other cellars of the mansions, hotel, and school for applied art that once stood here and became the SS and Gestapo buildings from 1933 to 1945 were excavated in the 1980s and have been integrated into a documentary exhibition that details the entire history of Nazi terror. All the texts are in several languages.

Just a few yards away from the northwestern corner of the site is the reconstruction of the Preussischer Landtag (Prussian Parliament Building), which, upon completion in 1994, will become the Berlin City-State Assembly Building.

Due north, between Potsdamer Platz and Toleranzstrasse (as Wilhelmstrasse is now called in eastern Berlin), municipal archaeologists have unearthed remnants of the **Führerbunker**, complete with furnishings and artifacts. It is part of the underground network in which Hitler, Goebbels, other Nazi bigwigs and their aides and guards had their headquarters during the last weeks of the war. Most of the labyrinth was blown up by the Soviets in 1945. The city has placed the bunkers under monument protection but sealed them off to public viewing.

Two blocks south of the Kochstrasse subway station (U-6 line) is the **Berlin Museum**, at Lindenstrasse 14. Its displays of art, furnishings, porcelain, handicrafts, and artifacts will tell you just about everything about Berlin and its history that you could possibly want to know. The building is a gem of Neoclassical architecture that was completed in 1735 and served as the city's supreme appellate court for two centuries. From 1816 to 1822 one of the justices was E. T. A. Hoffmann, the painter, composer, conductor, and author of fantasy tales, on whose life and stories the opera *Tales of Hoffmann* is based. The section on Jewish life in Berlin is now in the Martin-Gropius-Bau.

The museum is also a great spot for a snack or lunch. On its main floor is the **Alt-Berliner Weissbierstube**, a pub that serves seven varieties of Berlin Weisse, the local wheat beer, and an array of Berlin specialties such as *Soleier* (hard-boiled eggs pickled in salt brine), *Rollmops* (pickled herring), *Hackepeter* (sharply seasoned raw ground meat served on a piece of bread or crisp roll), and *Sülze* (jellied meat).

Near Kochstrasse station at Friedrichstrasse 44 on the corner of Kochstrasse and Friedrichstrasse, the **Haus am Checkpoint Charlie** contains an impressive collection of vehicles and equipment used by East Berlin refugees to flee over, tunnel under, ram through, and get around the Berlin Wall and the East-West German border. Among the exhibits are pint-size automobiles with hidden compartments for refugees, fake U.S. and Soviet army uniforms, and pieces of the balloon with which two East German couples and their four children flew over the border in 1979. The museum is a tribute to human wit, courage, and ingenuity. Though Checkpoint Charlie on Friedrichstrasse, the erstwhile crossing between the American and Soviet sectors, that is, from West to East Berlin, does not exist any more, many of its grim accoutrements—a watchtower, the turnpike, segments of the Wall, pillboxes, barbed wire—have been preserved and are under monuments protection. The museum acts as curator of these relics of the Cold War; they will be integrated into a new DM 800 million "American Business Center" on Friedrichstrasse, construction of which is expected to start in the summer of 1993, with completion planned for 1994.

Take the U-6 from Kochstrasse to Hallesches Tor and transfer there to the westbound U-1 to the Möckernbrücke stop near the **Museum für Verkehr und Technik** (Museum of Transport and Technology), at Trebbiner Strasse 9. Housed in Kreuzberg's 19th-century market hall, icehouse, and locomotive yard, the museum's exhibits include one of Otto Lilienthal's original gliders; Baron von Drais's wooden *Laufrad,* the world's first bicycle; and early steam locomotives.

A five-block walk eastward, along the Tempelhofer Ufer embankment of the Landwehrkanal, will take you to western Berlin's most important cemetery complex, the **Friedhöfe vor dem Halleschen Tor**, Zossener Strasse and the corner of Blücherstrasse. Inside the walls there are actually four graveyards belonging to four different church congregations, with the remains of some 80,000 dead, going back to the reign of Frederick the Great. The tombstones are the work of some of Berlin's greatest 18th- and

19th-century sculptors, and some of those buried here are
E. T. A. Hoffmann; the poet Adelbert von Chamisso; Arch-
duke Leopold Ferdinand of Austria; Frederick the Great's
chief architect, Georg Wenzeslaus von Knobelsdorff; and
the composer Felix Mendelssohn-Bartholdy, his parents,
and his sister Fanny.

Going south down Zossener Strasse, then west along
Bergmannstrasse, will take you through the gentrified
part of Kreuzberg and lead to **Viktoriapark**. The hill this
charming little park surrounds is topped by Schinkel's
Neo-Gothic, church-like monument commemorating the
Wars of Liberation (1813–1815) in which the alliance of
European powers—Russia, Prussia, Austria, and Britain—
defeated Napoléon. The iron cross atop the monument
gives Kreuzberg district its name: "Cross on the Mountain." The "mountain" is all of 220 feet high.

Just south of Viktoriapark, in what is actually the borough of Neukölln, is a monument that is the most sym-
bolic of the Cold War and of Berlin's division during
those years: the **Luftbrückendenkmal** (Airlift Monument)
on Platz der Luftbrücke at the entrance to Tempelhof
airfield. The 65-foot-high stone memorial, with three towering arches symbolizing the three air corridors that
linked West Berlin with the Western occupation zones of
Germany during the 1948–1949 blockade by the Soviets,
is a tribute not only to the airlift itself, which kept the city
alive, but also to the 31 American and 41 British service-
men who died in the line of duty during the operation.

The Soviet blockade of West Berlin had its roots in the
Western Allies' decision on June 20, 1948, to introduce the
deutsche mark of West Germany into the three western
sectors of Berlin. The Anglo-American answer to the blockade was "Operation Vittles," the airlift that lasted nearly 11
months until the U.S. and Soviet governments negotiated a
settlement of the dispute. During the operation American
transport planes alone made 277,728 flights to the city.
Tempelhof was the focal point of the operation.

Tempelhof airfield is virtually in the middle of the city,
and it has a history going back to the earliest days of
aviation. Indeed, it actually predates airplanes. In 1883
Arnold Böcklin, a Swiss landscape painter who was also
an inventor, experimented on the site with two motorless
biplanes, but he failed to get them off the ground because
of high winds. In 1908 the Wright brothers demonstrated
one of their planes here with a 19-minute flight. In 1923

Tempelhof, which takes its name from a 13th-century church built by the Knights Templar, became Berlin's central airport. In 1975 civil air traffic was routed to Tegel because the Tempelhof runways, surrounded by apartment houses, shops, office buildings, a public park, and even a sports stadium, could not be extended to accommodate wide-bodied jetliners. For the next 15 years it was used exclusively by the U.S. Air Force. Since early 1991 the airport has been used again for commercial flights, all of them regional and feeder lines.

SCHÖNEBERG

This borough, just west of Kreuzberg and Tempelhof and south of Tiergarten, was the "capital" district of West Berlin. Once a rich farming area, it became an independent city in 1898 and had a population of well over 200,000 when it was incorporated into Berlin in 1920.

Rathaus Schöneberg (also the name of a subway station on the U-4 and U-7 lines, which intersect here), the borough's city hall, is a massive structure that could easily be mistaken for a factory. It was the seat of West Berlin's city-state government from December 1948 until Berlin became one again. The mayor and his cabinet have already moved to the Rotes Rathaus near Alexanderplatz. The city-state parliament will continue to meet in Schöneberg, which also serves as the borough city hall, until the Prussian Parliament Building near the Martin-Gropius-Bau is completed.

In the building's 230-foot clock tower is the Liberty Bell, a replica of the bell at Independence Hall in Philadelphia. It is a gift of the American people to the people of Berlin, and the signatures of 17 million Americans who contributed money for it during the 1948–1949 Crusade for Freedom are preserved in a book in the tower. The ten-ton bell is rung every day at noon and on special occasions.

It was from the tower balcony, facing the square, that President John F. Kennedy delivered his memorable June 26, 1963, speech, in which he said: "All free men, wherever they may live, are citizens of Berlin, and, therefore, as a free man, I take pride in the words '*Ich bin ein Berliner.*' " Berliners have revered him ever since.

PRENZLAUER BERG

With a population of around 150,000 living in an area of 10.8 square km (about 4.2 square miles), this borough just northeast of Berlin Mitte is the most densely populateed in eastern Berlin. It is a consequence of the city's mid– to late–19th-century industrialization. As late as 1802 the whole district had only 100 inhabitants— farmers who tried to eke out a meager living by tilling the loamy soil.

Architecturally, Prenzlauer Berg resembles Kreuzberg: straight streets with rectangular blocks, lined by row upon row of five-story tenement houses, more of which survived wartime bombing than in any other borough, but are crumbling from decades of neglect. And in spirit Prenzlauer Berg also has much in common with Kreuzberg: Since the 1960s it has become a kind of "Berlin Montmartre," a center of artists, intellectuals, young dropouts from the ideological strictures and regimentation of Communism and of the "peace movement," the cradle of dissent and opposition that toppled the GDR regime in the peaceful revolution of November 1989. Three years after those events Prenzlauer Berg is still somewhat of a hotbed of opposition from those who feel steamrollered by the market economy and consumerism. Many are the "We Are the People" graffiti slogans on walls on which the "Are" has been crossed out and replaced with "Were." But at the same time the neighborhood is also becoming trendy, with an increase of boutiques, chic restaurants, and cafés, and "Wessies" buying up real estate.

The fastest and most comfortable way to get here from Berlin Mitte is on the U-2 subway from either the Stadtmitte station on Friedrichstrasse or the Alexanderplatz station, getting off at the Senefelderplatz stop. It's about a 15-minute ride and you will be right on **Schönhauser Allee**, the borough's main shopping street and also its most attractive boulevard. It is shaded by linden and chestnut trees, first planted in the 1740s when the avenue was laid out as the coach road to Schloss Niederschönhausen (in the northern borough of Pankow; see below), the Baroque château that Frederick the Great had assigned as a residence to the wife his tyrannical father forced him to marry.

Just north of the subway stop, in the triangle between

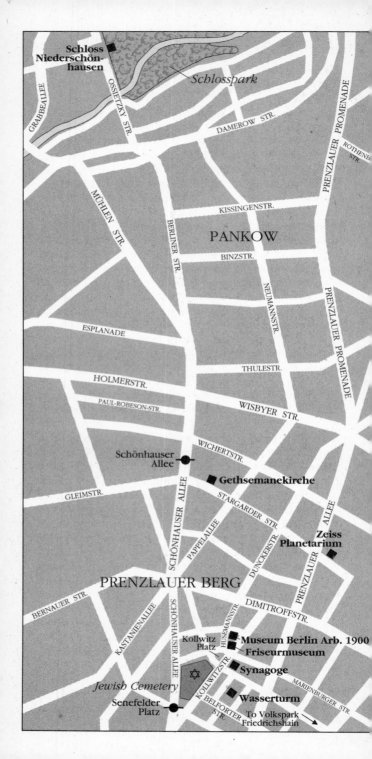

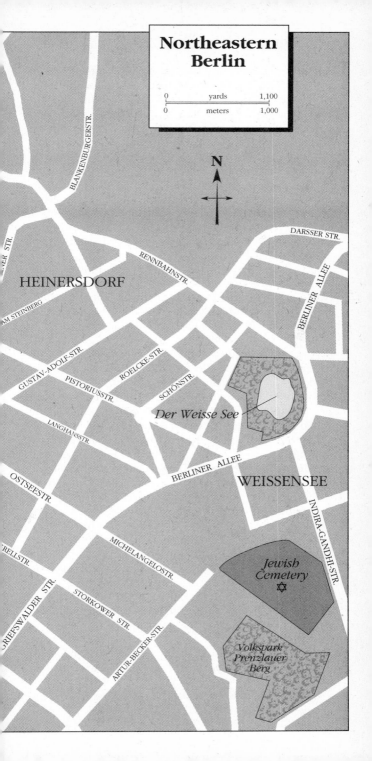

Schönhauser Allee, Kollwitzstrasse, and Wörther Strasse, is Prenzlauer Berg's **Jüdischer Friedhof** (Jewish Cemetery), with the graves and tombstones of prominent 19th- and 20th-century politicians, businessmen, artists, and scientists. Among them are the composer Giacomo Meyerbeer, the Impressionist painter Max Liebermann, and Gerson von Bleichröder, the Berlin banker who served as Bismarck's financial adviser and masterminded the financing that made possible Prussia's ascendency in the 1860s and the creation of the German Reich. There is also a bronze tablet in the cemetery commemorating a group of anti-Nazi resistance fighters who hid out here, were discovered by the SS, and then were hanged from the trees in the graveyard.

Just east of the cemetery, on Belforter Strasse, is the **Prenzlauer Wasserturm** (water tower), the district's landmark and one of the technological wonders of the mid-19th century. It was built in the 1850s in an eclectic Neo-Roman style and was the first of its kind in Berlin.

A brief stroll from Belforter Strasse's intersection with Kollwitzstrasse leads to the **Käthe-Kollwitz-Haus**, at Kollwitzstrasse 25, where the artist Käthe Kollwitz lived and worked for more than 50 years until 1943, two years before her death. Born in 1867 in Königsberg (now Russian Kaliningrad), East Prussia, as Käthe Schmidt, the daughter of a Protestant pastor, she studied art in Munich and Berlin. Shortly after their marriage in 1890 her physician husband, Karl Kollwitz, set up a general practice in this house in Prenzlauer Berg, treating the borough's poor. Käthe started to work as a graphic artist and sculptor, inspired by patients of her husband's. She first gained recognition with two cycles of etchings, *The Weavers' Uprising* (1894–1898) and *The Peasants' War* (1902–1904), in which the influences of Honoré Daumier, Edvard Munch, and Vincent van Gogh are apparent. From 1914 to 1932, among many other projects, she worked on her *Monument to the Dead,* a war memorial that was also a tomb for her son, Peter, killed in 1914 at the start of World War I. Though the house is not open to the public, there is a limestone copy of her sculpture *The Mother* in front of the house.

Just a few steps north of the house is Kollwitzplatz with the **Käthe Kollwitz Denkmal** (memorial), based on one of her self-portraits.

A block east of Kollwitzplatz, at Ryekestrasse 53, is the

only large Berlin **synagogue** that was not destroyed during the Crystal Night or the war. Built in 1904 in an eclectic Moorish-Art Nouveau style, it is used regularly for services.

Husemannstrasse, which starts at Kollwitzplatz and runs north for two blocks, was the last attempt by the East German authorities to preserve and restore some of East Berlin's architectural heritage. Beginning with the turn-of-the-century–style street signs and lampposts, and culminating in replica early-20th–century pubs and taverns, it looks a bit like a movie set—if you close your eyes to those tenement façades of crumbling houses whose ownership is in dispute. The **Restauration 1900**, a corner pub at Husemannstrasse 1, is a good place to stop, have a beer, wine, or coffee, and contemplate it all. They also serve light snacks and good steaks, and from the sidewalk tables in summertime you have a good view of the street and of Kollwitzplatz.

Two museums along the street are worth visiting: the **Friseurmuseum**, Husemannstrasse 8, which is devoted to the history of barbering, hairdressing, and wig-making, and the **Museum Berliner Arbeiterleben um 1900**, Husemannstrasse 12, a division of the Märkisches Museum, whose furnishings, artifacts, and documents reflect the life of a typical Berlin working-class family around the turn of the century.

A long walk up Schönhauser Allee or a two-stop ride farther north on the U-2 line from Senefelder Platz to the Schönhauser Allee station will take you to within a block of **Gethsemanekirche**, Stargarder Strasse 77. The church, an 1890s replica of a 13th-century March of Brandenburg Gothic brick basilica, is interesting not so much for its architecture as for the role it played in the 1989 East German revolution. It was here that the dissenters of the East German peace and ecology movement, hounded and harassed by the Stasi, held their meetings in the 1980s.

If astronomy is your interest, head southeast six blocks along Stargarder Strasse to the **Zeiss Planetarium**, entrance at Prenzlauer Allee 80. Built in 1987, it ranks as one of the most technologically advanced in Europe. There is seating for 290 during the projection demonstrations, which take place regularly between 2:00 and 8:00 P.M. daily except Mondays and Tuesdays.

From here the numbers 20 and 72 streetcars will take you back close to Alexanderplatz, or you can hop the elevated S-Bahn, adjacent to the planetarium, for one stop back to the Schönhauser Allee station, and there transfer to the U-2 subway for the ride back to Alexanderplatz or Friedrichstrasse.

AWAY FROM THE CENTER

THE DAHLEM MUSEUMS

From the inner city, it is a 20- to 30-minute subway ride southwest on the U-2 line to the Dahlem-Dorf station, the heart of the great museum area in the leafy residential district of **Dahlem**.

West Berliners love to confront visitors with a riddle: Who are the city's two most famous residents? The answer: Queen Nefertiti and The Man with the Golden Helmet. The bust of Nefertiti is the centerpiece of western Berlin's Ägyptisches Museum (Egyptian Museum), near Schloss Charlottenburg. Although its authenticity is now doubted, *The Man with the Golden Helmet* is by far the most popular of the "Rembrandts" in western Berlin's Gemäldegalerie (Picture Gallery), one of the main attractions in the Dahlem museums complex.

The Dahlem complex, one block south of the Dahlem-Dorf subway station, with entrances at Arnimallee 23 and Lansstrasse 8, includes the Skulpturengalerie (Sculpture Gallery), the Gemäldegalerie, the Museum für Völkerkunde (Ethnographic Museum), the **Museum für Indische Kunst** (Museum of Indian Art), the **Museum für Islamische Kunst** (Museum of Islamic Art), and the **Museum für Ostasiatische Kunst** (Museum of East Asian Art). But with the amalgamation of the western and eastern collections in the coming years, some of this will change.

The **Skulpturengalerie**, covering two floors in the Lansstrasse building, is full of spectacular pieces dating from the Early Christian-Byzantine period through the 19th century. Among the greatest treasures are wood carvings by Tilman Riemenschneider and other German masters and works by such Italian sculptors as Giovanni Pisano, Donatello, and Bernini.

The **Gemäldegalerie**, located on two floors and in three wings of the Arnimallee building, is a treasure trove of European painting of all schools from the Middle Ages through the Neoclassical period. The German masters section includes paintings by Albrecht Altdorfer, Lucas Cranach the Elder, Hans Holbein the Younger, and Albrecht Dürer. In the Dutch and Flemish division are 25 Rembrandts and 19 Rubenses. In addition there are major works by Hieronymus Bosch, the Brueghels, Van Dyck, Van Eyck, van der Goes, Hals, Memling, Vermeer, and van der Weyden. The Italian section includes a dozen paintings by the Bellinis—father Jacopo and sons Giovanni and Gentile—seven Botticellis, and Giottos, Tintorettos, Titians, and Raphaels. The Spanish school is represented by, among others, El Greco's haunting *Mater Dolorosa* and Velázquez's *Three Musicians*. The paintings, together with those on the Museumsinsel, will move to a new building on the Kulturforum site in 1996.

The **Museum für Völkerkunde**, whose entrance is on Lansstrasse, is one of the most important in Europe. Only a small portion of the collection is on display; it is divided into five sections: pre-Columbian American, African, Southeast Asian, East Asian, and Pacific South Seas art.

If, after you have visited these four museums, your legs, back, and eyes are still working, proceed to the museums of Indian, Islamic, and East Asian art.

About a half hour's walk from the Dahlem complex, at Bussardsteig 9, near the edge of Grunewald forest (see Green Berlin and the Lakes, below), you will find the **Brücke Museum**, named for *Die Brücke* (The Bridge), a group of early–20th-century German Expressionists. Virtually all of these artists, who collaborated between 1905 and 1913, are represented: Erich Heckel, Ernst Ludwig Kirchner, Otto Mueller, Emil Nolde, Max Pechstein, and, not least, Karl Schmidt-Rottluff, whose own collection of paintings, a gift to the city of Berlin, forms the foundation of this collection.

SCHLOSS CHARLOTTENBURG
AND THE MUSEUMS

It was not until the late 17th century that the electors of Brandenburg began to build grand residences, but once started they freely indulged in ostentatious pomp and

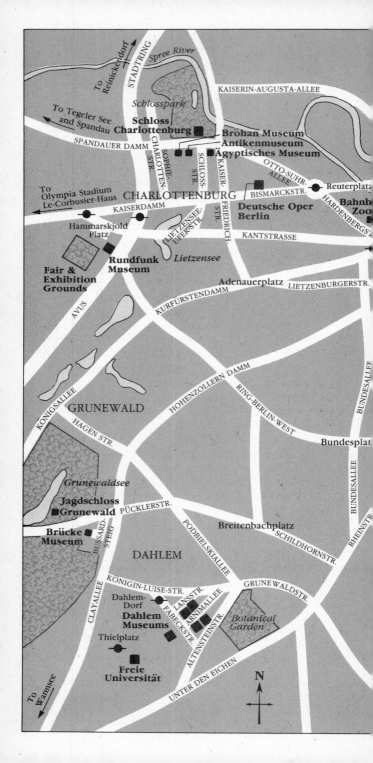

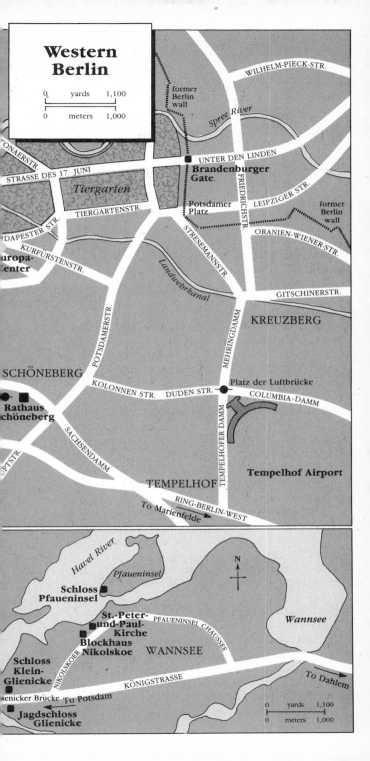

Western Berlin

0 yards 1,100
0 meters 1,000

STRASSE DES 17. JUNI

ÖNAERSTR.

Tiergarten

TIERGARTENSTR.

former Berlin wall

Spree River

UNTER DEN LINDEN

Brandenburger Gate

FRIEDRICHSTR.

WILHELM-PIECK-STR.

LEIPZIGER STR.

former Berlin wall

Potsdamer Platz

STRESEMANNSTR.

ORANIEN-WIENER-STR.

DAPESTER STR.

KURFÜRSTENSTR.

uropa-enter

Landwehrkanal

GITSCHINERSTR.

KREUZBERG

SCHÖNEBERG

POTSDAMERSTR.

KOLONNEN STR. DUDEN STR.

MEHRINGDAMM

Platz der Luftbrücke

COLUMBIA-DAMM

Rathaus chöneberg

SACHSENDAMM

TEMPELHOFER DAMM

Tempelhof Airport

PTSTR.

TEMPELHOF

RING-BERLIN-WEST

To Marienfelde

Havel River

Pfaueninsel

N

Schloss Pfaueninsel

St.-Peter-und-Paul-Kirche

PFAUENINSEL CHAUSSEE

Wannsee

Blockhaus Nikolskoe

NIKOLSKOER

WANNSEE

Schloss Klein-Glienicke

KÖNIGSTRASSE

To Dahlem

ienicker Brücke   To Potsdam

Jagdschloss Glienicke

0 yards 1,100
0 meters 1,000

conspicuous Baroque consumption. Most of their lavish digs were damaged during World War II; nearly all have been restored. The most dazzling palace is **Schloss Charlottenburg** in Charlottenburg borough, a half-hour walk north from Kurfürstendamm and its intersection with Adenauerplatz, or about ten minutes on foot northwest along Otto-Suhr-Allee from the Richard-Wagner-Platz subway station on the U-7 line.

The building was commissioned in 1695 by Elector Frederick III (King Frederick I) as a summer palace for his second wife, Sophie-Charlotte. Many wings were added in the 18th century, along with a manicured park, little pavilions, and various museums. Even a cursory visit takes half a day. The ornate historic apartments can be seen only on guided one-hour tours, starting about every 20 minutes; the last one begins at 4:00 P.M.

During the 220 years that the Hohenzollern clan used the palace, the interior decor and furnishings underwent many changes to suit changing tastes. But, as frugal Prussians, they never threw anything away. Instead, each generation stored its forebears' household goods in Berlin's environs. There, the furniture survived the 1943 air raid that almost completely destroyed Schloss Charlottenburg, and restorers could re-create the palace's interior as it had been during Sophie-Charlotte's time.

The queen was addicted to Oriental decor, which was then quite the rage. Therefore, as you are shepherded through the more than 70 rooms and hallways open to the public you'll see nearly a dozen decorated in East Asian motifs and one chamber whose walls are entirely covered with Oriental porcelain.

Charlottenburg began rather modestly. The original central building, crowned by an elegant 165-foot copper dome upon which stands a gilded figure of Fortuna, was a summer "cottage" by royal standards, with only a dozen rooms. But Sophie-Charlotte was a lavish hostess who gave brilliant parties and balls, for which she needed more space. Extension of the central building and the addition of the Orangerie began in 1701. Another wing was built between 1740 and 1746 by Frederick the Great's favorite architect, Georg Wenzeslaus von Knobelsdorff, and in 1790 a court summer theater was added. Today the façade of the entire palace complex, only two stories high, is a mind-boggling 1,666 feet long.

The immense bronze equestrian statue in the center of the courtyard is of Duke Frederick William of Brandenburg, the Great Elector. Unveiled in 1703, it ranks as one of the finest examples of Baroque bronze sculpture in Europe. Its present location, however, is strictly postwar. Originally it stood on the Lange Brücke in Berlin Mitte, and later in front of the royal palace that is no more. In 1943, just before the first devastating air raid on the city, the statue was removed by river barge to safety. Unfortunately, the barge sank in Tegel harbor. The statue was recovered in 1949 and erected in front of Schloss Charlottenburg in 1952.

When the **Schlosspark** was laid out in 1697 it was in the neatly manicured French Baroque style. In the 19th-century Lenné, the landscape architect of the Tiergarten, turned it into a less formal English-style garden. Part of it was restored to its original Baroque form after World War II. The two principal buildings in the park are the **Schinkel Pavilion**, in the style of a Neapolitan villa, and the **Belvedere**, completed in 1788, a late Rococo-style teahouse. The Schinkel Pavilion contains fine examples of late–18th-century furnishings. The Belvedere has a collection of 18th- and 19th-century china from Berlin's state-owned Royal Porcelain Manufactory.

The Charlottenburg Museums

Four museums that are part of the Prussian state collections are at Schloss Charlottenburg, two in the palace itself and two across the street in the former royal armory and the palace guards' barracks. Before visiting them you might want to fortify yourself with a light lunch in pseudo-royal surroundings at the **Kleine Orangerie**, Spandauer Damm 20, a moderately priced restaurant adjacent to the western Orangerie wing of the palace. Game dishes are among the specialties.

The **Galerie der Romantik**, a division of Berlin's Nationalgalerie, is in the long Knobelsdorff wing of the palace and contains a collection of fine examples of German Romantic painting. Caspar-David Friedrich (1774–1840) and Carl Blechen (1798–1840) are each represented by 23 pictures. Though best known as an architect, Karl-Friedrich Schinkel (1781–1841) was also a talented illustrator and painter; more than a dozen of his landscapes and pictures of imaginary Gothic cathedrals are on exhibit.

At the opposite end of the long palace façade, in the former court theater, is the **Museum für Vor- und Früh-**

geschichte (Pre- and Early History), displaying a collection of artifacts and art from the Paleolithic, Mesolithic, and Neolithic cultures of Asia Minor and of the Bronze and Iron ages in Brandenburg.

The **Ägyptisches Museum**, at Schloss Strasse 70, across the street from the palace, is the home of Queen Nefertiti, whose polychrome limestone bust draws an estimated half-million visitors a year. This 3,350-year-old sculpture alone is worth the visit, because Nefertiti, wife of Akhenaton, was surely one of the greatest beauties of all time, and also because the bust is one of the finest pieces of art extant from the Amarna period. But there is much else to see in the museum, including an ebony bust of Queen Tiy, a green stone head of a priest, several mummies, and artifacts of daily life from 2,000 to 5,000 years ago.

The **Antikenmuseum**, at Schloss Strasse 1, directly across the Schloss Strasse parkway from the Ägyptisches Museum, is a dazzling repository of art from the Minoan and Mycenaean periods through early Byzantine times, including Greek vases and amphoras, bronzes, jewelry, worked gold, and ivory carvings.

You can buy replicas of some of the best pieces in west Berlin's state museums at the **Gipsformerei** on Sophie-Charlotten-Strasse 17–18, just past the west end of the palace grounds. This workshop, run by the museums, has more than 7,000 molds of the most famous sculptures and bas-reliefs in Berlin (and elsewhere), from which copies in plaster, synthetic stone or resin, and bronze can be cast. It keeps some of the more popular items in stock. There's a catalogue, and the Gipsformerei will also ship. Small stock items start at around DM 40. A copy of the head of Nefertiti will cost about DM 1,500. Open Monday through Friday, 9:00 A.M. to 4:00 P.M., Wednesdays to 6:00 P.M.

Fans of Art Nouveau and Art Deco ought to take a look at the **Bröhan Museum**, Schloss Strasse 1a, adjacent to the Antikenmuseum. This is a stunning collection of paintings, furniture, china and glassware, and jewelry from the turn of the century to the 1930s that was amassed by Berlin businessman Karl H. Bröhan, and that he donated to the city in 1984.

There is more to Charlottenburg borough than the palace or the museums, and among the other sights to see, about four miles west, are the Olympiastadion (Olympic Stadium) and the Le Corbusier House. The best way to get there is to take the U-7 subway from Richard

Wagner Platz back one stop to Bismarckstrasse and there board the U-1 going west, getting off at the Olympiastadion stop.

The **Olympiastadion**, built for the 1936 games in dehumanizing Third Reich style, was the site of the first politicized Olympics. It became infamous when Hitler stormed out of the grandstand when Jesse Owens, the African-American track star, won the first of his four gold medals and thus disproved the Nazi claims of Nordic and Aryan racial superiority. Berliners have meanwhile paid tribute to Owens, who died in 1981, by naming a street south of the stadium complex for him. The stadium is still used and, with its seating capacity of 96,000, counts as the largest in Germany. It is destined to be used again if Berlin wins its bid to host the games in 2000.

The **Le-Corbusier-Haus**, Reichsportfeldstrasse 15, south of the stadium complex, is no less controversial architecturally. Built in 1957 as Le Corbusier's contribution to the international construction exhibition held in Berlin that year, it was patterned after his "Shining City" project in Marseilles, but raises doubts about the future of city life if it's going to be like this. The seven-story building, nearly 450 feet long and about 75 feet wide, is only 185 feet high, which means—taking away space for floors and ceilings—that the more than 1,500 tenants in its 527 apartments have relatively little headroom. This "city-within-a-city," conceived as a "machine for living," still rates as the largest apartment building in Europe.

OUTLYING AREAS

SPANDAU

The formerly independent town of Spandau, half a century older than Berlin itself, now one of its 20 boroughs, and best known perhaps for its Spandau prison, is situated at the westernmost edge of the city and is well worth a day's exploration. Getting there is easy. Take the U-7 subway westbound; the next-to-last two stops on the line, Zitadelle and Altstadt Spandau, are where the attractions are.

Zitadelle Spandau is a thick-walled medieval castle built on the foundations of one of Albrecht the Bear's 12th-century fortresses. The present 1,000-by-1,000-foot complex, moated on three sides and bordered on the fourth by the Havel river (more of a lake here) was begun by Elector Joachim II in 1560 and completed in 1594. Since then it has remained virtually unchanged, a perfect example of Italian military engineering—and indeed it was an Italian, Francesco Chiaramella di Gandino of Venice, who was its principal architect. Until the age of modern artillery it was virtually impregnable.

The citadel played a key role in all of the 17th- and 18th-century wars in which Brandenburg and, later, Prussia were involved. Twice it was captured—by the Swedes during the Thirty Years' War and by Napoléon in 1806—but each time without battle. The Juliusturm, the castle's central tower, is its oldest part, dating from 1200. The 19th-century kaisers used it as a kind of German Fort Knox, a storage depot for the five billion gold francs they wrested as "reparations" from France after the Franco-Prussian War of 1870–1871. What remained of the hoard after World War I was returned to France in accordance with the 1919 Versailles Treaty.

Most of the buildings in the complex are open to visitors. The most rewarding is the Renaissance-style **Palast**, once the main living quarters of the fortress and now the home of Spandau's **Heimatmuseum** of local history. The collection is actually far less parochial than its name suggests and includes objects dating from the tenth and eleventh centuries, when the Slavic Wends inhabited the area. The lower parts of the building incorporate thirteenth- and fourteenth-century tombstones with Hebrew inscriptions that were taken from Spandau's Jewish cemetery during a pogrom in 1348.

In the fortress commandant's house is the **Zitadellen-Schänke**, a rustic inn and restaurant that serves lunch and dinner as well as medieval-style banquets (the waiters and waitresses dress as knaves and wenches, etc.).

A ten-minute walk southwest from the citadel's main gate will take you to the heart of Spandau's **Altstadt** (Old City), where many 18th-century burgher houses have been restored in recent years. There are also remnants of the city's medieval defensive wall, and most streets are cobblestoned. The **Nikolaikirche**, on Reformationsplatz, is an early–15th-century brick Gothic structure built on the foundations of an even earlier church, and it is typical of the style of Brandenburg. The bronze baptismal basin was cast in 1398; the Renaissance altar dates from 1582.

KÖPENICK

Stronghold of the 12th-century Wendish Prince Jaczso, Köpenick predates even Cölln-Berlin. A separate city until its incorporation into Berlin in 1920, it is now the largest of the city's boroughs, and its most pastoral. The **Köpenicker Forst** and **Grosser Müggelsee** are, respectively, Berlin's largest municipal wood and lake: a vast area for hiking, boating, and escaping from the urban landscape. To get there take the eastbound S-3 S-Bahn from Bahnhof Zoo, Friedrichstrasse, Marx-Engels-Platz, or Alexanderplatz to the Köpenick stop.

Schloss Köpenick, south of the train station (walk or take the number 168 or 169 bus), occupies the site of Prince Jaczso's fortress and is the oldest surviving palace in Berlin. It was completed, in Renaissance style, in 1571 and served as a hunting château for Elector Joachim II. In the early 18th century Frederick I added two Baroque-style wings. The court-martial that condemned Frederick the Great and his friend Lieutenant Katte was held here in 1730. In October 1760, during the Seven Years' War, Russian troops plundered the château, and soon after that it went into a long decline. Virtually undamaged during World War II, the palace and its park have enjoyed a renaissance since 1963, when the East Berlin state museums turned the richly decorated structure into their **Kunstgewerbemuseum** (Museum of Applied Arts). The collection of furniture, porcelain, glass, and goldsmith work here includes more than 900 years of European decorative art from the Middle Ages to the present. The **Schlosscafé**, open daily except Mondays from 2:00 to 6:00 P.M., is a delightful place to take a coffee break and indulge in some calorific Berlin pastry.

Köpenick's Neo-Gothic red-brick **Rathaus**, a five-minute walk north of the palace toward the S-Bahn station, would hardly be worth a glance were it not for one Wilhelm Voigt and the playwright Carl Zuckmayer, who immortalized him in the drama *The Captain of Köpenick*.

In the fall of 1906, Voigt, a down-and-out shoemaker with a police record, found, in a pawn shop, a somewhat frayed, oversized uniform of a captain of the imperial guards. He put it on and strolled out of the shop, looking and feeling like a new man. And he was. On the street he spotted a squad of 12 soldiers under command of a lance corporal. Voigt took charge of the troop, marched it to the nearest train station, and rode with it to Köpenick. There Voigt and his soldiers proceeded to the Rathaus, arrested the mayor, and confiscated the municipal treasury. With the cashbox under his arm, the fake captain ordered his soldiers to release the mayor after half an hour and then take the rest of the day off. He strutted back to the station, boarded a train, and disappeared. The story of the Hauptmann von Köpenick, or "Copper Captain," as he was called in the Anglo-American press, made headlines around the world.

However, Voigt wasn't after the money: He wanted blank identity papers. When he didn't find any in the heavy cashbox, he surrendered to the police. He was tried for robbery and impersonating an imperial officer, was sentenced to four years in prison, and served two. For the rest of his life the cobbler earned a good living by appearing in uniform for a fee.

Zuckmayer turned the episode into a hit play in 1931 and in the 1950s wrote the script for a prizewinning movie starring Heinz Rühmann, then Germany's leading comic actor. The incident gave the German language a new word—*Köpenickade,* a caper that plays on gullibility and blind respect for uniforms and military authority. To Berliners east and west, the phony Captain of Köpenick is still a hero. The room with the Köpenick municipal safe has been turned into a small museum and is open daily, including weekends. The Rathaus is still the borough city hall.

TREPTOW

This borough, which stretches southeast from Berlin Mitte along the Spree, is named for a fishing village first documented in 1568. In the late 19th century the area around the old town was turned into the English-style **Treptower Park**, and it has been a popular recreation area ever since. Today one of its main attractions is the **Sowjetisches Ehrenmal** (Soviet War Memorial) and military cemetery. Created in the late 1940s, this is the largest Soviet military monument outside the former U.S.S.R. Five thousand Soviet soldiers killed in the Battle of Berlin are buried here. Although the sculpture is in strict Socialist Realist style and the architecture is monumentally Stalinist, the memorial is poignantly moving. On the avenue leading to the entrance is a figure of Mother Russia carved from a 50-ton block of granite. Birches line the broad path to a "Grove of Honor," and two walls of red granite symbolize flags lowered in mourning. Atop the cylindrical mausoleum stands a 38-foot-tall bronze figure of a Red Army soldier cradling a small child in one arm and brandishing a sword with which he has just smashed the Nazi swastika.

To get to the park, take any westbound S-Bahn via Friedrichstrasse and Alexanderplatz stations to the Ostkreuz stop and transfer to any southbound line (S-8, S-6, S-9, or S-10) to Treptower Park. It is a five-minute walk along Puschkinallee from the station to the memorial.

LICHTENBERG

What originally was the village of Lichtenberg, near the eastern edges of Berlin, northwest of Köpenick, has a documented history going back to 1288 and became a town in its own right in 1907, just shortly before it was incorporated into today's metropolitan Berlin as a borough. In the 18th century the area around the village became a kind of bedroom community for high-ranking Prussian officers and civil servants who built châteaux and grand mansions from which they commuted by coach into the inner city whenever their duties required it or the king wanted to see them. One of them was Benjamin Raule, chief of the royal navy, who built Schloss Friedrichsfelde, which you can reach by taking the U-5 subway from Alexanderplatz to the Friedrichsfelde station.

Schloss Friedrichsfelde, Am Tierpark 125, was built in 1694 by the architect Johann Nering in the style of a Dutch manor house, surrounded by a Baroque park with a canal system—which was not only fashionable in those days but especially fitting for the head of Prussia's navy. During the next century the *schloss* changed hands several times. Among the owners was Frederick the Great's youngest brother, Prince Ferdinand, who lived here for more than 20 years until the completion of Bellevue Palace in the Tiergarten. It also underwent some expansion and interior changes. Napoléon's Marshal Louis Davout made it his headquarters during the two-year-long French occupation of Berlin. From 1816 until 1945 it was the property of the von Tresckow family, one of whose more recent descendants, Major General Henning von Tresckow, was, together with Colonel Claus Schenk von Stauffenberg, one of the key conspirators and organizers of the plot against Adolf Hitler (von Tresckow committed suicide on July 21, 1944, the morning after Stauffenberg's assassination attempt). The Third Reich government expropriated the Tresckow family holdings as punishment, and Friedrichsfelde became East German government property after World War II.

The palace has been open to the public since 1981 and its rooms, appointed to give viewers an idea of aristocratic living conditions in the 18th and 19th century, can be seen on guided tours three times daily (11:00 A.M. and 1:00 and 3:00 P.M.) Tuesday through Sunday.

It was also the Tresckow family who in 1821 commissioned the landscape architect Peter Joseph Lenné to lay out and expand the park, with the idea of eventually turning it into a private zoo. The plan was finally realized in 1955 by the East German regime, which wanted to give its side of the city a zoo of its own.

Though the **Tierpark Berlin** is smaller than the Zoologischer Garten in number of animals and species— "only" 7,500 animals and 900 kinds—it is in area one of the largest zoos in the world (400 acres) and also ranks as one of the most beautiful because of its landscaping. It is open daily from 9:00 A.M. until dusk, though the ticket office closes at 6:00 P.M. in the spring and summer months (April through September), at 4:00 P.M. in winter.

PANKOW

This northernmost of Berlin's boroughs probably draws its name from the Panke, a little tributary of the Spree, that flows through its most bucolic areas. As a village Pankow was first mentioned in 1370, though it probably existed at least a century before then. The rural atmosphere is still here. Of the district's area of 30 square miles (78 km), some 10,000 acres are still used as farmland.

Pankow is known for two developments: its popularity in the 18th and 19th century as a site for summer châteaux and rich merchants' mansions, all surrounded by sprawling landscaped estates, of which Schloss Nieder-schönhausen is the grandest, and because of the takeover of the estates by Communist bigwigs after World War II. Indeed, because Niederschönhausen served as the official residence of Wilhelm Pieck, the German Democratic Republic's first president, from 1949 until his death in 1960, the popular Cold War expression for the East German government was "Pankow Regime."

The number 46 streetcar from the Friedrichstrasse S-Bahn and U-Bahn station will take you to within walking distance of the Niederschönhausen palace. (See also the map Northeastern Berlin in the Prenzlauer Berg section, above.)

Schloss Niederschönhausen, entrance at Ossietzky-strasse 65, is set amid a beautifully landscaped park and has origins going back to 1664 as a baronial estate. In 1691 Elector Frederick III (King Frederick I) bought it from a Countess Dohna and had it rebuilt and enlarged in Baroque style for use as a country estate. His grandson, Frederick the Great, used it for something else: to get the wife his father had forced him to marry out of his hair, or, more appropriate for the times, wig.

In 1740, seven years after his arranged marriage and a couple of weeks after he became king, he dispatched his wife to Niederschönhausen and made it her residence. Two decades later, during the Seven Years' War (which Frederick should never have started and almost lost), Russian troops occupied and laid waste to the estate. Elisabeth hired the architect Johann Boumann the Elder to rebuild and expand it in its present form, a blend of late Rococo and early Neoclassical style.

The interiors are opulent and typical of the life of the nobility and royalty in the second half of the 18th century. The surrounding park was landscaped by Peter Joseph Lenné in 1829 on the commission of King Frederick William III.

After Wilhelm Pieck's death in 1960 the East German regime turned the palace into an official government guest house for use by visiting foreign dignitaries and for formal receptions. The park surrounding it is now open to the public Saturdays and Sundays, but as we went to press the palace was still closed, with plans uncertain about what to do with it. It may continue to be used as a government guesthouse when Berlin really becomes the capital, but it might also be turned into a luxury hotel.

GREEN BERLIN AND THE LAKES

Vast expanses of Berlin are as pastoral as a landscape painting. The Grunewald is 12 square miles in area; the Spandau and Tegel forests are somewhat smaller. (Köpenicker Forst, discussed above, is the largest, at 22 square miles.) The tourist office in the Europa-Center provides guidebooks and maps of the marked trails.

The **Grunewald**, in the southwest corner of the city, is bordered in the west by the Havel river and one of the lakes, the **Grosser Wannsee**. The forest begins just beyond the western end of the Kurfürstendamm, which becomes Königsallee and winds southward through the eastern half of the forest. From the Dahlem museum area take the U-2 subway southbound, get off at Dahlem-Dorf, walk northwest to the Brücke Museum, and you are at the edge of the forest. The forest is rewarding not only for its greenery and excursion-boat facilities but also for sheltering several of Berlin's most interesting smaller châteaux and royal mansions.

Jagdschloss Grunewald is a hunting château built for Elector Joachim II in 1542. The château, situated idyllically on the shore of the little **Grunewaldsee**, was restored to its original Renaissance appearance in 1963 and is now a museum. Among its holdings are paintings by German and Flemish masters, including pictures by both Lucas Cranachs (the Elder and the Younger), Barthel Bryn, Jacob Jordaens, Antoine Pesne, and Rubens. There are also 16th- to 18th-century furnishings, hunting trophies, and weapons. For sustenance, try the delightfully rustic forest inn nearby, **Forsthaus Paulsborn**, right by the lakeside. It is open for lunch and dinner in the summer, lunch only in the winter, and for breakfast, starting at 9:00 A.M., every Sunday.

To see more châteaux and the Wannsee, head to the southern part of the Grunewald. Take either the S-3 elevated train from Bahnhof Zoo or the S-1 from Friedrichstrasse, Unter den Linden, or Anhalter Bahnhof; both lines stop at the Wannsee station. From there you can either walk due west along Königstrasse or north along the lakeshore, or board the number 116 or 114 bus.

A walk north along the shore on the street called Am Grossen Wannsee, or a ride on the number 114 bus, which you can board at the S-Bahn station and take to the Löwendenkmal stop, will lead you to the **Gedenkstätte**

Haus der Wannsee-Konferenz (House of the Wansee Conference Memorial), Am Grossen Wannsee 56–58. This is the mansion, built in 1915 for a Berlin industrialist, then sold to the security service of the SS as a guest house, where in January 1942 top Nazi officials, including Adolf Eichmann and Reinhard Heydrich, met to plan the systematic destruction of European Jewry. Since the end of World War II the manor house had served numerous purposes, including that of a boarding school. Plans to turn it into a memorial and study center with a permanent exhibition on the "Final Solution" were first made in the 1980s. It opened on January 20, 1992, the 50th anniversary of the awesome conference—the minutes of which were kept by Eichmann—in which the deportation and murder of Europe's Jews was implemented and organized. The exhibition documents the conference, the events prior to it, and its consequences: the Holocaust. There is also an educational department where seminars and workshops are held and a multimedia library on Jewish history, anti-Semitism, Nazism, and neo-Nazism.

The four main attractions at the western end of Königstrasse are the Glienicker Brücke, Jagdschloss Glienicke, Schloss Klein-Glienicke, and the DEFA Film Studio in Potsdam. The **Glienicker Brücke**, a bridge that crosses the Havel to Potsdam, became famous during the spy trading of the Cold War. This is where Soviet KGB Colonel Rudolf Abel went east (although he actually walked west by the compass) in exchange for U-2 pilot Gary Powers in 1963, and where Soviet human rights activist Anatoly Sharansky walked to freedom in 1983. Until November 1989 the bridge could be used only by Western and Soviet military and diplomatic personnel. Now it is a main route between southwestern Berlin and Potsdam.

The **DEFA Film Studio**, August Bebel-Strasse 26–52, in the Potsdam suburb of Babelsberg, just beyond the Berlin city limits, is an embodiment of movie history. Marlene Dietrich, Greta Garbo, Peter Lorre, Fritz Lang, Joseph von Sternberg, Billy Wilder, and Robert Siodmak were only a few of the stars and directors who worked at what is still one of the world's largest film production sites, making such classics as *The Blue Angel, Metropolis,* and *The Cabinet of Dr. Caligari* until Nazism and Hitler's rise to power forced them to emigrate or flee to Hollywood. In their day it was the Universum Film Studio (UFA). After World War II and nationalization by the East German regime it became known by its present name, DEFA. Reunification

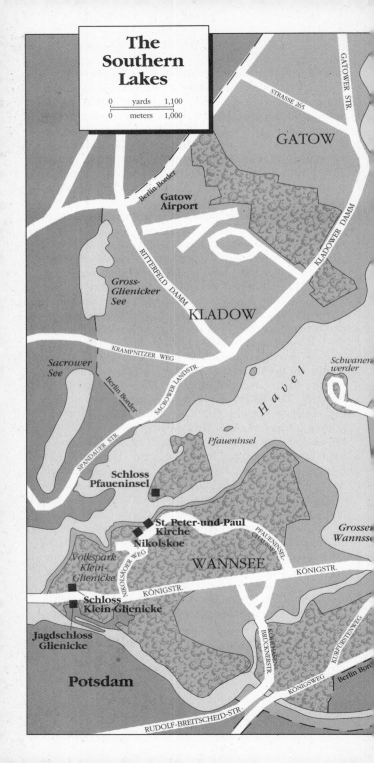

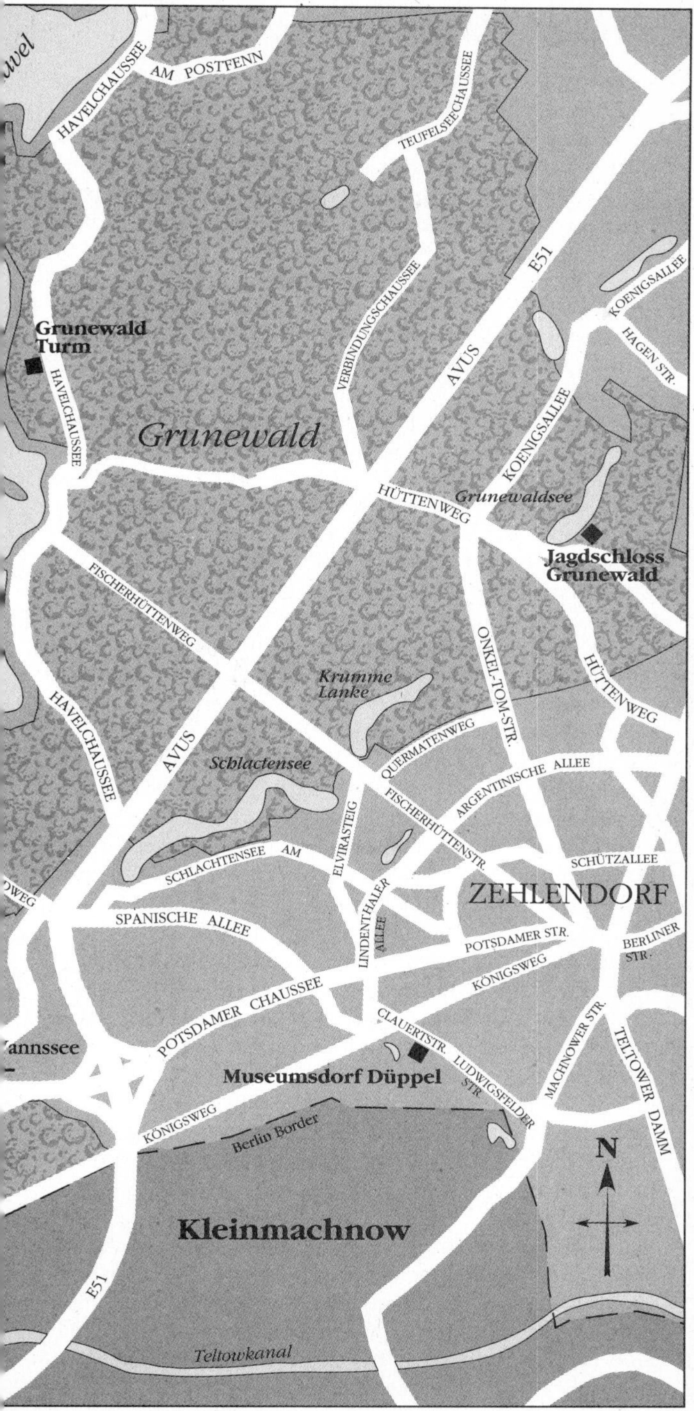

Havel
HAVELCHAUSSEE
AM POSTFENN
TEUFELSEECHAUSSEE
VERBINDUNGSCHAUSSEE
E51
AVUS
KOENIGSALLEE
HAGEN STR.
Grunewald Turm
HAVELCHAUSSEE
Grunewald
KOENIGSALLEE
HÜTTENWEG
Grunewaldsee
Jagdschloss Grunewald
FISCHERHÜTTENWEG
ONKEL-TOM-STR.
HÜTTENWEG
Krumme Lanke
HAVELCHAUSSEE
AVUS
QUERMATENWEG
Schlactensee
ARGENTINISCHE ALLEE
ELVIRASTEIG
FISCHERHÜTTENSTR.
SCHLACHTENSEE AM
SCHÜTZALLEE
LINDENTHALER ALLEE
ZEHLENDORF
SPANISCHE ALLEE
POTSDAMER STR.
BERLINER STR.
KÖNIGSWEG
POTSDAMER CHAUSSEE
CLAUERTSTR.
MACHNOWER STR.
TELTOWER DAMM
Wannssee
Museumsdorf Düppel
LUDWIGSFELDER STR
KÖNIGSWEG
Berlin Border
N
Kleinmachnow
E51
Teltowkanal

put a virtual end to film production here and eliminated more than two thirds of the 2,300 jobs, but a French investment conglomerate, Compagnie Générale des Eaux (GCE), has bought it and plans to turn it into a media center. Meanwhile, tours of the site, replete with visits to the props warehouses, cutting rooms, and sound studios; walks through sets; film showings; and demonstration shoots with actors and stuntmen have made the studio a magnet for busloads of visitors, especially on weekends. The best way to get here is to continue past the Wannsee station on the S-3 to the next stop, Griebnitzsee, and there either catch the number 693 bus, which drops you right in front of the main entrance, or walk west on Rudolf Breitscheid Strasse to its intersection with August Bebel Strasse; there turn left (it's about a 20-minute walk). Open daily from 10:00 A.M. to 6:00 P.M. with the last admission at 4:30 P.M. To enjoy the whole program, you are advised to arrive by 3:00 P.M.

Jagdschloss Glienicke, just south of the Glienicker Brücke, was built as a hunting lodge for Brandenburg's Frederick William, the Great Elector, in 1682. A gem of the Baroque style, it has served since 1963 as a live-in adult education center. Only the grounds are open to visitors.

Schloss Klein-Glienicke, just across the street, is currently closed to the public, although worth visiting as it is situated in one of Berlin's most beautiful parks, landscaped by Peter Josef Lenné in 1816. The château, originally a small country mansion belonging to a wallpaper manufacturer and then to a chancellor of Prussia, was enlarged and rebuilt in its present form by Schinkel to serve as a summer residence for Prince Karl, a son of King Frederick William III. Neoclassical in style, it has a central building with two wings that enclose an Italian-style courtyard. Prince Karl was an inveterate globetrotter who brought back hundreds of souvenirs from his travels to Italy, Greece, and Asia Minor. He had them all imbedded in the château's exterior walls, where they can be seen today. One is an old Persian gravestone. The late shah of Iran, on a visit to West Berlin in 1967, pointed out that it was upside down; apparently Prince Karl could not read Persian.

A stroll north through the park or on the path along the Havel river embankment will take you to **St.-Peter-und-Pauls-Kirche** and **Blockhaus Nikolskoe**. The onion-domed church and the log house, which looks as if it is right off the Siberian taiga, were built by King Frederick William III in honor of his son-in-law, Tsar Nicholas I, who married Prussia's Princess Charlotte in 1817. The church, consecrated in 1837, was a 20th wedding anniversary gift. The log house, named for Nicholas, was a present from the king to the couple in 1819. A fire destroyed it in 1984; it was reconstructed and is now a popular restaurant, serving strictly German, not Russian, food. This transplanted piece of Russia provides a panoramic view of the Havel, the Wannsee, and the Pfaueninsel (Peacock Island), site of one of Berlin's strangest châteaux, **Schloss Pfaueninsel**. A ferry will take you there; the landing is just below the Russian church.

For centuries the island has been a famous scenic spot. Toward the end of the 17th century it belonged to an alchemist named Johann Kunkel von Löwenstern, who was supposed to make gold here for the Great Elector. Instead he produced beautiful ruby-colored glasses and goblets, examples of which are on exhibit in the palace. When the Great Elector died, in 1688, Kunkel left to ply his trade in Sweden, and the island went into a long sleep until 1793. Then Frederick William II bought it from Kunkel's heirs, intending to use it as a hideaway for himself and his mistress, Wilhelmine Encke, the Countess Lichtenau. Together they designed the château to resemble the ruin of a Roman country house, with Romanesque elements. They did not have much use of it—the king died in 1797. But his son, Frederick William III, and his consort, Queen Louise, loved the place and used it as a summer retreat. During their reign peacocks were brought here, and Lenné landscaped the parks.

From the island you can catch the number 1 steamer, part of the city's public transit system, back to the landing at the Wannsee S-Bahn station, and from there transfer to the number 2 steamer route, which will take you all the way back north to Spandau for connections to the U-7 subway line. Or transfer to another boat to travel north to the **Tegeler See**, the Tegel forest and Schloss Tegel.

If you happen to be in the Wannsee area on a Sunday from May through October, be sure to visit the Düppel village museum, **Museumsdorf Düppel**, at Clauertstrasse 11, about a half-hour walk east of the Wannsee S-Bahn station (bus number 211 will also take you close). The museum consists of a reconstruction of a medieval farming hamlet, based on excavations made by archaeologists of the Museum of Pre- and Early History. The houses exhibit furnishings, tools, and artifacts of the period and there are demonstrations of 13th-century handicrafts and lifestyles.

Schloss Tegel, at Adelheidallee 19–20 (a half-mile north of the boat landing in Tegel and near the Tegel station on the U-6 subway line), is also called the **Humboldt Schlösschen**. Built in 1550 for the court secretary of Elector Joachim II, it was later used as a hunting château by the Great Elector. In 1766 it became the property of Georg von Humboldt, father of Alexander, the famous naturalist, and Wilhelm, the equally famous statesman, philosopher, and educator.

Wilhelm von Humboldt commissioned Schinkel to reconstruct the house in the Neoclassical style for his use as a private residence. He, Alexander, and many of their descendants are buried in the family mausoleum on the grounds, not far from an 800-year-old oak under which, according to legend, Margrave Albrecht the Bear often napped. The mansion and surrounding park are still owned by the Humboldt family. The house is full of family heirlooms and memorabilia documenting the life and work of both Wilhelm and Alexander.

Wilhelm von Humboldt established Berlin's university and created Germany's public education system. He was also an art collector, with a special interest in Greek and Roman sculpture. Unfortunately, many pieces in his collection were lost during World War II (although some mysteriously reappeared in East Berlin). Until mid-1990 most of the artworks in the mansion were copies, but the East Berlin authorities then began returning the originals and the collection is now again complete.

From the Humboldt mansion it is a 10- to 15-minute walk (or two minutes on any of the bus lines) back to the Tegel subway station, where you can catch the U-6.

SPECIAL SIGHTSEEING

VILLAGE CHURCHES

Within Berlin there are more than 50 stone *Dorfkirchen,* or village churches. Seven were built in the early 13th century, before the founding of Berlin itself, by Knights

Templar—for whom the Tempelhof area and airport are named.

Three interesting ones are in the districts of Marienfelde, Lichtenrade, and Buckow, all part of Tempelhof borough. To reach these, take the southbound S-2 elevated train from the Friedrichstrasse, Unter den Linden, or Anhalter Bahnhof S-Bahn stations to the Marienfelde station. From there, it's not far by bus to these little chapels (see below for specific directions).

The **Dorfkirche Marienfelde**, consecrated in 1220, is the oldest village church in Berlin. A Gothic structure built of massive granite blocks, it is located on the tree-shaded, cobblestone village square just off Marienfelder Strasse on a little street named, appropriately, An der Dorfkirche. To get there take the S-2 to the Marienfelde station, then transfer to the number 179 bus going south on Marienfelder Allee. The church is about one mile away from the station; the bus stops right at the corner leading to the square.

The 14th-century **Dorfkirche Lichtenrade**, another two miles southeast, is right in front of a farmyard, with a pond inhabited by quacking ducks. Next to the simple fieldstone church is the old village tavern, **Zum Alten Dorfkrug**, where you can lunch, snack, or have a beer. To get there, take the number 183 bus east from near the Marienfelde village square; it stops near the Lichtenrade village square.

The **Dorfkirche Buckow**, about three miles northeast of Lichtenrade, was built around 1250, and still has five 13th-century stained-glass windows. There are also wall frescoes and gravestones dating from the 14th century. To get here, take the S-Bahn back from Lichtenrade station, one stop to Buckower Chaussee, and there transfer to the number 172 bus going east, which stops right in front of the church.

To return to central Berlin, take the number 172 bus east to the Johannisthaler Chaussee subway station on the U-7 line, where you can catch a westbound train to the Adenauerplatz station on the Kurfürstendamm, a ride of about one-half hour.

Dahlem district's **St. Annen Kirche**, on the corner of Königen-Luise-Strasse and Pacelli Allee, just a few minutes' walk from the Dahlem museums complex, is a Gothic brick structure on a fieldstone base that dates from the late 13th or early 14th century. There are 14th-century frescoes and a carved altarpiece attributed to the artist of the Death Dance frescoes in central Berlin's St. Mary's church. St. Anne's was a major center of anti-Nazi resistance during the Third Reich, under the leadership of the Protestant Confessing Church and Reverend Martin Niemöller, who was its pastor from 1931 until 1937, when he was arrested and put into Dachau concentration camp. Among those buried in the adjacent churchyard is Rudi Dutschke, leader of the 1968 German students' rebellion, who died in 1979.

Reinickendorf borough, at the northwestern corner of Berlin, has two picturesque churches, both dating from the 15th century.

Dorfkirche Reinickendorf, on Alt Reinickendorf Strasse, is a late-Gothic fieldstone church, dated around 1480, with a spire from the early 18th century. The main altar, from 1520, shows scenes from the *Passion of Christ* that are based on woodcuts by Albrecht Dürer. The polychrome woodcarvings of Mary and St. Margaret here are late 15th century. To get here, take the U-8 subway north from Alexanderplatz to the Paracelsus-Bad station, the end of the line; the church and village common are just a few steps north of the U-Bahn stop.

Dorfkirche Wittenau, on Alt-Wittenau Strasse, dates from the second half of the 15th century but has had a number of alterations since, including the installation of Neo-Gothic stained-glass windows. The wood carvings of St. Anne, St. Nicholas, and Mary on the winged altarpiece count among the finest examples of late-Gothic ecclesiastical art in Berlin. The church itself stands idyllically surrounded by old linden, oak, and chestnut trees on the village green. To reach it, take the U-8 subway from Alexanderplatz to the Paracelsus-Bad station, as you would to get to the Reinickendorf church, and here transfer to the number 120 bus, which stops right in front of the church.

Two village churches in eastern Berlin are also noteworthy. Weissensee borough's **Dorfkirche Karow**, on Alt Karow, is a Romanesque fieldstone structure that probably predates the village's first documentary mention in 1244. In layout and structure it is similar to the churches in Marienfelde and Mariendorf. Except for a beam ceiling installed in 1830 the interior is original. The elaborate pulpit and carved choir stalls date from 1622 and are in the style of the late Renaissance. The church spire and belfry are Neo-Romanesque additions from the mid-19th century. The best way to get here is to take the U-2

subway from central Berlin (Stadtmitte station on Friedrichstrasse, or Alexanderplatz) in the direction of Pankow, and transfer to the S-8 elevated train, direction
Bernau, at the Schönhauser Allee station. From here it's
four stops to the Karow station. The church is five short
blocks southeast of the S-Bahn station.

Dorfkirche Hohenschönhausen, on the Hauptstrasse in
the Hohenschönhausen district near the eastern edge of
Berlin, also dates from the 13th century, but is notable
mainly for its medieval furnishings, including two carved
figures from around 1430, a 16th-century lectern, and an
intricately carved late Gothic chest. Again, take the U-2
and transfer at Schönhauser Allee to the S-8, but go *south*
in the direction of Grünau for three stops to the Lands-
berger Allee station, and there transfer to the number 15
or 63 streetcar to the center of Hohenschönhausen.
There is a stop on Hauptstrasse directly across from the
church.

INDUSTRIAL BERLIN

In the 19th century Berlin was *the* boom town of Europe.
Buoyed by the Industrial Revolution, its population ex-
ploded from 172,000 in 1801 to more than 1.9 million by
1900. Though the city was governed by the kings and
kaisers, its real power brokers were the barons of industry.
As symbols of their wealth and might they fashioned their
factories, office buildings, and warehouses after medieval
castles, palaces, and cathedrals. Surprisingly, scores of
these edifices—factories, railway stations, power plants,
warehouses, streetcar depots, town halls and courthouses,
and even breweries—have survived. As recently as a decade ago they were viewed as architectural monstrosities.
But now, in an age of Postmodern nostalgia, they are being
preserved, renovated, and restored. Many still serve their
original purpose, and some are of major architectural and
historical importance. Unless otherwise noted, they can
only be viewed from the outside.

The AEG electrical company's turbine plant in Tiergarten borough's Moabit section, **Turbinenfabrik der AEG**,
Huttenstrasse 12–16, was designed by the architect Peter
Behrens. Behrens started his career as a painter, and was a
member of Munich's Secession, the late 19th-century
movement that marked the beginning of the Art Nouveau
style. He ranks as one of the precursors of Modernism in

Germany. Walter Gropius and Ludwig Mies van der Rohe were among his pupils. In this building, which he designed in 1908 while serving as design consultant to AEG, he applied the concept of "form follows function." In the building, originally over 300 feet long then extended to more than 600 feet, he placed the emphasis on getting as much natural light into the structure as possible. It is still used for making electrical turbines, and now belongs to Kraftwerk Union Berlin, a local utility.

The waterworks in Köpenick, **Wasserwerk Friedrichshagen**, Müggleseedamm 301–308, right on the banks of the Müggelsee, built between 1889 and 1893, is a classic example of romanticizing Neo-Gothic forms in industrial architecture. With its turrets, crenellated walls, tracery windows, and steeply gabled roofs it looks like a medieval castle. It still pumps water, though two of the pumping houses do double duty as a machinery museum, and, thus, it is open to the public.

In Lichtenberg borough there's the **Knorr-Bremse-Werk**, Hirschberger Strasse 4, which was built as the main plant for this brake manufacturing company in the 1920s. It looks like a fortress.

Prenzlauer Berg district's **Wasserturm** (water tower) on Belforter Strasse, built in the 1850s, is a mix of Neo-Roman and Neo-Renaissance elements and looks like a Roman citadel.

The application of historical architectural styles was by no means limited to industrial buildings. The **Kriminalgericht** (Criminal Courts Building) in the Moabit district, part of Tiergarten, Turmstrasse 91, is more elaborately and ostentatiously Baroque than any Hohenzollern palace. It was built between 1902 and 1906.

A number of old industrial structures have been imaginatively converted to other purposes. In Moabit, for example, dozens of craft and artisan shops are now lodged in the original **Schultheiss brewery** at Stromstrasse 11–17. This biggest of the Berlin breweries (you'll see its name all over town) moved to a new site in 1981. The 110-year-old former brewing room, with its huge, gleaming copper vats, has been converted into a tavern, the **Sudhaus**, which features live jazz and folk music nightly except Monday starting at 8:00 P.M.

The Sorat hotel group has converted the **Humboldt Mühle**, a medieval grain silo in the district of Tegel, into a first-class hotel. And the **Hamburger Bahnhof**, Invalidenstrasse 50 (north of the Tiergarten), Berlin's first railway station, built in the 1840s, has been converted into an art museum and will house the Nationalgalerie's collection of contemporary works.

GETTING AROUND

Sightseeing

Even if it is not your thing, an introductory tour of two to four hours is a good way to get oriented in Berlin.

By bus. Besides a variety of English-language sightseeing tours of Berlin, lasting from two to four hours, a number of bus operators also offer tours to some of our day-trip destinations, notably Potsdam, Brandenburg, and the Spreewald.

The major operators are BBS-Berliner Bären Stadtrundfahrt GmbH, Rankestrasse 35, D(W)-1000 Berlin 30, Tel: 213-40-77, Fax: 2137354; Berolina Sightseeing, Meinekestrasse 3, D(W)-1000 Berlin 15, Tel: 882-20-91, Fax: 8824128; Severin & Kuhn, Kurfürstendamm 216, D(W)-1000 Berlin 15, Tel: 883-10-15, Fax: 8825618.

By boat. There are more than a dozen independent fleets that operate on the rivers, canals, and lakes of Berlin and Potsdam, offering a variety of sightseeing and excursion tours of the city as well as journeys on the Havel, the Spree, the canals, and smaller rivers to some of the day-trip destinations, notably Potsdam, Brandenburg, Neuruppin, and Niederfinow, from May through September. Beverages, snacks, and in some cases full meals are served on all vessels.

Some of the principal operators are Stern und Kreisschiffahrt GmbH, Sachtlebenstrasse 60, D(W)-1000 Berlin 37, Tel: 810-00-40, Fax: 8152016; Weisse Flotte Potsdam, An der Langen Brücke, D(O)-1560 Potsdam, Tel: 215-27; Reederei Triebler, Johannastrasse 24, D(W)-1000 Berlin 20, Tel: 331-54-14 or 371-16-71; Reederei Winkler, Levetzowstrasse 12a, D(W)-1000 Berlin 21, Tel: 391-70-10 or 391-70-70, Fax: 3918049.

Berolina Sightseeing and Stern-und-Kreisschiffahrt GmbH also collaborate for combination bus and boat trips to Brandenburg, Chorin and Niederfinow, and the Spreewald.

Driving

Though the sheer size of the city makes it seem inviting, it is also an invitation to headaches and heartaches. Not only is Berlin confusing to get around in, requiring you to

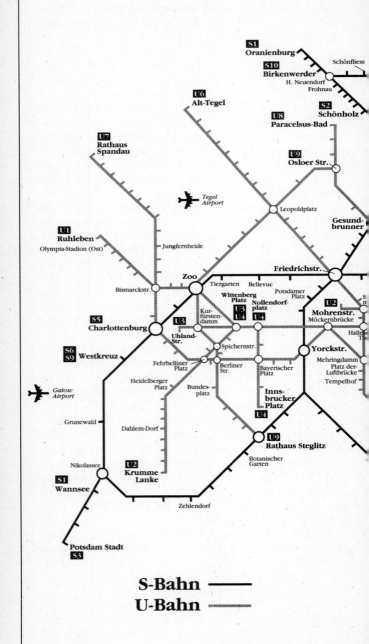

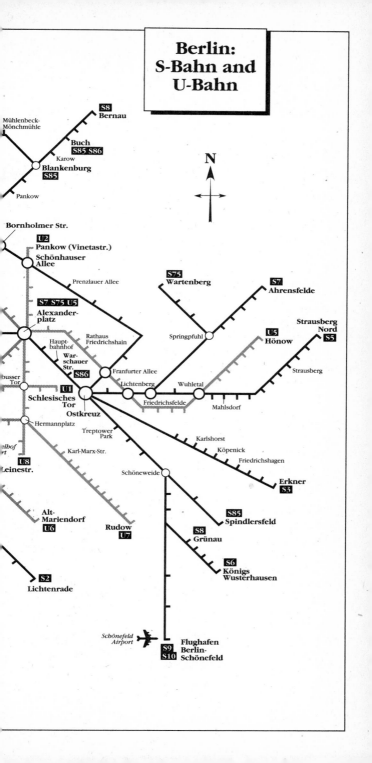

Berlin: S-Bahn and U-Bahn

N

stop frequently and check your map, but traffic is excruciating most hours of the day—nighmarish during rush periods—and parking spaces are as hard to find as gold nuggets on the street. If you have driven to Berlin and have found a place to park near your hotel, consider yourself lucky and leave the car there. You will, of course, need it or a rental car for day trips, but while in the city rely as much as you can on public transit.

Public Transit

Berliners claim theirs is the best in Germany, if not the world. Their penchant for boasting notwithstanding, the claim has some validity.

The system consists of U-Bahn subways, S-Bahn elevated trains, buses, including many double-deckers, streetcars in east Berlin only, and steamers on many rivers and lakes. Multiple-ride and 24-hour tickets provide free transfers among all systems.

The U-Bahn has nine lines. Service during peak hours is every two and one half minutes; off peak, trains run every five to seven and one half minutes. Late at night it slows to a train every ten minutes.

The network operates on an honor system, backed by spot inspections: You obtain tickets from dispensing machines or ticket windows and cancel them in meters at platform entrances or on buses. The fine for not having a canceled ticket is DM 60. A single ride costs DM 3, four-ride tickets DM 10.40. The best bargains are 24-hour tourist passes, costing DM 12. They give unlimited use of all conveyances, and are for sale at the tourist-office counter at Tegel airport, the BVG-Kiosk Zoo, on Hardenbergplatz, at most dispensing machines, and at ticket windows in the following subway stations: Zoo, Kurt-Schumacher-Platz, Richard-Wagner-Platz, and Rathaus Spandau.

Berliner Verkehrs Gesellschaft (BVG, the public transit company) has an information pavilion adjacent to Bahnhof Zoo, on Hardenbergplatz, open 8:00 A.M.–11:00 P.M., Tel: 256-24-62.

Taxis

Altough there are more than 6,000 cabs licensed in Berlin, you can never get one when you need it. They can be hailed on the street or ordered by phone at the following numbers: 69-02, 26-10-26, 21-60-60, and 24-02-02. A one-mile ride costs about DM 7.50. Tip by rounding up the fare.

MUSEUMS

Even if you just popped in and right out again without really seeing anything, you would need months to take in all of Berlin's museums: There are more than 160 within the city limits.

The list ranges from small *Heimatmuseen*—museums of local history—in almost each of the 20 *Bezirke* (boroughs), offbeat collections such as the Friseurmuseum, which deals with the history of barbering and hairdressing, and the Zuckermuseum, devoted to anything and everything you might want to know about sugar, to the world-renowned art museums of the Prussian Cultural Heritage Foundation on Museumsinsel, in the Kulturforum, in and around Schloss Charlottenburg, and in Dahlem. It includes a number of castles and palaces that are in themselves museums; exhibitions; *Gedenkstätten* (memorials), such as the Topographie des Terrors (Topography of Terror) on the grounds of the erstwhile Gestapo headquarters; and open-air museums of village life in medieval Brandenburg.

Of the State Museums of the Prussian Cultural Heritage Foundation there are two of almost each type—one in western, the other in eastern Berlin: a consequence of World War II, the formal dissolution of Prussia as a political entity by the Allied Control Council in 1947, and the Cold War. Though once a unified complex, these collections were evacuated during the war to protect them against bombing and stashed at various sites—salt mines, castles, bank vaults, cellars of monasteries, air raid bunkers—all over Germany. There they were recovered and confiscated by the various advancing armies—American, British, Soviet. But the evacuation had been hasty and haphazard, with the result, for example, that a painting would end up in a western cache, its frame at a deposit in the east. This is how Botticelli's original drawings for Dante's *Inferno,* part of the Kupferstichkabinett (Prints Collection), got divided.

When the occupation zones became the rival, divided Germanys in 1949, the British and American authorities began turning most of the treasures in their keep over to the Bonn government and West Berlin city-state administration, and the Soviets gave theirs to the Communist authorities in East Berlin. Two competing complexes of museums and collections on opposite sides of the Berlin Wall developed. Many objects, however, are still missing, and there is much mystery as to whether they were destroyed during the war or pilfered by Allied and Soviet soldiers and are now in secret repositories in the United States and Russia. Since the Wall came down and Berlin is again one city the museums and collections have been slowly moving toward reamalgamation. During the next decade this will require much moving about of collections, renovating of old museums, and building of new ones. Our listing is based on what is or will be where by summer 1993.

Hours and opening days of Berlin museums vary greatly. Almost all now charge admission, a policy inaugurated in 1992 to compensate for the reduction of government subsidies; this ranges from around DM 2 to DM 6, with special discounts for groups, students, senior citizens, the disabled, and, in the case of some museums, free admission on Sundays and holidays.

Our alphabetically arranged listing is based on the German name of the institution, with its English one, where appropriate, in parentheses. In the case of the dual State Museums in west and east, both locations are given.

Abgussammlung Antiker Plastik (Copies Collection of Ancient Sculpture), Schlossstrasse 69-B (across from Schloss Charlottenburg). Some 400 gypsum copies of Greco-Roman statuary, used in studies of classical archaeology at the Free University. Open Friday through Sunday 2:00 to 6:00 P.M.

Ägyptisches Museum (Egyptian Museum), Schlossstrasse 70 (across from Schloss Charlottenburg). This western Berlin section of the State Egyptian collection includes the famous bust of Queen Nefertiti. Open daily except Fridays 9:00 A.M. to 5:00 P.M.; Saturdays and Sundays from 10:00 A.M. The eastern Berlin division is in the **Bode Museum**, and shows bas-reliefs from tombs and temples, mummies, the Gold Treasure of Meroe, and the papyrus collection.

Altes Museum (Old Museum), Bodestrasse 1–3, Museumsinsel, entrance from the Lustgarten on Marx-Engels-Platz. This is Berlin's oldest museum, built by Karl Friedrich Schinkel and opened in 1830. Presently being used only for rotating and visiting exhibitions, it will be closed for renovation and repairs starting in 1994. After reopening it will house the entire Antiquities Collection. Open Wednesday through Sunday 10:00 A.M. to 6:00 P.M.

Antikenmuseum (Antiquities Museum), Schlossstrasse 1 (across from Schloss Charlottenburg). This is the western Berlin section, which shows Greek vases, Etruscan art, Roman gold jewelry, and the Silver Treasure from Hildesheim. Open daily except Fridays 9:00 A.M. to 5:00 P.M., Saturdays and Sundays from 10:00 A.M. The eastern Berlin division, one of the world's most important collections of architecture, sculpture, and applied art spanning 12 centuries of antiquity, is in the **Pergamon Museum** on Museumsinsel; see below.

Museum Berliner Arbeiterleben (Berlin proletarian life), Husemannstrasse 12, in Prenzlauer Berg borough, is a division of the Märkisches Museum (see below) and shows furnishings, artifacts, and other objects depicting the home life of working-class families in Berlin at the turn of the century. Open Tuesday through Thursday and Saturdays 10:00 A.M. to 6:00 P.M., Fridays to 3:00 P.M., holidays 1:00 to 6:00 P.M. Closed Mondays and Sundays.

Bauhaus-Archiv, Klingelhöferstrasse 14, in the Kulturforum. Built posthumously on the basis of designs by Walter Gropius, it shows architecture, art, and objects of design of the Bauhaus school from 1919 to 1933 and its successors, the New Bauhaus in Chicago and the Ulm School for Design. Works by Gropius, Ludwig Mies van der Rohe, Marcel Breuer, Lyonnel Feininger, Wassily Kandinsky, Paul Klee, Lazlo Moholy-Nagy, and Oskar Schlemmer are on exhibit. Open daily except Tuesdays, 11:00 A.M. to 5:00 P.M., Fridays until 8:00 P.M.

Berliner Dorfmuseum (Village Museum), Alt-Marzahn 31, in the Marzahn district of eastern Berlin. This division of the Märkisches Museum (for which see below) is in a 19th-century farmhouse and barn and exhibits furnishings, artifacts, tools, and machines depicting village life in Brandenburg and around Berlin in the 1800s. Open daily except Mondays and Tuesdays, 10:00 A.M. to 5:30 P.M.

Berliner Kinomuseum (Cinema Museum), Grossbeerenstrasse 57 in Kreuzberg. There are Wednesday to Saturday showings of old silent movies by Fritz Lang and F. W. Murnau and slapstick comedies with Charlie Chaplin and Buster Keaton. In addition, it exhibits old projectors and studio equipment, posters, programs, and still photos. Showings at 7:00 P.M. Wednesday through Friday, 5:00 P.M. Saturdays.

Berlinische Galerie, Stresemannstrasse 110, **Martin-**

Gropius-Bau, in Kreuzberg. Martin Gropius' 1870s Neo-Renaissance structure, rebuilt in the 1980s after wartime destruction, once home of Berlin's museum of applied art, is now used for various rotating and visiting shows and houses the permanent collection of the Berlinische Galerie—paintings and sculptures by Berlin artists of the 20th century, including key works by Lovis Corinth, George Grosz, Otto Dix, the Dadaists, Naum Gabo, Karl Hofer, Erich Heckel, Max Liebermann, and Leser Ury. The Martin-Gropius-Bau also holds a museum of Jewish life in Berlin. (See also Berlin Museum, below.) Open daily except Mondays, 10:00 A.M. to 8:00 P.M.

Berlin Museum, Lindenstrasse 14, in Kreuzberg. The former Prussian supreme court building, in which E. T. A. Hoffmann was once a justice, exhibits art, applied art, artifacts, furnishings, fashions, tools, machines, photos, books, and documents dealing with the history of Berlin and Brandenburg from the 16th through the 19th centuries. Max Beckmann, Lovis Corinth, Max Liebermann, and Max Slevogt are among the artists represented. (The section on Jewish life in Berlin, an independent museum, is in the Martin-Gropius-Bau; see Berlinische Galerie, above.) Open Daily except Mondays 10:00 A.M. to 10:00 P.M.

Bode Museum, Bodestrasse 1–3 (Museumsinsel, entrance by Monbijoubrücke). Built at the turn of the century, the Bode Museum currently houses the eastern Berlin divisions of the Ägyptisches Museum, *Gemäldegalerie* (Picture Gallery), Coin Collection, Sculpture Collection, Museum of Pre- and Early History, and Museum of Late-Ancient and Early Christian-Byzantine Art of the Prussian Cultural Heritage Foundation. The Gemäldegalerie exhibits Old Masters, notably Italian and Flemish, from the 13th through the 18th centuries. It and the western division, presently in the Dahlem complex (see below), will move to a new building in the Kulturforum in 1996. Open daily except Mondays and Tuesdays 10:00 A.M. to 6:00 P.M. (See also Ägyptisches Museum, above.)

Brecht-Weigel Gedenkstätte (Brecht house), Chausseestrasse 125 (at the northern end of Friedrichstrasse). The house in which Bertolt Brecht and Helene Weigel lived after returning to Berlin in 1949 has been turned into an archive of their work. Seven rooms, virtually unchanged, contain their furnishings and personal effects and can be seen on guided tours Tuesday through Friday at 10:00, 10:30, 11:00, and 11.30 A.M., Thursdays also at 5:00, 5:30,

6:00, and 6:30 P.M., Saturdays half-hourly from 9:30 A.M. to 1:30 P.M.

Bröhan Museum, Schlossstrasse 1a (across from Schloss Charlottenburg). The private collection of Karl H. Bröhan, donated to the city in 1981, shows art, sculptures, furnishings, and decorative art from the period 1890 to 1939, with special emphasis on Jugendstil, Art Deco, and modern Functionalism. Open daily except Mondays 10:00 A.M. to 6:00 P.M., Thursdays until 8:00 P.M.

Brücke Museum, Bussardsteig 9, in the Grunewald. *Die Brücke* was the name Germany's leading early–20th-century Expressionists—Erich Heckel, Ernst Ludwig-Kirchner, Emil Nolde, Max Pechstein, and Karl Schmidt-Rottluff—gave themselves when they began painting in a similar style in Dresden in 1905. Most later moved to Berlin, and all were declared "degenerate" and forbidden to paint by the Nazis during the Third Reich. The museum, founded in 1967 with Schmidt-Rottluff's own works and the works of his friends in his private collection, and enlarged with gifts and acquisitions since, is devoted entirely to their work. Open daily except Tuesdays, 11:00 A.M. to 5:00 P.M.

Schloss Charlottenburg (Charlottenburg Palace). Built at the end of the 17th century by King Frederick I for his wife Sophie Charlotte, and enlarged in the 18th and early 19th centuries, it is the largest and most spectacular of Berlin's surviving royal palaces. Every important Prussian architect contributed to it. It is open daily except Mondays from 9:00 A.M. to 5:00 P.M., Saturdays and Sundays from 10:00 A.M. Buildings in the park (the **Schinkel-Pavilion**, **Belvedere**, and **Mausoleum**—designed by Schinkel and containing the remains of various rulers, including Kaiser Wilhelm I) are closed November through March. In the palace wings are the **Galerie der Romantik**, a division of the Nationalgalerie, and **Museum für Vor- und Frühgeschichte** (pre- and early history) with the same hours as the castle, except the Museum für Vor- und Frühgeschichte, which is closed Fridays and open Mondays.

Haus am Checkpoint Charlie Museum, Friedrichstrasse 43–44. This is a collection of photos, documents, and objects dealing with the Berlin Wall and the East German resistance movement. Most spectacular are the paraphernalia and equipment used for daring escapes out of East Berlin and East Germany from 1961 to 1989. An outdoor exhibition of watchtowers, pieces of the Wall, barriers, and surveillance equipment, all under "monuments protection," is a block north of the museum. Open daily, 9:00 A.M. to 10:00 P.M.

Dahlem Museums, Arnimallee 23–27 and Lansstrasse 8, in Dahlem. This is the complex of museum buildings that houses the most important sections of the western Berlin collections of the Prussian Cultural Heritage Foundation: the *Gemäldegalerie* (Picture Gallery), the *Skulpturengalerie* (Sculpture Gallery), the Museum of Late Antiquity and Byzantine Art, the *Museum für Islamische Kunst* (Museum of Islamic Art), the *Museum für Ostasiatische Kunst* (Museum of East Asian Art), and the *Museum für Völkerkunde* (Ethnographic Museum) (see below). Open daily except Mondays 9:00 A.M. to 5:00 P.M., Saturdays and Sundays from 10:00 A.M.

Deutsches Historisches Museum (German Historical Museum), Unter den Linden 2 (in the *Zeughaus,* the Armory). The museum exhibits objects dealing with 900 years of German history. Open daily except Wednesdays 10:00 A.M. to 6:00 P.M.

Deutsches Rundfunk Museum (German Broadcasting Museum), Hammarskjöldplatz 1 (at the radio tower, the Funkturm). The museum gives an overview of radio and television broadcasting from the early 1920s through the 1960s and exhibits many objects, from the earliest microphones and loudspeakers to TV cameras and video recorders. Open daily except Tuesdays 10:00 A.M. to 5:00 P.M.

Museumsdorf Düppel (Village Museum), Clauertstrasse 11 (in the Düppel district of Zehlendorf, south of the Wannsee). This open-air museum, made up of reconstructions of peasant cottages, barns, and artisans' shops, depicts life in a Brandenburg village in the Middle Ages. Open April through September, Thursdays 3:00 to 7:00 P.M., with last admission at 6:00 P.M., Sundays and holidays 10:00 A.M. to 5:00 P.M., last admission at 4:00 P.M.

Ephraim Palais, Poststrasse 16, in the Nikolaiviertel. This division of the Märkisches Museum shows Berlin art from the 17th through early 19th centuries and Berlin portraits and busts from the Baroque to the Biedermeier periods. Open daily except Mondays 9:00 A.M. to 5:00 P.M., Saturdays until 6:00 P.M., Sundays starting 10:00 A.M.

Friedrichswerdersche Kirche–Schinkel Museum, Werderstrasse (south of and parallel to Unter den Linden). The Neo-Gothic brick church, built by Schinkel in the 1820s, houses a permanent exhibition of Neoclassical sculpture from 1780 to 1860 and displays documents pertaining to construction of the church and Schinkel's life and work. Open 10:00 A.M. to 6:00 P.M. Closed Mondays and Tuesdays.

Friseurmuseum (Barbering and Hairdressing Museum), Husemannstrasse 8 in Prenzlauer Berg. The little museum on the ground floor of a turn-of-the-century apartment house shows less than 10 percent of its 13,000 objects, all dealing with the history of barbering, hairdressing, and wig-making from the 18th through 19th centuries. Open Tuesdays and Wednesdays 10:00 A.M. to 12 noon, 1:00 to 5:00 P.M.

Galerie der Romantik, East Wing of Schloss Charlottenburg (see above). This important division of the Nationalgalerie exhibits early–19th-century German painting, with many works by Caspar David Friedrich, Schinkel, Carl Blechen, the Nazarenes, and other masters of the Romantic period. Open daily except Mondays 9:00 A.M. to 5:00 P.M., Saturdays and Sundays from 10:00 A.M.

Gedenkstätte Deutscher Widerstand (Memorial to German Resistance), Stauffenbergstrasse 13–14, in the Tiergarten borough. The former German army high-command building, from which Colonel Claus Schenck von Stauffenberg and other anti-Nazi officers attempted to organize the July 20, 1944, coup, after his abortive assassination attempt on Hitler, has a permanent exhibition of documents, photos, and objects dealing with German resistance against Nazism. Open daily 9:00 A.M. to 6:00 P.M. except Saturdays and Sundays, when it closes at 1:00 P.M.

Gedenkstätte Haus der Wannsee-Konferenz (House of the Wannsee Conference Memorial), Am Grossen Wannsee 56–58, on the Wannsee shore. This turn-of-the-century mansion was the site where top Nazi government and SS officials, including Reinhard Heydrich and Adolf Eichmann, met in January 1942 to organize the "Final Solution," the planned genocide of European Jewry. The permanent exhibition documents the conference, events prior to it, and its consequences. Open Tuesday through Friday 10:00 A.M. to 6:00 P.M., Saturdays and Sundays 2:00 to 6:00 P.M. Closed Mondays.

Gedenkstätte Plötzensee (Plötzensee Memorial), Hüttigpfad (between the Hohenzollern and Westhafen canals). This is part of the prison (still used as a juvenile reformatory) where more than 2,500 anti-Nazis, most of them implicated in the July 20, 1944, assassination attempt on Hitler, were executed in the fall and winter of 1944 and the spring of 1945. There is a documentary exhibition in a side room. Open daily 8:30 A.M. to 4:00 P.M.

Gemäldegalerie (Picture Gallery), Arnimallee 23 (Dahlem museums complex). This, the western Berlin division of the Gemäldegalerie, is the more important, showing hundreds of Old Master paintings from the 13th through 18th centuries, including many Rembrandts and Rubenses, Botticellis, Correggios, Tintorettos, Titians, and Veroneses. It ranks as one of the world's leading museums. Open daily except Mondays, 9:00 A.M. to 5:00 P.M., Saturdays and Sundays from 10:00 A.M. The eastern section in the **Bode Museum** on Museumsinsel has major works by 13th- to 14th-century Italian masters, Dutch and Flemish painting from the 15th through 17th centuries, French and English from the 17th and 18th century—including Nicolas Poussin's famous *Self Portrait*—and important works by Thomas Gainsborough. Open 10:00 A.M. to 6:00 P.M. Closed Mondays and Tuesdays (Some 400 paintings from the combined collection have been missing since World War II.)

Schloss Klein-Glienicke, Königstrasse 1 (adjacent to Glienicker Brücke, the bridge to Potsdam), in the Wannsee area. This Italian villa-style château, built by Schinkel for Prussia's Prince Karl in the 1820s, is set in a beautifully landscaped garden. It will be closed through 1993 for renovation and conversion into a museum, but the park is open.

Jagdschloss Grunewald (Grunewald Hunting Château), Am Grunewaldsee 29, in the Grunewald. Built in the 16th century as a hunting lodge for Elector Joachim II, the château now houses a gallery of more than 200 paintings by 14th- to 19th-century German and Dutch masters, including major works by Lucas Cranach the Elder, Rubens, Jordaens, and Jan Lievens. Closed Mondays. Open 10:00 A.M. to 6:00 P.M. April to September, until 5:00 P.M. in March and October, until 4:00 P.M. November through February.

Hamburger Bahnhof, Invalidenstrasse 50–51, north of the Tiergarten. Berlin's oldest railway station, built in 1847, closed in 1884, and used from 1906 until World War II as the museum of technology, is currently being used for visiting exhibitions and will become the Nationalgalerie's division of contemporary (late–20th- and soon enough, 21st-century) art upon completion of the present restoration, late 1993 or early 1994. Open daily except Mondays, 10:00 A.M. to 6:00 P.M.

Haus der Kulturen der Welt (House of World Cultures), John-Foster-Dulles-Allee 10 (in the Tiergarten). The former Kongresshalle, a gift of the United States to Berlin, presents exhibitions of art from Africa, Latin America, and parts of Asia. Hours vary depending on the exhibit.

Hugenottenmuseum (Huguenot Museum), Gendarmenmarkt 5 (in the French Cathedral). The early-18th-century church of Berlin's French Protestant community, patterned on that of Charenton, France, has in its tower a small museum on 17th- through 19th-century Huguenot life in Berlin. Closed Mondays and Fridays. Open 10:00 A.M. to 5:00 P.M. Tuesdays, Wednesdays, Saturdays; until 6:00 P.M. Thursdays; 11:30 A.M. to 5:00 P.M. Sundays.

Museum für Indische Kunst (Indian art), Lansstrasse 8 (Dahlem complex, see above). This is a collection of Indian, Indonesian, and Central Asian sculptures, bronzes, miniature paintings, and applied art covering almost two millennia, from the second century B.C. to the eighteenth century. Open daily except Mondays, 9:00 A.M. to 5:00 P.M., Saturdays and Sundays from 10:00 A.M.

Museum für Islamische Kunst (Islamic art), Lansstrasse 8 (Dahlem complex; see above) for the western division; in the Pergamon Museum (on Museumsinsel) for the eastern section (see below). Both show important eighth-through nineteenth-century works of Islamic art, including miniature figures, calligraphy, carpets, architectural elements, works of glass, ceramic, gold, silver, and ivory. Dahlem complex open daily except Mondays, 9:00 A.M. to 5:00 P.M., Saturdays and Sundays from 10:00 A.M.; eastern Berlin division closed Monday and Tuesday, otherwise 10:00 A.M. to 6:00 P.M., Fridays to 10:00 P.M.

Käthe Kollwitz Museum, Fasanenstrasse 24, just off the Kurfürstendamm. A fine private collection of 100 graphic works, 70 drawings, 15 bronze casts, and virtually all her original sculptures. This museum, begun and directed by Berlin artist and gallery owner Hans Pels-Leusden, ranks as a major repository of Käthe Kollwitz's work. Open daily except Tuesdays 11:00 A.M. to 6:00 P.M.

Knoblauchhaus, Poststrasse 23, in the Nikolaiviertel. The Knoblauchs were a well-to-do bourgeois family, several generations of whom played a key role in 18th- to 19th-century Berlin life. The Neoclassical building is one of the few originals that survived World War II. The exhibition in ten rooms, with furnishings from the time, depicts the family's history in relationship to the city's development. Closed Mondays. Open Tuesday through Friday 9:00 A.M. to 5:00 P.M., Saturdays to 6:00 P.M., Sundays 10:00 A.M. to 5:00 P.M.

Kunstgewerbemuseum (Museum of Applied Arts), western section, Matthäikirchstrasse 10, Kulturforum area; eastern division in Schloss Köpenick, Schlossinsel in Köpenick. The western Berlin section, in a modern building, exhibits works of European decorative art from the Middle Ages to the present, including the beautifully crafted silver objects of the Lüneburg town council. The eastern Berlin division shows objects covering ten centuries of craftsmanship, including gold jewelry from the time of Holy Roman Emperor Otto I, around the year 1000. The entire collection was in the Martin-Gropius-Bau before World War II. The Kulturforum building is open daily except Mondays, 9:00 A.M. to 5:00 P.M., Saturdays and Sundays from 10:00 A.M. Schloss Köpenick, Berlin's oldest surviving palace, is closed Mondays and Tuesdays, otherwise open from 10:00 A.M. to 6:00 P.M.

Kupferstichkabinett (Print Collection), Matthäikirchplatz (Kulturforum). The entire collection of 600,000 drawings, etchings, engravings, woodcuts, lithographs, and other forms of graphic art, up to now divided between western and eastern Berlin (with 40 of the Botticelli drawings for Dante's *Inferno* in the east, 80 in the west) will move into this new museum in the Kulturforum in summer 1993.

Märkisches Museum, Am Köllnischen Park 5 (south of Alexanderplatz). This turn-of-the-century museum, built to look like a Gothic brick church, is devoted to the cultural history of Berlin and the March of Brandenburg, beginning with the first traces of human settlement in the Stone Age and continuing to the present. It maintains a number of branches around the city, such as the Ephraim Palais, Knoblauchhaus, Nikolaikirche, Museum Berliner Arbeiterleben, and the Dorfmuseum in Marzahn (see individual listings). Open 10:00 A.M. to 6:00 P.M. Closed Mondays and Tuesdays.

Münzkabinett (Coin Collection), Bodestrasse 1–3 (in the Bode Museum, Museumsinsel, entrance via Monbijoubrücke). This numismatic collection of 500,000 pieces covers coinage from its beginnings in the seventh century B.C. to the present. Open 10:00 A.M. to 6:00 P.M. Closed Mondays and Tuesdays.

Musikinstrumenten Museum, Tiergartenstrasse 1 in the Kulturforum. The collection includes rare and artfully crafted musical instruments—woodwinds, strings, pianos, and organs—from the 16th through 20th centuries. Open 9:00 A.M. to 5:00 P.M., Saturdays and Sundays from 10:00 A.M. Closed Mondays.

Nationalgalerie, Bodestrasse 1–3, Museumsinsel. Begun in the 1860s, the Nationalgalerie is the architectural centerpiece of Museumsinsel and presently shows Neoclassical German sculptures, 18th- through early-20th-century painting (including some fine Goyas and German and French Impressionists), as well as works of the modern (pre-World War II) period. It will be closed for repairs and total renovation December 1993, and after reopening will house the Prussian Cultural Heritage Foundation's entire 19th-century collection, including works now in the Galerie der Romantik in Schloss Charlottenburg. Open 10:00 A.M. to 6:00 P.M. Closed Mondays and Tuesdays.

Neue Nationalgalerie, Potsdamer Strasse 50, in the Kulturforum. Ludwig Mies van der Rohe's last work, completed in 1968, a year before his death, contains painting and sculpture of the late 19th century to the present, including major works by modern and contemporary artists. Starting some time in 1994 or 1995 the collection will be 20th-century art only, bolstered by special shows. Open 9:00 A.M. to 5:00 P.M., from 10:00 A.M. Saturdays and Sundays. Closed Mondays.

Neues Museum, Museumsinsel. This building, destroyed during the war, remains a ruin. Reconstruction is scheduled to start in 1995, and after completion will house both the western and eastern Egyptian collections.

Museum für Ostasiatische Kunst (East Asian art). The western Berlin collection is in the Dahlem complex, Lansstrasse 8 (see above); the eastern one in the Pergamon Museum, Bodestrasse 1–3, entrance from the Kupfergraben, on Museumsinsel (see below). The two collections show thousands of archaeologically excavated objects of Chinese, Japanese, and Korean art and decorative art, including stone, wood, and ivory engravings, bronze sculpture, ceramics and porcelain, paintings, calligraphy, and woodcuts from 3000 B.C. to the present. The Dahlem section is closed Mondays. Hours 9:00 A.M. to 5:00 P.M., from 10:00 A.M. Saturdays and Sundays; the section in the Pergamon Museum is open 10:00 A.M. to 6:00 P.M., Fridays until 10:00 P.M., closed Mondays and Tuesdays.

Otto-Nagel-Haus, Märkisches Ufer 16–18 (near the Märkisches Museum). This division of the Nationalgalerie exhibits revolutionary, proletarian, and anti-Nazi paintings and sculptures, including works by the Berlin artists Otto Nagel, Käthe Kollwitz, and Ernst Barlach. Open 10:00 A.M. to 6:00 P.M. Closed Fridays, Saturdays, and Mondays.

Pergamon Museum, Bodestrasse 1–3, entry via Kupfergraben, on Museumsinsel. Besides the other divisions in the building, (Islamic, East Asian) it houses the eastern Berlin section of the Antiquities Museum, including the Pergamum Altar and the Roman market gate of Miletus, and portions of the throne room of Nebuchadnezzar in the Eurasian division. The halls containing the major architectural exhibits are open daily from 10:00 A.M. to 6:00 P.M. Smaller halls open Wednesday through Sunday.

Schloss Pfaueninsel (Peacock Island Château), Pfaueninsel (in the Wannsee). The landscaped island with its fake ruins and romantic little château was laid out in the 1790s. The Neoclassical rooms of the palace are the original, as planned by King Frederick William II, and show murals, paintings, stucco reliefs, and furnishings. Open 10:00 A.M. to 4:00 P.M. April through October, closed November through March. Closed Mondays year-round.

Postmuseum (Postal Museum), of which there are two. The one in western Berlin is at An der Urania 15 in Schöneberg, the eastern one at Leipziger and Mauer Strassen, near the former Checkpoint Charlie. The western museum concentrates on the history of the Brandenburg and Prussian mail system, the eastern section on the history of mail and postal systems from their earliest beginnings. There are philatelic exhibitions in both. The western museum is open 9:00 A.M. to 5:00 P.M., from 10:00 A.M. Saturdays and Sundays; closed Fridays. The eastern division is open 10:00 A.M. to 6:00 P.M., closed Sundays and Mondays.

Skulpturengalerie (Sculpture Collection), Arnimallee 23–27 in the Dahlem complex for the western Berlin section; Bode Museum, Bodestrasse 1–3, on Museumsinsel for the eastern parts (see above for both). The Dahlem division shows sculpture from early Christian times to the 19th century, divided into five art-historical periods. Exquisite wood carvings by Tilman Riemenschneider are among the treasures. The eastern section is strong on works from the tenth through eighteenth centuries, with the best here being Italian Renaissance pieces, especially of the Florentine school. The Dahlem section is closed Mondays, otherwise open 9:00 A.M. to 5:00 P.M., from 10:00 A.M. on Saturdays and Sundays. The Bode

Museum exhibits are closed Mondays and Tuesdays, otherwise open from 10:00 A.M. to 6:00 P.M.

Schloss Tegel, Adelheidallee 19–21, near the Tegel stop on the U-6 subway line. Built in the 16th century and renovated in Neoclassical style by Schinkel for the family of Alexander and Wilhelm von Humbolt, it is still privately owned by the Humboldt family and contains Wilhelm von Humboldt's stunning collection of Greco-Roman sculptures. Open Mondays only 10:00 A.M. to 12 noon, 3:00 to 5:00 P.M.

Topographie des Terrors (Topography of Terror), Stresemannstrasse 110, adjacent to the Martin-Gropius-Bau, in Kreuzberg. This is the site of Gestapo and Nazi security service headquarters, all since razed. The pavilion and the excavations of building cellars, with their interrogation and torture cells, present a documentary exhibition of secret-police terror and surveillance during the Third Reich. Open 10:00 A.M. to 6:00 P.M. Closed Mondays.

Museum der Verbotenen Kunst (Museum of Forbidden Art), corner Pushkinallee and Schlesische Strasse, along the former Berlin Wall, Treptow borough. Located in a former watchtower of the Berlin Wall, this unusual museum shows paintings, graphics, and sculptures by artists banned or ostracized during the Communist regime. The museum's café is called *Im Todestreifen*—"In the Death Strip." Open daily Monday through Friday 4:00 to 10:00 P.M., Saturdays and Sundays from 11:00 A.M. to 11:00 P.M.

Museum für Verkehr und Technik (transport and technology), Trebbiner Strasse 9, in Kreuzberg. Located on the grounds of an old freight railway station and wholesale warehouses, the museum, founded in 1983, now has more than 100,000 square feet (10,000 square meters) of display space and is still being enlarged, with completion expected in the late 1990s, after which it will be one of the world's largest museums of its kind. It exhibits originals of all types: old locomotives, cars, ships, and rail and air transport memorabilia, including 1930s airplanes. Also on display are objects of household and industrial technology, such as old office machines, printing presses, computers, precision instruments, and implements for energy production, e.g., windmills. Open Tuesday through Friday 9:00 A.M. to 5:30 P.M., Saturdays and Sundays 10:00 A.M. to 6:00 P.M. Closed Mondays.

Museum für Völkerkunde (Ethnographic Museum),

Lansstrasse 8 (Dahlem complex). It started as long ago as the 17th century when Brandenburg's Frederick William, the "Great Elector," began collecting odds and ends of objects from places so far from Berlin that no one was sure they even existed. Now the museum's trove of pre-Columbian, African, Southeast Asian, Far Eastern, and South Pacific art, applied art, and artifacts is one of the world's richest. Open 9:00 A.M. to 5:00 P.M., from 10:00 A.M. Saturdays and Sundays. Closed Mondays.

Museum für Ur- und Frühgeschichte (pre- and early history), Langhans wing of Schloss Charlottenburg for the western section; Bode Museum, Bodestrasse 1–3, Museumsinsel for the eastern Berlin division (see above for both). Also once a single museum, then divided, now reuniting, its collections of art and decorative art from the Paleolithic Age to the Dark Ages are among the most important in the world, though also the most plundered. Among the gems missing since World War II and now known to be held in Russia are Priam's Treasure, which Heinrich Schliemann excavated at ancient Troy, and the Bronze Age Gold Treasure of Eberswalde. Charlottenburg section is open 9:00 A.M. to 5:00 P.M., Saturdays and Sundays from 10:00 A.M., closed Fridays. Bode Museum exhibits are closed Mondays and Tuesdays, otherwise open 10:00 A.M. to 6:00 P.M.

Zitadelle Spandau, Am Juliusturm, in Spandau. The 800-year-old citadel, once a Slavic stronghold, houses Spandau's *Stadtgeschichtliches* (municipal history) *Museum,* which shows art and objects dealing with the town's and Brandenburg's pre- and early historical development, its fishing and trade, the medieval Jewish community, the citadel's role as a military bastion, and Spandau's 19th-century industrialization. Open 9:00 A.M. to 5:00 P.M., Saturdays and Sundays from 10:00 A.M. Closed Mondays.

Zuckermuseum (Sugar Museum), Amrumer Strasse 32, in Wedding borough. Prussia was the cradle, Berlin the historical capital, of Europe's sugar-beet production. This museum, subsidized by the industry, tells and exhibits everything anyone might want to know about sugar—both beet and cane: from its planting, harvesting, refining, and production, to its marketing and consumption. Open Mondays and Tuesdays 9:00 A.M. to 6:00 P.M., Sundays 11:00 A.M. to 6:00 P.M.

BERLIN MUSEUMS BY INTEREST

Ancient Art
Abgussammlung Antiker Plastik (Copies Collection of Ancient Sculpture)
Ägyptisches Museum (Egyptian Museum)
Antikenmuseum (Antiquities Museum)
Bode Museum's Ägyptisches Museum
Dahlem complex's Museum of Late Antiquity and Byzantine Art
Pergamon Museum
Schloss Tegel
Museum für Ur- und Frühgeschichte (pre- and early history) in Schloss Charlottenburg

European Art
Bode Museum's Gemäldegalerie (Picture Gallery)
Dahlem complex's Gemäldegalerie and Skulpturengalerie (Sculpture Gallery)
Jagdschloss Grunewald (Grunewald Hunting Château)
Kupferstichkabinett (Print Collection; opening summer 1993 in Kulturforum)
Nationalgalerie (closing for renovation late in 1993)

International Art
Haus der Kulturen der Welt (House of World Cultures)
Museum für Indische Kunst (Indian art)
Museum für Islamisches Art (Islamic art)
Museum für Ostasiatische Art (East Asian art) in both Dahlem complex and Pergamon Museum
Museum für Völkerkunde (Ethnographic Museum)

German Art and Architecture
Bauhaus Archiv
Berlinische Galerie
Bröhan Museum
Brücke Museum
Ephraim Palais
Freidrichswerdersche Kirche-Schinkel Museum
Galerie der Romantik in Schloss Charlottenburg
Hamburger Bahnhof (opening late 1993 or early 1994)
Käthe Kollwitz Museum
Neue Nationalgalerie
Otto-Nagel-Haus

Museum für Verbotenen Kunst (Museum of Forbidden Art)

Palaces
Schloss Charlottenburg
Schloss Pfaueninsel
Schloss Tegel

German History
Museum Berliner Arbeiterleben (Berlin proletarian life)
Berliner Dorfmuseum (Village Museum)
Berlin Museum
Brecht-Weigel Gedenkstätte (Brecht house)
Deutsches Historisches Museum (German Historical Museum)
Museumsdorf Düppel (Village Museum)
Knoblauchhaus
Märkisches Museum (March of Brandenburg Museum)
Zitadelle Spandau

World War II and Nazi History
Haus am Checkpoint Charlie Museum
Gedenkstätte Deutscher Widerstand (Memorial to German Resistance)
Gedenkstätte Haus der Wansee-Konferenz (House of the Wannsee Conference Memorial)
Gedenkstätte Plötzensee (Plötzensee Memorial)
Topographie des Terrors (Topography of Terror)

Technology
Berliner Kinomuseum (Cinema Museum)
Deutsches Rundfunk-Museum (German Broadcasting Museum)
Museum für Verkehr und Technik (transportation and technology)

Unusual Interests
Friseurmuseum (Barbering and Hairdressing Museum)
Münzkabinett (Coin Collection)
Musikinstrumenten Museum (Musical Instrument Museum)
Postmuseum (Postal Museum)
Zückermuseum (Sugar Museum)

ACCOMMO-DATIONS

By John Dornberg

Berlin's appeal as a tourist destination and growing importance as a convention, trade-fair, and business city pose two problems for travellers: a scarcity of hotels and rates that for value given are even higher than elsewhere in Germany. As of fall 1992 there were about 365 establishments in all categories, with about 37,000 available beds, in both western and eastern Berlin. Although new places to stay are sprouting up and there is hardly a major international chain that isn't trying to get a piece of the action, it will be another few years before these are completed and visitors will get the feeling that they have a choice of where to stay during the peak periods and seasons. Meanwhile, making reservations well in advance is imperative.

A Berlin specialty is the *Pension,* a small, privately and individually run abode, usually on an upper floor of a turn-of-the-century bourgeois apartment house. It is a bed-and-breakfast spot that can range from barely minimal comfort—albeit at budget rates—to sumptuous appointments and an ambience of elegance. Another variation is the *Hotelpension,* with the reception and lobby areas usually on the second floor (in German called the first floor, or *erster Stock*), of one of those old buildings. The distinction between them is not always immediately discernible, but there *is* a difference. Hotels, even those called *garni,* meaning they have no restaurant but serve breakfast and *maybe* light snacks, have key desks and concierges on duty around the clock; in a Pension you are

141

handed room and front-door keys for the duration and left to your own devices. The Hotelpension is a hybrid of the two: with a part-time concierge, usually from 8:00 A.M. to 8:00 or 9:00 P.M. and a few hotel amenities, such as direct-dial telephones in the rooms. Pensionen and Hotelpensionen abound on and around the Kurfürstendamm. All hotels, Pensionen, and Hotelpensionen serve breakfast.

Though postal codes in western and eastern Berlin will remain divided for another year, meaning you should precede correspondence to addresses in western boroughs with "W" and those in eastern districts with "O," Berlin's and Germany's phone system has been "re-united" since the summer of 1992. The country code for all of Germany is 49. The city code for all of Berlin is 30, though when phoning Berlin from elsewhere in Germany the 30 should be preceded by a zero.

Eight of the luxury and first-class hotels listed below (Bristol-Hotel Kempinski, Inter-Continental, Schweizerhof, Grand-Maritim, Hilton-Dom, Steigenberger, Metropol, and Radisson Plaza) can be booked toll-free in the United States by calling (800) 237-5469. This is the number of an agency called "Dial Berlin." It also has a Fax connection: (314) 432-0512. If you call the hotels listed here directly, you can expect most, if not all, hotel personnel to be able to respond to you in English—though it is, of course, always polite to ask first.

The rates listed here are 1993 projections for double-occupancy rooms, with a range from low to high whenever possible. Basic rates are always subject to change, so please verify price when you are booking. Service charges and taxes are *always,* breakfast *usually,* included in the price of a room. Breakfast is included in all prices given below. Many smaller hotels and Pensionen do not accept credit cards.

The Kurfürstendamm Area

If you can afford it, *die beste Adresse* in town is the **Bristol-Hotel Kempinski**, in the center of all the action. Totally destroyed during the war, rebuilt in 1952, and thoroughly renovated in 1980, it has all the ambience of a grand hotel, and its guest list reads like pages from *Who's Who*.

Kurfürstendamm 27, D(W)-1000 Berlin 15. Tel: 88-43-40; Fax: 8836075. DM 530–600.

East on the boulevard, and easy to miss because terrace cafés flank the entrance, is the **Hotel am Zoo**, a favorite among visiting journalists, and not just because it's close to where some of them have Berlin editorial offices. It's the size—130 rooms—and the courteous, efficient service. Rooms have a pleasing modern elegance. The best face the avenue, and some even have little balconies from which to watch the show down below.

Kurfürstendamm 25, D(W)-1000 Berlin 15. Tel: 88-43-70; Fax: 88437714. DM 300–370.

Meinekestrasse is a small side street that intersects the Ku'damm just across the avenue from the Hotel am Zoo. In what used to be an upper-class apartment house you'll find the **Hotel Meineke**, a small, family-run establishment with some of the advantages of a Pension and none of the disadvantages. The 60 rooms are high-ceilinged and large, the furniture comfy, the breakfast chamber a delight of Neo-Baroque decor with crystal chandeliers.

Meinekestrasse 10, D(W)-1000 Berlin 15. Tel: 88-28-11; Fax: 8825716. DM 215–240.

Right next door, in a splendid Belle Epoque building, is the moderately priced **Hotel Residenz**, a reincarnation of old Berlin. Although functionally modern, all of the 85 rooms are agreeably large, and many have elaborate stucco ceilings. Its **Grand Cru** dining room is one of the city's better French restaurants.

Meinekestrasse 9, D(W)-1000 Berlin 15. Tel: 88-44-30; Fax: 8824726. DM 300.

Joachimstaler Strasse, which intersects the Ku'damm just west of the Gedächtniskirche and the Europa-Center, is noisy, but you couldn't be more centrally located. And nothing beats the **Art Hotel Sorat** here for living with and in an ambience of modern art and design. In fact, German designer Wolf Vostell has turned the entire establishment into a kind of live-in avant-garde gallery

Joachimstaler Strasse 28/29, D(W)-1000 Berlin 15; Tel: 88-23-07; Fax: 8844700. DM 260–285.

Right at the corner of the Ku'damm and Joachimstaler Strasse, in a recently renovated Jugendstil building, is the **Hotel Frühling am Zoo**, each of whose 69 rooms is individually appointed with period furniture and resuscitated turn-of-the-century antiques and crystal chandeliers. Though it has a noisy location, double-pane windows help to keep out the din.

Kurfürstendamm 17, D(W)-1000 Berlin 15; Tel: 881-80-83; Fax: 8816483. DM 256–280.

The atmosphere is strictly more old-worldly up the street in the **Hotel Hardenberg**, a converted and modernized turn-of-the-century Berlin burgher house with only 34 rooms, each appointed differently.

Joachimstaler Strasse 39/40, D(W)-1000 Berlin 12; Tel: 881-41-83; Fax: 8815170. DM 260–290.

Going north along Joachimstaler Strasse takes you to Bahnhof Zoo, and northwest from there into Hardenbergstrasse and toward the Technical University. About halfway along is the **Berlin Hotel Excelsior**. Though strictly functional-modern, and likely to be crowded with busloads of visitors speaking a Babel of languages, the hotel has rooms facing the courtyard at the back—about 200 of the total 320—that are pleasantly quiet; and, given the hotel's size, the staff is exceptionally friendly and helpful. The breakfast buffet, which includes hot dishes prepared continuously, is one of the most abundant in town.

Hardenbergstrasse 14, D(W)-1000 Berlin 12; Tel: 319-91 or 319-93; Fax: 31992849 or 31992295. DM 350.

Moving west on Kurfürstendamm you will find a number of medium-category to first-class hotels along the avenue and on side streets, and a number of Pensionen, Hotelpensionen, and smaller, quieter hotels on the many streets intersecting and paralleling the boulevard.

The **Savoy Hotel** on Fasanenstrasse between Kantstrasse and the Ku'damm is close to the most important commercial art galleries and has ranked as a favorite among more successful contemporary artists since the 1950s. All 116 rooms are appointed in furnishings that give you a feeling of timeless elegance. Its Belle Epoque main restaurant is good for French and German dishes prepared nouvelle style.

Fasanenstrasse 9, D(W)-1000 Berlin 12; Tel: 31-10-30; Fax: 31103333. DM 450–520.

If you want to be right on the boulevard, the **Mondial** is a good choice in the upper price range. Though modern with functionally appointed rooms, it is small enough— 75 rooms—for personal and friendly service. It was designed especially to meet the needs of the physically handicapped. All corridors, rooms, and public areas can be easily negotiated by those in wheelchairs.

Kurfürstendamm 47, D(W)-1000 Berlin 15; Tel: 88-41-10; Fax: 88411150. DM 290–500.

Farther up the Ku'damm, between Schlüter and Wielandstrasse, you'll find the **Askanischer Hof**. Established in 1925 by the connection of two grand *belle-étage* apartments in adjacent houses, it has been a favorite of film and stage folk for decades. Arthur Miller was a guest not too many years ago, as was Heinz Rühmann, the character actor who played in the film *The Captain of Köpenick.* Many movies have been made in its opulent Art Nouveau salon and suites. All 17 rooms have private baths or showers, but two are without private toilet.

Kurfürstendamm 53, D(W)-1000 Berlin 15; Tel: 881-80-33; Fax: 8817206. DM 240–400.

The most interesting and rewarding cross streets for smaller, less expensive hotels, Pensionen, and Hotelpensionen are (moving west) Knesebeck, Schlüter, Wieland, Giesebrecht, and Albrecht-Achilles streets.

The **Berlin Plaza Hotel**, just off the Ku'damm on Knesebeckstrasse, is part of the same local chain as the Excelsior. Its 131 functionally modern rooms are all equipped with cable television, radio-alarm clocks, direct-dial phones, minibars, room safes, and hair dryers and makeup mirrors in the bathrooms. The Plaza may be somewhat faceless, but the staff is especially friendly and attentive, and for location and value in the medium-to-first-class category it's hard to match.

Knesebeckstrasse 63, D(W)-1000 Berlin 15; Tel: 88-41-30 or 88-41-34-44; Fax: 88413754. DM 320.

The **Hotel Bogota**, in a reconstructed early 20th-century apartment house, and strictly functional in its decor, is located on a quiet cross street of the Ku'damm. Only 60 of the 120 rooms have private showers and toilets; 13 have showers only and 47 have no bath or WC.

Schlüterstrasse 45, D(W)-1000 Berlin 15; Tel: 881-50-01; Fax: 8835887. DM 100–180.

The **Hotelpension Dittberner**, on the fourth floor of a turn-of-the-century building on Wielandstrasse, will give you the impression that you've entered an art gallery, for it is full of works by contemporary Berlin painters that proprietress Elly Lange and her husband Ludwig, an art dealer, collect and exhibit. Among the keys handed to guests is one to the cagelike elevator. Eighteen of the twenty rooms have private baths or showers, but thirteen of them are without private toilet.

Wielandstrasse 26, D(W)-1000 Berlin 15; Tel: 883-33-26 or 881-64-85. DM 120–180.

Just one floor below, and even more moderate in price, is the **Hotelpension Modena**, most of whose twenty rooms face the building's quiet courtyard. Six of these have private baths or showers and WCs, twelve have showers only (installed as cubicles in a corner of the room), and two have merely wash basins. As at the Dittberner upstairs, you'll be handed a key to the building elevator in addition to the ones to the outside door, the pension, and your room.

Wielandstrasse 26, D(W)-1000 Berlin 15; Tel: 883-54-04; Fax: 8815294. DM 100–170.

Giesebrechtstrasse is a quiet residential street that runs diagonally northwest off the Ku'damm for just two short blocks, starting at Olivaer Platz. The **Hotel Charlot**, in an early-20th-century apartment house here, gives the impression of being a private home, and with only 24 rooms—14 of those without private WC—it almost is. The rooms are all pleasantly and cozily appointed with an eclectic mix of functionally modern and traditional furniture.

Giesebrechtstrasse 17, D(W)-1000 Berlin 12; Tel: 323-40-51; Fax: 3240819. DM 110–220.

Hotel Steiner, also just off the Ku'damm and Olivaer Platz, is known as Berlin's version of New York City's Chelsea Hotel—a favorite among artists and literati who are still waiting for the big commercial breakthrough and may be in arrears on the rent. It's young, trendy, and avant-garde, though some of the furnishings are reminiscent of yesteryear. Only three of the thirty-three rooms have both showers and private WCs, eleven have shower stalls only, and the rest are equipped merely with washbasins.

Albrecht-Achilles-Strasse 58, D(W)-1000 Berlin 31; Tel: 891-16-15 or 891-90-16. DM 100–150.

On and Around Pariser Strasse

This relatively short street starts—if you are looking east— just south of the Ku'damm at Olivaer Platz and runs for six blocks southeast to as far as Fasanenstrasse. In a sense it is part of the Kurfürstendamm area, but it is more a neighborhood unto itself: trendy and fashionable with a profusion of art galleries, antiques and upscale bric-a-brac shops, the boutiques and showrooms of local designers and craftspeople, macrobiotic food stores, sidewalk cafés, and ethnic restaurants, including an ersatz-American one called **Jimmy's Diner** (see Dining: Eclectic and Eccentric, below).

Hotel Alexander, which opened only in September 1991 in a renovated and converted Jugendstil apartment house, expresses the mood and environment. It is a small Postmodern establishment with burnished steel-tubing designer furnishings, a warm paprika-and-black color scheme, contemporary graphics on the walls, and such amenities as bathrobes and hair dryers in its tile bathrooms. A trendy café on the ground floor doubles as the room for breakfast, which is not included in the price for the room.

Pariser Strasse 37, D(W)-1000 Berlin 15; Tel: 881-60-91; Fax: 8816094. DM 320–370.

The **Pension Austriana**, almost adjacent, is one of the city's bargains. The twenty-four rooms—five with private baths, eighteen with shower stalls but no WC, and one with just a sink—are cozy, comfortable, and invitingly appointed, and the atmosphere is friendly and homelike.

Pariser Strasse 39–40, D(W)-1000 Berlin 15; Tel. 885-70-00; Fax: 88750088. DM 120–220.

Farther along the street, at the corner of Uhlandstrasse, is the **Hotel Domus**, a bed-and-breakfast establishment in the moderate price range. All 50 rooms, some of which are designated as nonsmoking, have private bathrooms and are appointed in unobtrusive blond wood. Some— rare in Berlin and the rest of Germany—have French-style double beds without the usual canyon-like crack down the middle. Buffet breakfast is served from 7:00 to 11:00 A.M.

Uhlandstrasse 49, D(W)-1000 Berlin 15; Tel: 88-20-41; Fax: 8820410. DM 180–220.

South of the Tiergarten

Budapester Strasse, south of the Tiergarten, became a hotel street not long after the building of the Wall, specializing in the luxury and first-class category. Among the establishments the **Schweizerhof** is popular, in part because it can boast Berlin's largest indoor hotel pool, replete with ozone-bubble thermal baths, and a balneological department to cure whatever you think ails you. All 430 rooms were recently renovated and redecorated. The atmosphere is a bit sterile, but the Swiss cuisine in the main dining room is great.

Budapester Strasse 21-31, D(W)-1000 Berlin 30; Tel: 269-60; Fax: 2696900. DM 460–600.

The **Inter-Continental**, Berlin's largest luxury hotel (580 rooms) which began life in the early 1960s as a Hilton, was a deliberate statement of capitalist defiance close to the Wall and the no-man's-land that World War II and the Cold War had created in this part of central Berlin. Though the street and ownership have changed, the hotel has lost none of its functionally modern yet elegant cachet. Its **Zum Huguenotten** restaurant is one of the city's best French eateries. Moreover, the hotel is so close to the zoo that if you sleep with an open window you can hear the lions roar at night.

Budapester Strasse 2, D(W)-1000 Berlin 30; Tel: 260-20; Fax: 260280760. DM 460–630.

Just south of Budapester Strasse is another group of first- and luxury-class hotels. The **Ambassador** offers the best in service and amenities at manageable prices. Whatever the 200 rooms may lack in spaciousness is compensated for by the bathrooms. The pool on the top floor is decorated in "tropical Caribbean" style, and there is also a fitness center with solarium.

Bayreuther Strasse 42-43, D(W)-1000 Berlin 30. Tel: 21-90-20; Fax: 21902380. DM 340–420.

The **Steigenberger-Berlin,** part of the luxury and first-class hotel group that shows its flag in other key German cities, is a business travellers' favorite. The building itself is a facelessly modern shoe-box construction that stretches the width of Los Angeles Platz between Ranke and Marburger Strassen, and is virtually within shouting distance of the Europa-Center. But rooms are appointed with period furniture, and once inside the lobby you get a little more "Old Berlin" feeling. There are 234 doubles.

Los Angeles Platz 1, D(W)-1000 Berlin 30; Tel: 210-80; Fax: 2108117. DM 450–600.

The **Hotel Brandenburger Hof,** just a block southwest of Los Angeles Platz, is a welcome break from the functional modernism that characterizes so many of Berlin's top-category establishments. This is a turn-of-the-century burgher house that has been totally renovated and modernized. The grand lobby and conservatory, with its beautifully landscaped winter garden, give it a tone of quiet elegance. Furnishings in the style of the Classical Modern—Corbusier leather sofas and chairs, Frank Lloyd Wright chairs—provide a harmonious contrast to the original 1890s architectural details in the public areas and in the 88 rooms.

Eislebener Strasse 14, D(W)-1000 Berlin 30; Tel: 21-40-50; Fax: 21405100. DM 270–390.

Though the Landwehrkanal, an artificial channel of the Spree, cuts through the southern corner of the Tiergarten, its embankments and the neighborhood surrounding it are hardly idyllic. Small wonder Berliners guffawed when the luxury-class **Grand Hotel Esplanade** opened here in 1988. But reunification, close proximity to the

Kulturforum and Postdamer Platz, and hopes that the city will shift its center eastward in the 21st century now make the site a promising location. The structure is a gem of Postmodern architecture, with splashes of polished granite everywhere. Among the amenities are the hotel's own river yacht, on which you can have Sunday brunch while cruising along Berlin's waterways.

Lützowufer 15, D(W)-1000 Berlin 30; Tel: 261-01-1; Fax: 2629121. DM 440–600.

On and Around Unter den Linden

For reasons having to do with the Cold War there was a long-held opinion that East Berlin couldn't possibly have a hotel worth recommending (except maybe to your worst enemy). But long before the Wall crumbled the then state-owned Interhotel chain had been doing its utmost, and with considerable success, to dispel that idea.

Indeed, the grandest and most luxurious of all hotels in all Berlin is the **Grand-Maritim**, on Friedrichstrasse between Behrenstrasse and Unter den Linden. Opened in 1987, it is built in an eclectic blend of Belle Epoque and Postmodern. The Grand is everything its name implies. A splash of marble, thick carpeting, beautifully crafted period furniture, warm wood paneling, exquisite filigree stucco work, crystal chandeliers, and subdued lighting from polished brass lamps with silk shades are some of its best details. Fresh flowers, mostly orchids from the hotel's own greenhouse, decorate the 350 rooms, apartments, and suites. Down pillows and comforters complement soft linens on the beds. Guests have use of the marble swimming pool, saunas, solarium, and squash courts. Classical music plays around the clock on one of the four in-house channels.

Friedrichstrasse 158-164, D(O)-1080 Berlin; Tel: 232-70; Fax: 23273361. DM 490–640.

The latest addition to hotels in and near Berlin's historic center is the splendid **Hilton-Dom Hotel**, a Postmodern-style building with cozily furnished rooms, adjacent to the Gendarmenmarkt, the French and German cathedrals, and the Schauspielhaus. There are seven different restaurants here—from a beer cellar with bowling alley to a top-rated gourmet eatery.

Mohrenstrasse 30, D(O)-1080 Berlin. Tel: 238-20; Fax: 23824269. DM 410–580.

In the more moderate price range, yet right at the

center of everything, there is the **Hotel Unter den Linden** at the corner of Unter den Linden and Friedrichstrasse. Rooms are functionally modern with few frills.

Unter den Linden 14, D(O)-1080 Berlin; Tel: 220-03-11; Fax: 2292262. DM 240–280.

North of Unter den Linden, along Friedrichstrasse and directly across the street from the International Trade Center, is the **Metropol Hotel**. The functionally modern structure, designed and built by Swedish architects at the height of the Cold War, was for many years *the* Western-style establishment in East Berlin. Though without much character, it still rates high among business travellers, and the 340 rooms, all alike in their so-called international-style appointments, are comfortably efficient.

Friedrichstrasse 150–153, D(O)-1080 Berlin; Tel: 238-75; Fax: 20307509. DM 360–450.

Right across from the Palast der Republik you will see the huge, modern, Swedish-designed **Radisson Plaza Hotel**. The ambience in the 600 rooms is uniformly modern, with a warm Scandinavian touch. You have a choice of ten restaurants in the house.

Karl-Liebknecht-Strasse 3, D(O)-1020 Berlin; Tel: 238-28; Fax: 23827590. DM 370–440.

With nearly 1,000 rooms and a height of 40 stories, the **Forum Hotel Berlin** is not only the city's biggest hotel but, after the TV Tower, which is almost adjacent to it, the tallest building. When it was built in the 1960s the Communist regime wanted to best the West, while simultaneously trying to give Alexanderplatz a modicum of cosmopolitan flair. The hotel is strictly functional and modern, though mercifully the Inter-Continental chain's Forum division, which bought it, has replaced its drab East German furnishings and spruced it up with a massive interior renovation. The biggest attraction here is the **Panorama Restaurant** on the 37th floor, from which you have a spectacular view of the entire city.

Am Alexanderplatz, D(O)-1020 Berlin; Tel: 238-90; Fax: 23894305. DM 270.

The **Spreehotel**, practically across the street from the Märkisches Museum, has what will some day be one of eastern Berlin's most idyllic locations: right on the banks of the river facing the eastern tip of the island on which the city of Cölln was founded in the early 13th century. The establishment itself is considerably younger: a 1980s Communist afterthought to provide accommodations for party functionaries. So it's a bit sterile, but rates are moderate and the location, a block from a subway stop, is good.

Wallstrasse 59, D(O)-1020 Berlin. Tel: 391-73-79; Fax: 2002109. DM 200–270.

Smaller, individually run hotels are starting up gradually in eastern Berlin, and one of them is **Hotel Fischer-insel** near the Märkisches Museum and the Otto-Nagel-Haus gallery of revolutionary art. The decor is still a bit reminiscent of the waning days of the East German regime, but rooms are comfortable and clean, and there's a subway stop just around the corner.

Neue Ross Strasse 11, D(O)-1020 Berlin. Tel: 238-07-50; Fax: 23807800. DM 170.

Out of the Center

One of the newer additions to the first-class category is the 78-room **Seehof**, just east of the trade-fair grounds and idyllically situated on the banks of the Lietzensee, one of Berlin's smaller lakes. The rooms could be a little larger, but they have all the conveniences and amenities, and when the city is not overcrowded you can choose between a room with modern or with traditional furnishings. The service is personal, there's a terrace restaurant and garden bar facing the lake, and for all the pastoral ambience you are within easy walking distance of Schloss Charlottenburg and the museums there and only a block from a subway station with a connection to the Ku'damm.

Lietzensee-Ufer 11, D(W)-1000 Berlin 30. Tel: 32-00-20; Fax: 32002251. DM 380–450.

Kreuzberg may not strike most people as the kind of neighborhood in which to stay, no matter how well worth visiting or how many worthwhile museums. But there are a couple of exceptions to that caveat. One of them is the **Hotel Riehmers Hofgarten** on Yorckstrasse, just one subway stop north from Tempelhof airport. Wilhelm Riehmers was an architect who between 1881 and 1892 built a complex of 20 pricey apartment houses here in the style of town mansions around a landscaped courtyard. The entire ensemble is under "historical monuments" protection, and it is in one of the structures that this delightful little 25-room hotel has been installed. All rooms are furnished in period pieces of precious wood and offer such little extras as private safes for valuables, pants presses, minibars, and hair dryers in the bathrooms, which have either full baths or shower stalls.

Yorckstrasse 83, D(W)-1000 Berlin 61; Tel: 78-10-11; Fax: 7866059. DM 230–265.

Also in Kreuzberg, the **Hotel Stuttgarter Hof**, almost adjacent to the Martin-Gropius-Bau, Berlinische Galerie, Topographie des Terrors, and remaining remnants of the Wall, actually has a pedigree going back to the turn of the century, when it ranked as one of the main establishments near the Anhalter Bahnhof, Berlin's rail gateway to western and southern Germany. The station itself is no more; only a segment of its façade stands as a monument. And little of the hotel survived wartime destruction, either, but those elements that did, have been integrated into a new 110-room hotel. The ambience is a blend of modern and traditional decor, with some rooms in light period furnishings, others in rich palisander veneers. The Kochstrasse subway station is just two blocks east.

Anhalter Strasse 9, D(W)-1000 Berlin 61; Tel: 26-48-30; Fax: 26483900; Best Western Reservations in the U.S., (800) 268-1234. DM 315–340.

Outlying Areas

Because of Berlin's efficient public transit system you will find that staying in some of the boroughs on the periphery, along the lakes, or even in Potsdam will leave you no more than 30 minutes' ride by U-Bahn or S-Bahn from the center. And there are some charming hotels in these locations.

Spandau, at least 50 years older than Berlin itself, seems almost like a separate city, despite its incorporation into Berlin in 1920. Right in its colorful medieval old quarter you'll find the **Hotel Benn**, set in a 200-year-old half-timbered and brick artisan's house. Family-owned and -run, it is something like an inner-city Pension—except that you'll feel as if you're in a village. Of the thirty rooms seventeen have private bathrooms, three have shower stalls but no private WC, ten have washbasins only. The nearest subway stop is three blocks away.

Ritterstrasse 1a, D(W)-1000 Berlin 20; Tel: 333-10-61; Fax: 3339978. DM 100–170.

The **Tegeler See** in the northwestern corner of the city is one of Berlin's most popular lakes, dotted with sailboats on a balmy day. But the community of Tegel on the lake shore was also an important industrial port with mills and granaries. One of these medieval storage silos is now the **Hotel Sorat Humboldt Mühle**, which ranks as the city's most successful conversion of ancient industrial architecture to modern use while still preserving its value as a historical monument. Of the 107 rooms, all decorated in a pleasant blend of timeless Postmodern furniture and subdued pastel fabrics, 77 are in the 500-year-old, seven-story brick silo itself; 30 more are in a functionally modern annex. From many of the rooms you have a spectacular view of the lake and port. The hotel has its own motor yacht, berthed right by the entrance, which can be rented for excursions on Berlin's and Brandenburg's waterways. It is a ten-minute walk to Schloss Tegel, the mansion of the Humboldt family, and two minutes to the Tegel U-Bahn station for a 20-minute ride to Unter den Linden.

An der Mühle 5–7, D(W)-1000 Berlin 27. Tel: 43-90-40; Fax: 43904444. DM 275–320.

When Berliners go hiking or biking in the **Grunewald** forest, one of their favorite stops for lunch, supper, or Sunday brunch is the **Forsthaus Paulsborn**, at the southern tip of the Grunewaldsee, just a few hundred yards from Jagdschloss Grunewald and about ten minutes' walk from the Brücke Museum. But the 120-year-old hunting château is also a delightful little hotel, set idyllically in a dark green wood a stone's throw from the water. The ten rooms, most of them with beamed wood ceilings, are all appointed in a rustic country decor and have such facilities as color television, direct-dial phones, and minibars.

Am Grunewaldsee, D(W)-1000 Berlin 33. Tel: 813-80-10; Fax: 8141156. DM 170–200.

Although **Potsdam** is one of our day-trip destinations, it actually shares city boundaries with Berlin, and is so close by S-Bahn to the center of the city that staying there is an option, especially if Berlin is overbooked. And *the* place to stay in Potsdam is **Hotel Schloss Cecilienhof**. Built in 1913 as a copy of an English Tudor-style country mansion for Kaiser Wilhelm II's son, Crown Prince William, and his wife, Cecilia, this was the palace where Harry Truman, Winston Churchill (and then Clement Attlee), and Joseph Stalin met for the Potsdam Conference and decided how to occupy Germany in the summer of 1945. Thirty-six rooms were used for that purpose, and many of them are part of a museum. But forty-two others and the dining and banquet chambers were converted into a hotel and restaurant already under Communist rule, and that is still what it is today. Many of the rooms are quite elegant and have views of the landscaped gardens surrounding the palace.

Neuer Garten, D(O)-1560 Potsdam; Tel: (331) 231-41; Fax: 22498. DM 260–360.

The **Müggelsee** at the southeastern corner of the city in Köpenick is the largest of Berlin's lakes, and, according to many Berliners, the most beautiful. Small wonder that East Germany's Communist leadership built government and party resort complexes along its shores. One of these is now the **Hotel Müggelsee**, a 175-room establishment directly on the lake, with such amenities as a yacht of its own for use by guests. Its only disadvantage is that it is somewhat remote from public transportation, but there is a nearby bus line that ultimately connects with the S-Bahn at Köpenick station.

Am Grossen Müggelsee, D(O)-1170 Berlin; Tel: 660-20; Fax: 6602263. DM 260–440.

DINING
AND
BERLIN AT NIGHT

By John Dornberg and June Carolyn Erlick

John Dornberg, who has contributed the Dining section of this chapter, is the editorial consultant for this book. June Carolyn Erlick, the author of the Berlin at Night section, is a correspondent for Fairchild News Service who arrived in Berlin shortly before the fall of the Wall. She has written on travel and other subjects for many publications, including the New York Times, Newsday, *the* Wall Street Journal, *and the* Miami Herald, *from both Latin America and Europe. She is a contributing editor to* World Press Review.

Berlin has more than 7,500 restaurants, cafés, pubs, dives, and eateries of various kinds—6,000 in western Berlin, 1,500 in eastern. Berliners, it seems, never eat at home. It also seems they need no sleep. In no other city in Germany do establishments stay open and serve food as late. There are no closing laws, no final drink calls. Most places call it quits at 1:00 or 2:00 A.M.; some stay open much later.

There is a distinct Berlin cuisine; it sticks to the ribs and is not to everyone's liking. A *Boulette* is a cold meatball, or Berlin's version of the hamburger, usually eaten as a snack. *Eisbein*—with sauerkraut, naturally—is pickled pig's feet. *Bockwurst* is a very chubby hotdog, smothered in curry-ketchup sauce or served with potato salad. *Erbsensuppe,* sometimes called *Erbspüree,* is thick pea soup, frequently served with pieces of bockwurst or

155

bacon in it. The *Schlachtplatte* is a platter of blood sausage, liverwurst, boiled beef, and hunks of pork kidney.

On a slightly more sophisticated level you will find *Schlesisches Himmelreich,* consisting of either roast goose or roast pork with potato dumplings and sweet-sour gravy containing dried fruit. *Königsberger Klopse* are veal meatballs, sometimes with pieces of herring ground in, in a caper sauce. *Aal grün mit Gurkensalat* consists of stewed eel in an herb, onion, and sour-cream sauce, accompanied by cucumber salad. A *Berliner* is a person and also a doughnut without a hole, filled with jam and sprinkled with sugar.

Beer is the beverage of Berlin, specifically *Weissbier,* brewed with wheat instead of barley malt and officially called a *Berliner Weisse.* Less officially it is known as a *Molle* or *Kühle Blonde* (cool blonde). With a dash of raspberry syrup it becomes a *Berliner Weisse mit Schuss.* Besides modifying the tartness of the beer, the syrup gives it a Champagne-like effervescence, which may explain why it is always served in a bowl-like chalice.

In addition to Berlin cuisine you will find a profusion of restaurants serving *gut-bürgerliche Küche,* which translates loosely as "good plain food" and "home-cooked simple fare." It is a euphemism for "German food," which in itself is a misnomer because there never was such a thing. Germany, even after its unification under the Hohenzollerns in 1871, has had *regional* cuisines: Bavarian, Swabian, Baden, Rhineland, Westphalian, Northern, Saxonian, and Thuringian, to name some. There are no fewer than 1,000 kinds of bread, several hundred distinct *types*—not just brands—of beer, and scores of hams, sausages, and smoked meats, each one a local specialty. No Stuttgarter could survive without a helping of *Spätzle* to accompany the noonday meal. *Labskaus,* a mush of corned-beef hash mixed with red beets, may be the dish of the gods for a native of Hamburg or Bremen, but anathema to the Münchener, who swoons over *Weisswürste,* plump "white sausages" made of minced veal, various herbs, and grated lemon peel.

Nonetheless, in too many restaurants local cuisines are neutralized and amalgamated as "German," and menus offer such standbys as *Sauerbraten* (a Rhineland specialty), *Wiener Schnitzel* (which originated in Vienna), *Gulaschsuppe* (a Hungarian invention), or *Tafelspitz* (thinly sliced beef served with horseradish and cream sauce and, usually, spinach, rooted in Bavaria and Austria).

The city probably has more foreign than German or Berlin restaurants, due in part to the large proportion of foreigners living here, and in part to the Berliners' predilection for vacationing outside Germany and yearning for a bit of the holiday atmosphere when back home. This has encouraged foreigners to start eateries that satisfy the local nostalgia. The ethnic spectrum ranges from simple Turkish kebab stands to stand-up (and take-out) sushi bars, from a flood of Italian pizzerias and ristorantes to some very fine French restaurants. The multitude of French places should come as no surprise in light of the role the Huguenots played here in the 17th and 18th centuries.

However, although Berlin is again Germany's capital, it is not the culinary one. At the top level, where eating is more than just satisfying hunger and cooking is an art, the choice is very limited. The Gault-Millau guide for Germany awards toques to only 27 Berlin restaurants (compared to 29 in Munich, a city with one third the population) and only 12 of these have two or more chef's hats. And of those a number are in residential areas or hard-to-reach edges of the city. The Michelin Germany is far less charitable; it gives a mere four Berlin establishments stars, and only one of those a two-star rating.

There is no special restaurant area, although most of the restaurants, and the better ones, are in Charlottenburg, Wilmersdorf, Kreuzberg, Tiergarten, and Mitte boroughs. There is still a large difference in the number of recommendable eateries between west and east, and some difference in prices. But both gaps are narrowing— the price one rather quickly.

Restaurant prices are high in Berlin by the standards of other German cities. Even open carafe wines are on average 15 to 20 percent more expensive in Berlin than elsewhere in the country. In the top gourmet restaurants dinner for two will cost at least DM 300, not including any beverages. On the other hand, two can still their hunger in a Berliner *Kneipe* (see below) for as little as DM 30.

The following selection is arranged by types of food and restaurant, with listings covering various parts of the city, though restaurants in eastern Berlin will be listed toward the end of each group. A listing by geographical area follows at the end of the chapter.

Telephone numbers are listed when reservations are recommended. For these restaurants, you can usually expect that people will be able to respond to you in English when you call for reservations.

GOURMET AND CREATIVE

The German neologism "gourmet temple" resulted from the discovery in the 1970s that eating is more than just satisfying a bodily need and that good food means more than just plenty of it. The restaurants in this group practice the principles of nouvelle cuisine: the best, freshest ingredients, prepared to order, and cooked more briefly, lightly, less calorifically than mother or grandmother did; changing daily menus in accordance with what is available on the market and the season; smaller portions served with the idea that food is also a feast for the eyes; quiet, restful, elegant surroundings in which the cuisine, not the furnishings or china, glass, and tableware, is on center stage.

Though it may seem like a journey to the end of the world, **Rockendorf's Restaurant**, at Düsterhauptstrasse 1 in Waidmannslust, Reinickendorf borough, 12 miles north of the city center, is certainly worth the trip. (With the high prices you'll be paying here, you might as well add in cab fare, though the restaurant is a half a block from the Waidmannslust station of the S-1 S-Bahn.) There, Siegfried Rockendorf has converted a lovely villa into what is indubitably Berlin's finest—and also most expensive—restaurant. The moment you have been seated by Rockendorf's wife, Ingeborg, as if you were a family guest, the maestro himself approaches your table to describe the menu. There are no à la carte choices, only multicourse prix-fixe menus that change daily. At lunch you can select either the three- or the six-course presentation, at dinner the six- or nine-course program. The wine list has more than 200 selections. Closed Sundays and Mondays, from Christmas through New Year's, and three weeks in summer. Tel: 402-30-99.

Frühsammer's Gasthaus, at Matterhornstrasse 101, near the Grosser Wannsee at the southern tip of the Grunewald, is almost as far away. (Again, you can take a cab, or the S-3 or S-1 to the Nikolassee stop.) Young Peter Frühsammer, whose wife, Antje, is the hostess and oversees the service staff, approaches German and French dishes in a creative, nouvelle style. You are not bound to a prix-fixe menu here, though one or two are offered daily, and 300 wines are listed. Open for dinner only. Closed Sundays and two weeks in January, three in July. Tel: 803-27-20.

Grand Slam, Gottfried-von-Cramm-Weg 47 at the north-eastern edge of the Grunewald, takes its name from the fact that it is on the ground floor of Berlin's most exclusive tennis club, and its chef, Johannes King, has been slamming his way up the gourmet listings to where he now ranks like a Boris Becker among Berlin cooks. The ambience is strictly clublike: lots of mahogany paneling, old etchings on the walls, an open fireplace, and the atmosphere of an English country house. What King creates in the kitchen is haute cuisine prepared to perfection: lobster and grapefruit salad with a curry cream sauce, roast quail with savoy cabbage, escalope of baby veal in a coriander sauce, honey ice cream with mango fruit and slivers of almonds—to mention some recent specialties. The service is equally perfect. The wine list has 200 labels. And you need be neither a club member nor a tennis freak to go there. Closed Sundays and four weeks of July and August. Tel: 825-38-10.

Franz and Dorothea Raneburger, both Austrians, moved to Berlin in the early 1980s and opened the **Bamberger Reiter** at Regensburger Strasse 7, a turn-of-the-century corner wine tavern in a residential/commercial neighborhood just two subway stops south of Bahnhof Zoo. Now their restaurant is one of the city's best, frequented by young professionals and intellectuals, scientists, and musicians. The late Vladimir Horowitz was served Dover sole when he ate here, but Raneburger's repertoire, which he performs with a staff of five in the kitchen, goes far beyond simple fare. The decor is rustic, with parquet flooring and a growing collection of antiques to make the maximum of 35 diners feel at home. Dinner only; closed Sundays and Mondays, January 1–15, and most of August. Tel: 24-42-82.

Karl Wannemacher came from a town on the Saar-Luxembourg border in the mid-1970s and eventually opened his own restaurant, the 25-seat **Alt Luxemburg**, at Windscheidstrasse 31, Charlottenburg. The exquisite fare is a blend of French, Luxembourgian, and Saarland cuisine, with occasional touches of Berlin nouvelle style to remind you where you are; the room is wood paneled, with lots of mirrors and antique furnishings that hostess Ingrid Wannemacher has collected. Dinner only; closed Sundays, Mondays, the first three weeks in January, and three weeks in July. Tel: 323-87-30.

Trio is also the name of the Villeroy und Boch china on which dishes are served in this small but elegant restaurant at Klausener Platz 14, diagonally across the boulevard from Schloss Charlottenburg. The ambience is more that of a cozy café—plain white walls with a few modern graphics, over each of the eight tables simple modern

ceiling lamps that can be pulled down to provide inti-
macy, starched linen, gleaming modern crystal. The nouvelle cuisine—German, French, and a touch of eclectic
internationalism—is prepared exquisitely, and prices are
moderate (a three-course dinner for two will cost about
DM 120 plus beverages). Dinner only; closed Wednesdays
and Thursdays, three weeks in June and July. No credit
cards. Tel: 321-77-82.

Maxwell, Helmstedter Strasse 9, is decorated in the
same simple low-key style, but will put a somewhat big-
ger dent in your billfold. But then, this is nouvelle German cooking at its most imaginative and creative, using
the best and freshest ingredients, with the idea that they
should be prepared and seasoned as naturally as possible. Gault-Millau raves about coowner and chef Uwe
Popall's "steadfastness and consistency" and awards him
three toques, one of the highest ratings in Berlin. A few
years ago this restaurant was in the heart of Kreuzberg,
but it moved to a strictly residential neighborhood, three
subway stops south of the Ku'damm. Open evenings only;
closed Mondays and Tuesdays. Tel: 854-47-37.

Aphrodite, Schönhauser Allee 61, in Prenzlauer Berg
(just north of the Eberswalder Strasse station of the U-2
subway), is proof that the gap between east and west is
starting to close, indeed that eastern Berlin wasn't entirely the culinary wasteland it appeared to be even in
Communist days. This elegantly appointed restaurant—
stucco ceilings and walls, crystal chandeliers—actually
made its debut three years before the Wall came down.
But since then chef Ortwin Hartwig and proprietor
Benno Ferch, who serves as maitre, have succeeded in
modernizing and lightening the fare because they now
have access to the fresh, high-quality ingredients that
sophisticated cuisine demands. They offer a daily three-
course prix-fixe menu for DM 60 and most entrees are
under DM 35. Open evenings only; closed Sundays, Mondays, and in July. Tel: 448-17-07.

TRADITIONAL BERLIN
There are hundreds upon hundreds of restaurants, inns,
and pubs serving what is generally called *Berliner* or *gut-
bürgerliche Deutsche Küche*. Prices in most are moderate,
as, alas are culinary skills. On or near the Ku'damm there
are quite a few, many of which stay open until 1:00 or 2:00
A.M.

The **Schultheiss Bräuhaus**, at Kurfürstendamm 220, is

the main beer hall of Berlin's leading brewery. The surroundings are rustic and so is the food—strictly stick to
the ribs.

Hardtke, at Meinekestrasse 27, just off the Ku'damm, is
typical of old Berlin restaurants, with its bare wood
benches, chairs, and tables—and its huge portions. The
waiters tend to be as robust as the food, and if you flinch
at the vast amounts of it on your plate you'll be instantly
typed as a wimp. Specialties are homemade black sausage
and liverwurst on sauerkraut with potatoes; pea soup; and
Eisbein with sauerkraut.

The **Spreegarten**, at Uhlandstrasse 175, just off the
Ku'damm, embodies the atmosphere of old Berlin: Its
dark, wood-paneled interior, with turn-of-the-century furnishings, will give you the feeling of being back in the
kaiser's days.

The **Mommseneck** in Charlottenburg, at Mommsenstrasse 45, was established in 1905 and is famous for its
100 brands of beer, many of them on tap, which you can
enjoy out in the beer garden.

A little farther afield, in Wilmersdorf borough, just
south of Charlottenburg, the **Wirtshaus Nussbaum**, at
Bundesplatz 4, is a bargain if you're looking for Berlin
specialties such as *Schlesisches Himmelreich* or potato
pancakes served with onions, bacon, and pumpkin purée.

For a combination of history and real *Kneipen* atmosphere (see below for a discussion of *Kneipen*), it's hard
to equal Kreuzberg's **Grossbeerenkeller**, Grossbeerenstrasse 90, north of Victoria park, open from 4:00 P.M. until
2:00 A.M. In business since 1862, the year of Bismarck's
appointment as Prussia's prime minister, the place is
filled with bric-a-brac souvenirs and odds-and-ends collectibles. Besides Bismarck herring and schnitzel à la
Holstein, specialties include fried potatoes (a main dish
by itself) with onions, and Silesian egg pancakes with
bacon and onions. The portions are huge.

The turf for real local and regional food is better in
eastern Berlin because, until the Wall came down, for
better or worse, it remained closer to "Germany as it
used to be."

You will find historic surroundings and honest food at
Zur Letzten Instanz (Waisenstrasse 14–16, south of Alexanderplatz). The name means "Court of Last Resort" and
comes from the location of this 360-year-old house next
to the former appeals court. The menu reads like a legal
proceeding: *Anklage* (indictment), *Kreuzverhör* (cross-

examination), *Plädoyer* (closing argument). Among the specialties are fried herring with onions, fried potatoes and cole slaw, and jellied meat with hash browns.

A number of such establishments can also be found in the **Nikolaiviertel**, although all are housed in reconstructions.

Though a 1980s replica, **Zur Rippe**, Poststrasse 17, at the corner of Mühlendamm, has a pedigree going back to the 14th century, when fossils of whales and mammoths were found around Berlin-Cölln, and indeed has had a whale's rib as its symbol for some 500 years. The simple fare is based on historic Berlin recipes.

Zum Paddenwirt, Nikolaikirchplatz 6, at the back side of the Nikolaikirche, smokes its own herrings, and serves *bouletten* and chunks of roast pork to go with the beer and the schnapps.

The **Bierschänke in der Gerichtsklause**, Poststrasse 28, provides an ambience of vaulted ceilings and medieval furnishings as the setting for its traditional Berlin dishes, such as *Eisbein* and pork roasts, with lots of sauerkraut.

Mutter Hoppe, Rathausstrasse 21, opens at 11:00 A.M. and closes when the last guest leaves. That could be in the wee hours; playing cards as long as you want, provided you order an occasional beer, is one of the amenities.

The **Spreeblick**, Probststrasse 9, with a terrace overlooking the river, boasts that its potato pancakes, traditionally served with apple sauce, are the best in town.

TRADITIONAL AND REGIONAL GERMAN

This is an arbitrary category, indicating restaurants and pubs that serve more than just simple Berlin food, and, while not necessarily imaginative or creative, prepare their dishes in a thoughtful manner. Among them are some real Berlin favorites, frequented by locals and regulars, and a number of spots that are popular with Berliners because they serve specialties from other regions of Germany.

Mampes Gute Stube, Kurfürstendamm 14–15, is one of the few old Berlin eateries whose interior furnishings survived both world wars; it was a favorite of the greats of literature, among them Kurt Tucholsky, Hermann Kesten, Thomas Wolfe, and Joseph Roth, the Austrian novelist and critic who wrote his *Radetzky March* at one of the restaurant's tables. Though the furnishings were preserved, the entire building was reconstructed in the 1980s and little of the original atmosphere is left. The establishment is now part of the Swiss Mövenpick operation, which puts the emphasis on 'international' cuisine, combining Swiss, German, French, American, even Italian dishes.

Hecker's Deele, Grolmanstrasse 35, north of Ku'damm, looks like a Westphalian farmhouse inside, and Westphalian dishes are the thing here: stick-to-the-ribs creations like broiled pork loin with thick beans and heaps of potatoes or a plate of cold cuts—black sausage, liverwurst, smoked ham, and bacon—accompanied by an orange-sized liver dumpling, sauerkraut, and mashed potatoes, all washed down with beer and corn schnapps.

Lutter & Wegner, Schlüterstrasse 55, off Ku'damm, west of Grolmant Strasse, has a pedigree going back to 1811, when it was founded as a wine tavern and wine dealership. Among past guests were E. T. A. Hoffman of *Tales of Hoffmann* fame, the poet Heinrich Heine, the German Shakespearean actor Ludwig Devrient, and, in more recent times, Joan Baez. The ambience is strictly "old Berlin"—dark walls, lots of wood, and rustically cozy. Main dishes such as *Zurich Geschnetzeltes,* stuffed breast of guinea hen, or broccoli salad with strips of beef fillet go for between DM 20 and 30, and portions are overgenerous. Open evenings only, and it is wise to reserve. Tel: 881-34-40.

Specialties from southwestern Germany, notably food from the Rhineland Palatinate (Chancellor Helmut Kohl's home turf) and wines from Württemberg (hard to find anywhere because the Swabians themselves drink most of them up), are found at the rustic **Beiz** restaurant, Schlüterstrasse 38. Open evenings only, and as it's usually crowded, reserve. Tel: 883-89-57.

Restaurant Heinz Holl, Damaschkestrasse 26 (the street runs northwest off the Ku'damm), has a tradition going back to 1945 when Holl, then not yet 30, was freed from Theresienstadt concentration camp, where he had been incarcerated as a half-Jew. He returned to Berlin, began a career as a movie actor, opened his bar, and taught himself to cook. He and his pub, where he can squeeze in 77 seated imbibers and diners like sardines in a can, have been a Berlin institution ever since. It's more than a VIP and personalities spot: Holl really can cook. His specialties are potato soup, stuffed beef roulade, and *rote Grütze*—a jellied dessert of red currants served with vanilla sauce. Open evenings only, closed Sundays. Reservations suggested. Tel: 323-29-93 or 323-14-04. No credit cards.

Out west in **Spandau**, the **Restaurant Kolk**, Hoher Steinweg 7, offers what you might term "international-ized" German food: for example, smoked chicken breasts with asparagus tips as a starter, followed by roast leg of lamb with a creamy sauce, and for dessert a chocolate mousse with exotic fruits as garnish. Open daily except Mondays.

Pichelsdorf, south of Spandau's old quarter, was once, like so many of Berlin's little neighborhoods, an indepen-dent village, and a few of its historic houses have sur-vived. One of them is the cottage-like mid–18th-century **Historischer Weinkeller**, Alt-Pichelsdorf 32. This thatch-roofed wine and beer cellar, crammed with antiques and bric-a-brac, looks like what you'd expect of an old Ger-man village inn. The menu runs the spectrum of roasts, schnitzels, steaks, duck, goose, and lake and river fish, with main courses in the DM 30 to DM 35 range. It's cozy in winter and relaxing in the summer, when you can sit in a leafy garden with a bubbling fountain. Sunday brunch, with an eat-as-much-as-you-like buffet, is a popular neigh-borhood attraction. Evenings you are advised to reserve. Tel: 361-80-56.

If Pichelsdorf gives you the feeling of being light-years from the hustle and bustle of Central Europe's largest city, you'll feel even more rural in the nearby **Grunewald** at the **Forsthaus Paulsborn**, Am Grunewaldsee. This Neo-Gothic hunting lodge with its wood-paneled, beam-ceilinged din-ing rooms, splendid garden, and terrace overlooking the little Grunewald Lake, was built in 1871. The cuisine is refined *gut-bürgerlich,* with a great selection of game dishes in season. In the spring, summer, and early fall months it is open for lunch and dinner; in the winter for lunch only. Brunch is served Sundays year-round 9:30 A.M. to 2:00 P.M. Closed Mondays and Sundays for dinner. For reservations, Tel: 813-80-10.

In eastern Berlin the most centrally located place for ambitiously prepared and presented German and Berlin regional food is the **Opernpalais**, Unter den Linden 5, in the former Princesses' Palace. The Opernpalais is actually a whole complex of restaurants and cafés: The **Königin Luise Restaurant** serves nouvelle German cuisine in ele-gant Baroque surroundings and is open for dinner only, Wednesday through Sunday; the **Fridericus** specializes in regional Berlin and Brandenburg dishes and fish and is open daily for lunch and dinner; the **Schinkelklause** offers more rustic Berlin specialties and beer on tap, for lunch and dinner, Tuesday through Saturday. For all, Tel: 200-22-69 or 238-40-16.

The **Ephraim Palais Restaurant,** Spreeufer 1, in the reconstructed banker's mansion at the southern tip of the **Nikolaiviertel,** presents refined German and international cuisine, prepared by an Italian woman who won her culinary spurs in the United States and says she is applying "upper category New York restaurant culture to Berlin." Among some of the pricey specialties here are *Tafelspitz* with lentils as a vegetable, and saddle of hare in a pastry crust. Open for lunch and dinner daily except Sundays. Tel: 242-51-08 or 242-51-53.

If you wish to dine in genuine Rococo surroundings, go to the **Ermeler Haus,** Märkisches Ufer 10–12, right on the Spree canal about five blocks south of Museumsinsel. This 16th-century mansion was renovated in the 18th century, and in the 1960s turned into the Communist regime's poshest restaurant. The culinary skills here are a bit uneven, as the management has tried with varying success to sail through the storms of political and economic transition, but the ambience is matchless. Open for lunch and dinner. Tel: 279-40-28.

Offenbach-Stuben, Stubbenkammerstrasse 8, in the Prenzlauer Berg borough, has been a favorite of eastern Berliners since Lutz König opened it as a private restaurant in 1979, and has been discovered by Wessies since the Wall came down. The rooms are decorated with sets and props from the Komische Oper and the Metropol Theater, and many music stars are among the regular clientele. The menu follows the themes of E. T. A. Hoffmann's stories and Jacques Offenbach's opera *Tales of Hoffmann.* Thus Orpheus in the Underworld is a veal escalope stuffed with ham and cheese. The Prince of Arcadia is saddle of veal with chanterelles. Fillets of beef in various versions are appropriately called Antonia, Olympia, and Guilietta. Open evenings only. Tel: 448-41-08.

HOTEL RESTAURANTS

Western Berlin

The best are: **Zum Huguenotten,** in the Inter-Continental Hotel (near the Zoologischen Garten at Budapester Strasse 2), where the cuisine is classically French, Tel: 26-02-12-52; **Park Restaurant,** in the Steigenberger Hotel

(Los Angeles Platz 1, south of the Kaiser-Wilhelm-Gedächt-nis-Kirche), serving French and sophisticated German cuisine, Tel: 210-80; **Kempinski Grill**, in the Bristol-Hotel Kempinski (Kurfürstendamm 27), serving international cuisine, Tel: 88-43-40; **Schweizerhof Grill**, in the Hotel Schweizerhof (Budapester Strasse 21–31, across from the zoo), serving Swiss cuisine, Tel: 269-60; **Grand Cru**, in the Hotel Residenz (south of Kurfürstendamm at Meineke-strasse 9), offering French cuisine, Tel: 88-44-30; and **Berlin Grill**, in the Hotel Berlin (south of the Landwehr-kanal in Tiergarten at Lützowplatz 17), specializing in French and international cuisine in nouvelle style, Tel: 25-05-25-62.

The **Harlekin** in the Grand Hotel Esplanade, Lützo-wufer 15, in the southern Tiergarten, takes a nouvelle approach to German, French, and international dishes. The **Restaurant Au Lac** in the Hotel Seehof, Lietzensee-Ufer 11, also serves French and German cuisine with a nouvelle touch, and besides offers the pleasure of having lunch or dinner on the terrace overlooking the little Lietzensee. It's near Schloss Charlottenburg and a block from a subway station with a connection to Ku'damm.

Eastern Berlin

The Grand-Maritim Hotel's **Le Grand Restaurant Silhou-ette**, at Friedrichstrasse 158–164, matches the best in the west, in both decor and creative, impeccably prepared nouvelle-style French and German cuisine. And it sur-passes all western competitors in friendliness and ser-vice. Lunch or dinner here is memorable, but very expen-sive. Besides the à la carte selections, you will be offered a daily six-course prix-fixe menu. The wine list has 300 labels, among them some otherwise unobtainable whites from eastern Germany's own wine-growing region along the Saale and Elbe rivers. There is low-key piano music until 10:00 P.M., and after that a combo with singer always performs, usually until 2:00 A.M. Tel: 232-70.

For acceptable French cuisine and very good charcoal-broiled specialties, try the Radisson Plaza Hotel's **Rôti d'Or**, at Karl-Liebknecht-Strasse 5. You'll dine by candle-light, with soft piano music in the background. Tel: 238-28. **La Coupole** in the Hilton-Dom Hotel, Mohrenstrasse 30, next to the Gendarmenmarkt, is in the superior category for its sophisticated German and international cuisine, prepared nouvelle style.

FRENCH

The Huguenots left an indelible mark on Berlin, and so did Frederick the Great's Francophile predilections. Germanized French words and expressions weave their way through Berlin slang and dialect, much to the delight of etymologists, and in few other German cities will you find as many restaurants serving French food at affordable prices.

One example is the **Restaurant Le Paris**, at Kurfürstendamm 211, in the Maison de France, the French cultural center, and adjacent to the best French bookshop in Germany. Open daily for lunch and dinner. In summer the thing to do here is eat out on the sidewalk, Paris style. The homemade pâté is always excellent; the cooking is classic French. No credit cards. Tel: 881-52-42.

The **Paris Bar**, at Kantstrasse 152, north of the Ku'damm, is not a bar but a restaurant, and *the* hangout of artists, writers, filmmakers, and theater people. The place is reminiscent of a French working-class bistro. The daily prix-fixe menu averages DM 50 per person. Open from noon to 2:00 A.M. No credit cards. Tel: 313-80-52.

Though there's no French chef in the kitchen, **November**, Schöneberger Ufer 65, south of the Tiergarten, in an old burgher house with Neoclassical interiors, offers imaginative nouvelle French cooking. Fish and seafood dishes and saddle of lamb reminiscent of Provence are among the specialties. But it's pricey. Open evenings only, closed Mondays and Tuesdays. No credit cards. Tel: 261-38-82.

Abricot, Hasenheide 48, in the heart of Kreuzberg, is a culinary version of Franco-German relations. Yvette Kurt, French wife of proprietor Thomas, and Simon François do the waiting, whereas a German, Andreas Staack, presides in the kitchen of this small bistro-style place. Fish is always meticulously prepared nouvelle style. Be sure to try the breast and liver of Barbary duck served with lentils. Open evenings only, closed Tuesdays. No credit cards. Tel: 693-11-50.

For elegant dining in a stunning setting, right on eastern Berlin's Gendarmenmarkt, with a view of the French Cathedral with its Huguenot Museum, the **Französischer Hof**, Jägerstrasse 56, is hard to top. Though a Communist-era reconstruction, the dining room seems genuinely Art Nouveau. The cuisine is classically French, bolstered by a few "international" dishes on the menu. The wine list is predominantly French, but it includes some hard-to-get-elsewhere vintages from the eastern German vineyards along the Elbe and Saale-Unstrut rivers. Tel: 229-39-69.

ITALIAN

Every Berliner has a favorite Italian restaurant among the nearly 800 in the city, which range in price, choice of dishes, and quality from simple pizzerias to haute cuisine.

Ironically, one of the best, **Fioretto**, Carmerstrasse 12, just off Savignyplatz and Kantstrasse, west of the zoo, is owned and run not by an Italian but by a German: Doris Burneleit, who moved from her original location in East Berlin's Köpenick borough to the glitzy part of western Berlin two years after the Wall came down, taking her three Gault-Millau toques with her. When she opened her original, simply decorated little establishment in 1987 she had never been to Italy, and prospects of ever going there were dim: the Wall still closed her in. What she knew of Italian cuisine she had heard from her father, a German Wehrmacht POW there during World War II, and read in books. But even before the Wall opened people were talking about her eatery, one of the few examples of private enterprise in the Communist part of the city. As soon as Berlin started moving toward reunification, she began travelling to Italy, looking into the best kitchens there, and, like western Berlin chefs, suddenly had access to the best and freshest ingredients. But ruthless competition and envy in the western part of the city, complicated by the long journey her clientele had to take to Köpenick, persuaded her to move into what for many years to come will remain the culinary epicenter of Berlin. Her new place is splashier—northern Italian "designer modern" with lots of chrome, marble, and mirrors—but her Italian country-style cuisine remains delectably unchanged. Closed for lunch Saturdays and all day Sundays, and several weeks in the summer. Tel: 312-31-15.

No less recommendable is **Ponte Vecchio**, at Spielhagenstrasse 3, not far from Schloss Charlottenburg. Proprietor-chef Valter Mazza is from Tuscany, and he stresses Tuscan regional cuisine. His restaurant is one of the few Italian restaurants in Germany with a Michelin star, not to mention three Gault-Millau toques. Open for dinner only. Closed Tuesdays and most of August. Tel: 342-19-99.

Ugo, Sophie-Charlotten-Strasse 101, across from Schloss Charlottenburg, is as spontaneous and experimental in its decoration as it is in its cuisine. Mementoes of musical and operatic performers and performances adorn the walls; wherever you look there are shelves bending under bottles as a reminder that this was once a Berlin *Kneipe*. There's no printed menu; instead, proprietor Bruno Pellegrini announces what chef Riccardo Paoli is offering that day on a blackboard near the entrance. The wine card lists an amazing 200 Italian labels. Open evenings only, closed Mondays and three weeks in summer. Tel: 325-71-10.

Anselmo Bufacchi has the distinction of being the first in Berlin to offer Italian grand cuisine in his restaurant, simply named **Anselmo**, Damaschkestrasse 17, off the Ku'damm. Top cooking it remains, though one yearns for a little more imagination and creativity. The ambience makes up for that: mirror walls, splashy neon lighting, bubbling water in glass pillars, and, wherever you look, Anselmo's own action art, influenced by the Fluxus movement, whose goal is to shock the complacent into a heightened awareness of their surroundings. Closed Mondays. Tel: 324-62-28.

Bacco, Marburger Strasse 5, near the Europa-Center, is as amazing for its rustic, dark-wood decor as for the consistency of its Tuscan cuisine. It's a favorite among business diners and diplomats. Closed for lunch on Sundays, otherwise open noon and evenings, often until 2:00 A.M. Tel: 211-86-87.

La Cascina, Delbrückstrasse 28, not far from the Grunewald, is a cozy little country house with a garden that's ideal for summer dining. Though not particularly creative, the cuisine is solidly upper class, with a wide range of excellent pasta dishes, fish that is perfectly charcoal-broiled, and sauces that are a delight of herbal and garlicky aromas. Closed Wednesdays. Tel: 826-58-83.

Cristallo, Teltower Damm 52, half an hour's walk southwest of the Dahlem museums complex, is a neighborhood spot that is not afraid to experiment. Many dishes are prepared with taragon vinegar, red lentils, sage juice, and mascarpone. The tortellini stuffed with ricotta cheese in a Champagne butter sauce are a delight. Closed Tuesdays. Tel: 815-66-09.

La Vernaccia, Breitenbachplatz 4, about 15 minutes north of the Dahlem museums, offers Sardinian cooking at its best, and Sardinia is where owner-chef Salvatore Brai, married to a German, is from. Unadulterated simplicity is the rule of the kitchen on that rocky, cliffy island, and that's what Brai emulates in Berlin. Another specialty:

Sardinian wines. Closed Mondays and three weeks in summer. Tel: 824-57-88.

Italians are also trying to close the culinary gap left in eastern Berlin by Doris Burneleit's move to western Berlin, with some success. **La Riva**, Spreeufer, is an Italian-run restaurant in the Ephraim Palais, in Nickolaiviertel. The fare is rather standard, but an added attraction is sitting outside on the banks of the Spree on a summer day. Tel: 832-68-70. The **Ristorante dell' Arte**, Palais am Festungs-graben 1, just off Unter den Linden and near Museums-insel, is in a Rococo palace built in the 18th century for Johann Gottfried Donner, Frederick the Great's chamberlain, who sold it to the Prussian royal finance ministry in 1787. The building, reconstructed after World War II, served as the seat of the German-Soviet Friendship Society until Berlin's reunification. Now, in addition to a theater and small concert hall, it is home for Sotheby's, the art auctioneers, Barclay's Bank, Salomon Brothers, the investment bankers—and this pleasant Italian restaurant, which is open for lunch and dinner daily except Sundays. Tel: 208-08-43.

ECLECTIC AND ECCENTRIC

Some Berlin eateries doggedly defy attempts to categorize them, although they're recommendable. Here are a few.

Diekmann, Meinekestrasse 7, just off the Ku'damm, is still lined with the pale green wooden shelves of the grocery and dry-goods store that occupied the premises many years ago. It's a charming environment. The cuisine is pragmatically seasonal. A few samplers: salads topped with grilled salmon or a salmon terrine; ground veal in a cream sauce; roast beef in a remoulade sauce with fried potatoes; pastry desserts. No credit cards. Tel: 883-33-21.

Jimmy's Diner, Pariser Strasse 41, the trendy galleries and designer boutiques street south of the Ku'damm, looks inside exactly like a 1940s or 1950s American diner complete with all the chrome and plastic, booths, and jukebox selectors. For Berliners it is a bit of *American Graffiti* and *Route 66* ambience. The food is a mélange of American—super hamburgers and cheeseburgers nothing like the fare of local MacDonalds and Burger Kings—and Tex-Mex. Open evenings only, until 3:00 A.M. weeknights, 5:00 A.M. weekends. No credit cards. And a sign above the counter makes it clear: "If You Think You've Got a Reservation, You're in the Wrong Place."

Storch, Wartburgstrasse 54, near Schöneberg Rathaus, is a bistro-type spot with sea-green walls, dark wood paneling, bare floors, and massive banquet-sized tables that you'll have to share when it gets crowded—which it usually is. On the menu you'll find Austro-Bavarian *Tafelspitz,* veal or lamb stews with Swabian spätzle, roast game dishes, and steamed fish. Open evenings only, no credit cards. Tel: 784-20-59.

Hakuin, Martin-Luther-Strasse 1, on the northern edge of Schöneberg, southeast of the Europa-Center, is vegetarian in the tradition of Zen master Hakuin, for whom it is named. It looks pseudo-Japanese, and there are exotic fish swimming in an artificial pond. As an apéritif you may want a cocktail of carrot juice; main dishes include such exotic concoctions as a curry ragout with a side order of coconut flakes. Meditation is part of the dining routine. Closed Thursdays; open evenings only except Saturdays and Sundays, when lunch is also served. No credit cards. Tel: 24-20-27.

Zitadellen Schänke, Am Juliusturm, Spandau, is a historic cellar restaurant right in Spandau's medieval citadel, and as genuinely medieval in its decor as it is in its food. The attraction here, while you sit among armor, old weapons, and other mementoes of the days when Spandau was an impregnable fortress on the frontier of the Holy Roman Empire, is the rustic medieval feast, served by knaves and wenches. You eat using your fingers and a dagger, while listening to ballads of minnesingers. Tel: 334-21-06.

ETHNIC

Berlin abounds with ethnic restaurants, ranging the alphabet from Afghani to Zambian. Turkish, Greek, Chinese, Indian, Thai, Vietnamese, and Japanese spots are the most numerous, to which one could add the plethora of Argentinian steak houses, all parts of Germany-wide chains and, except for the beef itself, very un-Argentine. Here are a few selections:

Asian

Ming's Garden, Tauentzienstrasse 16, directly across the street from the Europa-Center, is by consensus the best Chinese restaurant in town, and would be even better if German authorities would give the cooks, who come from China, longer residence and working permits. The menu is mercifully smaller than in most Chinese spots and, for those who like it, also has a good selection of

Szechuan dishes. But it's pricey, with main courses around DM 30 at dinner. Reservations are recommended; Tel: 211-87-28.

Ho Lin Wah, Kurfürstendamm 218, has the distinction of being in the building that, during the kaisers' days, the Weimar Republic, and the Third Reich, was the Chinese embassy in Berlin. It was empty for years, then sold in the 1970s and subsequently renovated. The ambience is pseudo-Chinese, like all too many restaurants in Germany and Berlin, but the food is a cut above average. Tel: 882-11-71.

Indian restaurants have only recently started to become popular in Berlin, and there are now about two dozen. The top of the lot, also in price, is the **Kashmir Palace,** Marburger Strasse 14, near the Europa-Center. The atmosphere is quiet and discreet: You are greeted at the door by a hostess in a sari and escorted to your table silently; a waiter in a turban soon arrives to ask your before-dinner drink wishes. Walls and tablecloths are in a soothing dove gray, though napkins, alas, are paper. Unless you are familiar with Indian cuisine, ordering one of the prix-fixe multicourse dinners is probably best. Count on around DM 100 for two. Closed Mondays. Tel: 214-28-40.

Thailand has become a popular tourist destination for Berliners, so restaurants back home are a natural consequence. Sasitorn Nakornsri's **Thai Palace,** Meierottostrasse 1, just off Fasanenstrasse and close to Fasanenplatz, is as near to the original cuisine as you can get. On request the seasoning will be toned down a bit, but that takes away from the fun. Open evenings only. Tel: 883-28-23.

The Japanese, entrenched in the business centers of Düsseldorf, Frankfurt, and Munich, have thus far only been testing the water in reunified Berlin. But with Sony corporation planning to rebuild half of Potsdamer Platz that will soon change. Meanwhile there is already a little advance guard in the form of a few Japanese restaurants, of which **Udagawa,** Feuerbachstrasse 24, in Steglitz borough, owned and run by T. Udagawa, S. Takahara, and T. Yasui, even rates a Gault-Millau toque. The DM 50 menu includes sushi, sashimi, and tempura. Open evenings only, closed Tuesdays; no credit cards. Reservations recommended: Tel: 792-93-73.

Vietnam, Suarezstrasse 61, in Charlottenburg, is the longest established and best Vietnamese restaurant in Berlin. Tel: 323-74-07.

Greek

Greek restaurants seem to be almost as common as Italian in Berlin, and in residential neighborhoods have become virtually corner *Kneipen*. Highly recommendable is **Kara-giosis**, Klausenerplatz 4, near Schloss Charlottenburg. It has none of the usual imitation Athenian-Cretan decor; the *tsatziki* is reputed to be the most garlicky in town; the wines are honest and reasonably priced; and the cooking is great. No credit cards. Tel: 321-20-05.

Fofi's Estiatorio, Fasanenstrasse 70, off the Ku'damm, is not only considerably more expensive than Karagiosis but also highly popular with Berlin's cultural and artistic circles, which explains the prices and the fact that it's hard to get a table here. If you succeed, you'll find the cooking good. Main courses such as a mixed-grill plate or souvlaki will cost around DM 35. Open evenings only; the kitchen is open until 1:00 A.M. No credit cards. Tel: 881-87-85.

Turkish

With a presence of almost a quarter million, Turks, originally recruited to Germany as "guest workers" in the 1960s, now account for Berlin's largest ethnic minority, and boroughs like Kreuzberg are virtually Little Istanbuls. Simple little eateries abound. Though **Istanbul**, Knesebeckstrasse 77, not far from the Ku'damm, is hardly where most Kreuzberg Turks would and could afford to go, it's popular among the better heeled, and still just as genuine for ambience and food. Tel: 883-27-77.

By contrast, **Merhaba**, Hasenheide 39, *is* in the heart of Kreuzberg. The name means "Good Day!" and you are definitely welcome. More than that, you will find it a pleasant blend of two cultures. The ambience tends a little toward the Casablanca look, with odds and ends of Oriental kitsch, but the food is honest and very reasonably priced. A starter of baked artichoke hearts stuffed with feta cheese will cost a mere DM 9, and a main course of döner kebab around DM 16. Open daily from 11:00 A.M. to midnight. No credit cards. Tel: 692-17-13.

Russian

There were times—around the turn of the century and again after the Bolshevik revolution—when there were so many Russian artists and literati in Berlin that the city was also a Little Moscow and St. Petersburg. That changed during the Third Reich and the Cold War, but is changing again with the influx of Russian emigrés. Meanwhile the supply of Russian restaurants is a bit thin, but there are some.

Mirnik's, Kantstrasse 153, close to the Paris Bar and the Theater des Westens, north of the Ku'damm, would like to be viewed as Berlin's version of New York's Russian Tea Room. The vaulted, warmly lit restaurant, with photos of VIP guests on the walls, is frequented by Russian exiles who have made good. They would have had to, to eat here: The prices are astronomical. Borscht or solyanka soup will set you back DM 12 per small bowl, an order of blinis with a dab of caviar and sour cream almost DM 50. And it was that way long before runaway inflation hit the Motherland. Evenings only. Tel: 313-31-62.

For a stark contrast, head east to what was once called Stalin-Allee, now Karl Marx-Allee, where the June 17, 1953, uprising started, and the **Moskau**, Karl Marx-Allee 34, east of Alexanderplatz. This was once East Berlin's showcase eatery of German-Soviet friendship, subsidized by the Kremlin. The interior of this 1960s Socialist-modern shoebox looks like an airport waiting room, its walls decorated with folkloristic Socialist-realist kitsch. The menu offers the classic standbys: smoked salmon, smoked sturgeon, blinis, borscht, solyanka, chicken Kiev, beef Stroganoff, and desserts such as *nalistinki* (a crepe filled with blackberries and covered with whipped cream and vanilla ice cream). Prices are moderate. Tel: 279-16-70.

KNEIPEN

More than 4,000 spots in Berlin come under the general heading of *Kneipe*. The term originally meant a corner tavern in a blue-collar neighborhood, but today it includes just about any place where people eat, drink, meet friends, or simply hang out—cafés included. In the summer months the action in Berlin is on the sidewalk, and makes this city, unlike any other German city, look and feel like Paris. Some *Kneipen* are always in and others are in for a while and then fall out. Keeping up with the scene is a science unto itself. Some of the restaurants we have already mentioned count as "in" *Kneipen*. Others are mentioned in our section on Berlin at Night, below. Even some of the breakfast places we list farther down count as *Kneipen,* if breakfast round-the-clock—or at least until late afternoon—is one of the attractions. What they all have in common is that they stay open until the wee hours, in many cases until dawn, and in some cases never close at all. Here is a sampler, with western and eastern Berlin presented separately.

Western Berlin
Kneipen close to and around the Kurfürstendamm are the **Cour Carree** (Savignyplatz 5), where billiard and card tables are among the attractions; **Zwiebelfisch** (Savignyplatz 7), which is popular with literati; **Die Kleine Kneipe** (Wielandstrasse 45), popular for its billiard tables as well as its stews and sandwiches; **Dicke Wirtin** (Carmerstrasse 9), which serves good, thick soups; **Rosalinde** (Knesebeckstrasse 16), where theater folk, journalists, and students read newspapers, gossip, or dream of their careers while nibbling at Swabian snacks; **Reste Fidèle** (Bleibtreustrasse 41), known for its very friendly service; and **Zillemarkt** (Bleibtreustrasse 48a), popular for breakfast, late-night drinks and snacks, and for its billiard room.

Among the places that are likely to stay popular for a while, also around the Ku'damm, are the already mentioned **Paris Bar** and **Heinz Holl**; the **Ax Bax** (Leibnizstrasse 34), popular among the artist set for its cold buffet; **Dschungel**, or Jungle (Nürnberger Strasse 53), which continues to attract the Neue Wilden painters; **Café Untreu** (it means "unfaithful") at Bleibtreustrasse ("stay faithful") 13; **Chez Alex** (Kurfürstendamm 160), favored for its piano bar, but rather pricey; **Schwarzes Café** (Kantstrasse 148), a hangout for those who think they're somebodies, open 24 hours daily; and **Café Wintergarten** (Fasanenstrasse 23, in the *Literaturhaus*), a 10:00 A.M. to 1:00 A.M. breakfast-lunch-dinner-coffee-snacks meeting place for everybody who's somebody on the literary scene.

Some distance from the center of the city, is **Exil**, an expensive eatery for successful artists and literati in Kreuzberg (Paul-Linke-Ufer 44a). Also in Kreuzberg is **Café Übersee** (Paul-Linke-Ufer 44), popular with artists aspiring to become successful.

Café EinStein (Kurfürstenstrasse 58) is where the upper-crust leftist intellectual crowd gathers and the novelist Günter Grass may show up to read from work in progress; near the Kurfürstenstrasse station on the U-1 line.

Eastern Berlin
Communist rule and the Wall may have left their mark on Berlin in many ways, but *Kneipenleben* (pub life) remains unchanged here.

The **Brandenburger Keller** (Mittelstrasse 29, just north of Unter den Linden) is indeed a cellar spot, furnished with stand-up tables and counters, and popular with journalists. The **Trichter** (Am Schiffbauerdamm) is the favorite *Kneipe* of the adjacent Berliner Ensemble Theater, off Friedrichstrasse, as popular with actors and staff as it is with the after-theater crowd.

Venturing a bit north of Unter den Linden, along Friedrichstrasse, you'll find the **Hafenbar** (Chausseestrasse 20, on the extension of Friedrichstrasse). Dimly lit, it attracts the younger generation, who come to dance. Across the street is the Brecht Haus museum, in whose basement is the **Brecht Keller-Restaurant** (Chausseestrasse 125), serving hardy Viennese cuisine to theater people, writers, and other Brecht fans.

The **Scheunenviertel**, Berlin's old Jewish quarter, east of Chausseestrasse and Friedrichstrasse, is fast turning into a popular neighborhood of cafés and *Kneipen,* especially along Tucholskystrasse and Oranienburger Strasse, where the main synagogue is being rebuilt. **Silberstein** (Oranienburger Strasse 27) draws the chic from western Berlin, many of whom stick it out until 3:00 A.M. **Café Oren** (Oranienburger Strasse 28, adjacent to the synagogue) serves kosher and Israeli food in a trendy Postmodern setting.

Still farther afield, in Prenzlauer Berg borough, there's the **Alt-Berliner Bierkneipe** (Saarbrücker Strasse 17, near the Senefelderplatz subway station), which attracts a counterculture crowd. Also in Prenzlauer Berg, the **1900** (Husemannstrasse 1, across from Kollwitzplatz) is a popular hangout for actors, painters, television people, and folks from the neighborhood. **Metzer Eck** (Metzer Strasse 33, near Senefelderplatz), open until 3:00 A.M. weekends, draws the prominent from east and west who lubricate with beer and still their hunger with pea soup and pork steaks.

BREAKFAST

Breakfast, definitely not of the "power" variety, has been a Berlin craze since the late 1980s. At latest count some 300 cafés, bistros, and pubs serve variations of the morning meal at the oddest of hours.

At **Lützower Lampe** (in Charlottenburg at Behaimstrasse 25, close to the Richard-Wagner-Platz U-Bahn station) the emphasis is on macrobiotic vegetarian breakfasts, with such offerings as grain coffee, rice with tahini cream, and full-kernel rolls. **Café Voltaire** (near the Char-lottenburg S-Bahn stop at Stuttgarter Platz 14) serves a choice of European breakfasts. **Zillemarkt** (Bleibtreu-strasse 48, next to the Savignyplatz S-Bahn stop) is re-nowned for gourmet ice-cream concoctions and offers Champagne breakfasts until 2:00 P.M. **Miami** (Kurfürsten-damm 100), with billiard and card tables, is open around the clock and starts serving breakfast at 4:00 A.M. **Café Leysieffer** (Kurfürstendamm 218) helps start the day with a breakfast of smoked salmon, Parma ham, fresh baguettes, and Champagne.

Schwarzes Café (Kantstrasse 148, north of Ku'damm) is open and serves breakfast around the clock. In Kreuzberg, **Café Alibi** (Oranienstrasse 166) offers breakfast at what is considered a proper neighborhood time: from 10:00 A.M. to 4:00 P.M. The **Café am Ufer** (Paul-Lincke-Ufer 42–43, Kreuzberg) follows similar hours.

The odd-hours breakfast craze has also reached east-ern Berlin. The **Café-Restaurant im Zeughaus**, at the Museum of German History (Unter den Linden 2), offers Huguenot (French Continental) and Prussian (boiled egg, ham, cheese, cottage cheese, rolls, butter, jam) breakfasts, among other variations, from 10:00 A.M. until 1:00 P.M.

In addition, most hotels have scrumptious breakfast buffets included in the price of your room.

CAFÉS

The word is overused in Berlin, where it can apply to anything from a gay bar or jazz cellar to a place serving *Kaffee und Kuchen*—coffee and calorific German past-ries. We have the last in mind here.

The ideal incarnation of the Berlin café is still the **Café Kranzler** (Kurfürstendamm 18), which is usually crowded with matronly ladies wolfing down two (never just one) pieces of cake topped by mounds of whipped cream. **Café Möhring** (Kurfürstendamm 213) was not only a favorite hangout of the bohemian and bourgeois Kurfür-stendamm crowd in the early part of this century, but has two other locations on the avenue: at Kurfürstendamm 234 and Kurfürstendamm 161–163. **Café Leysieffer** (Kur-fürstendamm 218) is an earthly paradise for chocoholics and anyone else not concerned with calories. **Café Huth-macher** (Hardenbergstrasse 29d, second floor, right by Bahnhof Zoo) offers daily teatime dancing at 3:30 P.M. in addition to fine pastries.

There are also a number of choices in eastern Berlin. The **Operncafé** on Unter den Linden is a great spot for coffee and pastries; in nice weather the terrace and garden, affording a splendid view of the avenue, are open. At **Café Bauer**, in the Grand Hotel at the corner of Friedrichstrasse and Unter den Linden, the pastries are divine; in the afternoon there is a string orchestra. The **Rathaus Café** in the Nikolaiviertel, at the corner of Spandauer Strasse and Rathaus Strasse, right by the city hall, is splendid for coffee, cake, and people-watching.

If you're strolling in Prenzlauer Berg borough, stop in at the **Kaffeestube** (Husemannstrasse 6), a copy of a turn-of-the-century Berlin café. The **Kyril Café** (Lychenerstrasse 73, also in Prenzlauer Berg), amid dilapidated turn-of-the-century apartment houses, is an intellectual hangout. And if you're out in Köpenick at the Museum of Applied Art in Köpenick Schloss, the **Schloss Café**, in one of the castle's outbuildings, is the place to try pastries and ice creams.

RESTAURANTS BY GEOGRAPHICAL AREA

South and East of Alexanderplatz
Moskau (Russian)
Zur Letzten Instanz (Traditional Berlin)

Charlottenburg
Alt Luxemburg (Gourmet)
Karagiosis (Greek)
Mommseneck (Traditional Berlin)
Ponte Vecchio (Italian)
Restaurant Au Lac (Hotel)
Trio (Gourmet)
Ugo (Italian)
Vietnam (Vietnamese)

Northern Friedrichstrasse
Brandenburger Keller (*Kneipen*)
Brecht-Keller (*Kneipen*)
Hafenbar (*Kneipen*)
Trichter (*Kneipen*)

Köpenick
Schloss Café (Cafés)

Kreuzberg
Abricot (French)
Café Alibi (Breakfast)
Café Übersee (*Kneipen*)
Café am Ufer (Breakfast)
Exil (*Kneipen*)
Grossbeerenkeller (Traditional Berlin)
Merhaba (Turkish)

On and around Kurfürstendamm
Anselmo (Italian)
AxBax (*Kneipen*)
Bacco (Italian)
Beiz (Traditional/Regional German)
Café Huthmacher (Cafés)
Café Kranzler (Cafés)
Café Leysieffer (Breakfast; Cafés)
Café Möhring (Cafés)
Café Untreu (*Kneipen*)
Café Wintergarten (*Kneipen*)
Chez Alex (*Kneipen*)
Cour Carree (*Kneipen*)
Dicke Wirtin (*Kneipen*)
Die Kleine Kneipe (*Kneipen*)
Diekmann (Eclectic and Eccentric)
Dschungel (*Kneipen*)
Fioretto (Italian)
Fofi's Estiatorio (Greek)
Grand Cru (Hotel)
Hardtke (Traditional Berlin)
Hecker's Deele (Traditional/Regional German)
Heinz Holl (Traditional/Regional German, *Kneipen*)
Ho Lin Wah (Chinese)
Istanbul (Turkish)
Jimmy's Diner (Eclectic and Eccentric)
Kashmir Palace (Indian)
Kempinsky Grill (Hotel)
Lutter & Wegner (Traditional/German)
Mampe's Gute Stube (Traditional/German)
Miami (Breakfast)
Ming's Garden (Chinese)
Mirnik's (Russian)
Paris Bar (French; *Kneipen*)

Park Restaurant (Hotel)
Restaurant Le Paris (French)
Reste Fidèle (*Kneipen*)
Rosalinde (*Kneipen*)
Schultheiss Bräuhaus (Traditional Berlin)
Schwarzes Café (*Kneipen; Breakfast*)
Schweizerhof Grill (Hotel)
Spreegarten (Traditional Berlin)
Thai Palace (Thai)
Zillemarkt (*Kneipen; Breakfast*)
Zum Huguenotten (Hotel)
Zwiebelfisch (*Kneipen*)

Nikolaiviertel
Bierschänke in der Gerichtsklause (Traditional Berlin)
Ephraim Palais (Traditional/Regional German)
Ermeler Haus (Traditional/Regional German)
Mutter Hoppe (Traditional Berlin)
Rathaus Café (Cafés)
La Riva (Italian)
Spreeblick (Traditional Berlin)
Zum Paddenwirt (Traditional Berlin)
Zur Rippe (Traditional Berlin)

Prenzlauer Berg
Alt-Berliner Bierkneipe (*Kneipen*)
Aphrodite (Gourmet)
Kaffeestube (Cafés)
Kyril Café (Cafés)
1900 (*Kneipen*)
Offenbach-Stuben (Traditional/Regional German)

Reinickendorf Borough
Rockendorf's Restaurant (Gourmet)

Scheunenviertel
Café Oren (*Kneipen*)
Silberstein (*Kneipen*)

Schöneberg
Hakuin (Eclectic and Eccentric)
Storch (Eclectic and Eccentric)

Spandau
Historischer Weinkeller (Traditional/Regional German)

Restaurant Kolk (Traditional/Regional German)
Zitadellen Schänke (Eclectic and Eccentric)

Steglitz Borough
Udagawa (Japanese)

Tiergarten Borough
Bamberger Reiter (Gourmet)
Berlin Grill (Hotel)
Café EinStein (*Kneipen*)
Harlekin (Hotel)
Leydicke (*Kneipen*)
November (French)

Unter den Linden Area
Café Bauer (Cafés)
Café-Restaurant Im Zeughaus (Breakfast)
La Coupole (Hotel)
Französischer Hof (French)
Le Grand Restaurant Silhouette (Hotel)
Operncafé (Cafés)
Opernpalais—Königin Luise, Fridericus, Schinkelklause
   (Traditional/Regional German)
Ristorante dell' Arte (Italian)
Rôti d'Or (Hotel)

Wilmersdorf
Maxwell (Gourmet)
Wirtshaus Nussbaum (Traditional/Regional German)

Zehlendorf/Grunewald/Dahlem
La Cascina (Italian)
Cristallo (Italian)
Forsthaus Paulsborn (Traditional/Regional German)
Frühsammers Gasthaus (Gourmet)
Grand Slam (Gourmet)
La Vernaccia (Italian)

BERLIN AT NIGHT

With three opera houses, six symphony orchestras, scores of theaters, and some of the country's wildest nightlife, there is no way to run out of after-sightseeing things to do in Berlin. Language may be a bit of a problem for the theater, but in both western and eastern Berlin you will find musical and revue theaters where the spoken word is not so important.

To find out what's doing and where, check the monthly *Berlin Programm,* available at the tourist office in the Europa-Center, at newsstands, in large bookstores, and from hotel concierges, or the fortnightly program magazines *Zitty* and *Tip,* sold at newsstands. *Prinz,* a monthly, is geared to the under-25 set, and also lists gay activities. Even though these are in German, the listings are easily understood—as long as you can figure out that "Konzert" is "concert," "theater" is "theater."

All theaters, opera houses, concert halls, and cabarets have box offices where you can buy tickets up to an hour before performances. You can also reserve by phone. Hotel desks and any of the central ticket agencies will also obtain tickets for you, but they charge a small fee.

Ticket agencies close to the Kurfürstendamm are **Theaterkasse Centrum**, Meinekestrasse 25, Tel: 882-76-11; **Theaterkasse im Europa-Center**, Europa-Center, Tel: 261-70-51; **Ottfried Laur**, Hardenbergstrasse 6, Tel: 31-70-41; **Theaterkasse Kiosk am Zoo**, Kantstrasse 3, Tel: 881-36-03; **Wertheim** department store, Kurfürstendamm 231, Tel: 882-53-54; **KaDeWe** department store, Tauentzienstrasse 21, Tel: 218-10-28.

Tickets for performances in eastern Berlin can be ordered in western Berlin at any of the above, as well as through **Theaterkasse Zehlendorf**, Teltower Damm 22, Tel: 801-16-52. In eastern Berlin, order through the **Theaterkassen im Radisson Plaza Hotel**, Spandauer Strasse 2, open Tuesday through Friday 10:00 A.M. to noon and 1:00 to 7:00 P.M., on Saturdays 11:00 A.M. to 2:00 P.M.; Tel: 212-52-58 or 212-59-02 for theater tickets, 212-71-82 for concert tickets.

Classical Music

Berlin offers a vast amount of classical music. Topping the list is the **Philharmonic**, under the new and competent direction of Claudio Abbado. Concerts are given in the main Philharmonic Hall, as well as in a smaller chamber music hall on the same premises. Tickets can be obtained through major ticket agencies (see above) or by going directly to the box office at Matthäikirchstrasse 1, open Tuesday through Friday 3:30 P.M. to 6 P.M., and Saturdays, Sundays, and holidays from 10 A.M. to 2 P.M. Take bus 129, which stops along the Ku'damm, going toward Kreuzberg, and get off at Kulturforum.

If both ticket agencies and the box office tell you a concert is sold out, don't give up. Instead, show up an hour or two before the concert with a little cardboard sign: "Ich suche eine karte" ("I am looking for a ticket"). Almost inevitably, you will get one. These are not scalpers' tickets but are sold for their market value or even lower—usually unused portions of season tickets. The system also works at other concert halls and theaters, but seems to have the best batting average at the Philharmonic.

Another Berlin classical treat is the elegant Schauspielhaus, built by Schinkel in 1818, on the Gendarmenmarkt in what used to be East Berlin. The house orchestra is the **Berlin Symphony Orchestra**, but the hall frequently hosts Berlin's **Radio Symphony Orchestra**, the **Rundfunkchor**, the **Berlin Symphoniker** and visiting groups such as Kiev's Ukrainian National Symphony Orchestra. You can get tickets at major ticket offices or at the box office, open Monday through Friday, 10 A.M. to 6 P.M. (To get there take the U-6 to Französische Strasse.)

Concerts in castles and churches are a special part of the Berlin classical scene. Many châteaux in the outlying areas of Berlin offer first-rate concerts in the summertime, but two, Schloss Charlottenburg and Schloss Friedrichsfelde, host concerts all year long. **Schloss Charlottenburg** is in the western part of the city (take bus 109 or U-1 or U-7 to Bismarckstrasse), while **Schloss Friedrichsfelde** is in the east (take the U-5 to Friedrichsfelde). Major ticket outlets are your best bet for tickets, but it's also fairly easy just to show up an hour before the concert.

Classical music in churches is fun and often free, especially around Christmas and Easter. **St. Hedwig's Choir** at the cathedral by the same name in the eastern part of the city is superb. Many churches sponsor concerts of nonreligious music to promote the arts in general. Large concerts sell tickets through established agencies. Otherwise, just show up early.

To find out what's going on in castles and churches,

look under "Musik-Klassik" or "Kirchenmusik" in *Tip* or *Zitty,* entertainment magazines that come out on alternate Wednesdays, or in the *Berlin Programm*. Many churches also advertise their concerts on subway posters or on the omnipresent kiosks throughout the city.

Opera and Musical Theater

The **Deutsche Oper Berlin** (Bismarckstrasse 35, Charlottenburg) is western Berlin's opera house. The season runs for ten months, with repertory performances nightly. The ticket office is open Monday through Saturday 11:30 A.M. to 5:30 P.M., and Sundays 10:00 A.M. to 2:00 P.M., as well as one hour before performances. Tel: 341-02-49. The Deutsche Oper subway stop is virtually at the door. Write for reservations to: Kartenbüro der Deutschen Oper Berlin, Richard-Wagner-Platz 10, D(W)-1000 Berlin 10.

Theater des Westens (Kantstrasse 12) is an operetta and musical theater. The box office is open 10:00 A.M. to 6:00 P.M. Monday through Saturday, Sundays 3:00 to 6:00 P.M., and one hour before performances. Tel: 31-90-31-93.

East Berlin's **Deutsche Staatsoper** (Unter den Linden 7) also has a ten-month season. Daniel Barenboim is its general music director. The box office is open Tuesday through Saturday noon to 6:00 P.M. and one hour before performances. Tel: 200-47-62.

The **Komische Oper** (Behrenstrasse 55–57, off Friedrichstrasse, adjacent to the main entrance of the Grand-Maritim Hotel) is in a league all its own, thanks to Walter Felsenstein, who, as general manager and director from 1947 until his retirement in the 1980s, built it into one of the world's greatest houses. Box-office hours are Tuesday through Saturday noon to 6:00 P.M. and one hour before performances. Tel: 229-25-55.

The **Friedrichstadtpalast** (Friedrichstrasse 107) is eastern Berlin's variety and musical revue theater. Box-office hours are Tuesday through Saturday 1:00 to 3:30 P.M. and 4:00 to 6:00 P.M. and one hour before performances. Tel: 283-64-74 and 283-64-36.

Musicals and operettas are performed on a repertory basis in the **Metropol-Theater** (Friedrichstrasse 100–102). The box office is open Monday through Saturday 10:00 A.M. to 6:00 P.M., Sundays from 3:00 to 6:00 P.M., and one hour before performances. Tel: 208-27-15.

Dance and avant-garde international performances, often in English, can be found at the **Hebbel Theater** in

Kreuzberg (Streseman 29, S-Bahn to Anhalter Bahnhof; Tel: 251-01-44). The box office is open from 3:00 P.M. to 6:00 P.M., and one hour before performances.

NIGHTLIFE

Variety Shows and Cabaret

Variety shows are the latest wave of Berlin nightlife. The most popular is the **Chamäleon Varieté** in an old turn-of-the-century factory building in eastern Berlin (Rosenthaler Strasse 40/41, U-8 subway station Weinmeisterstrasse, Tel: 282-71-18; reservations strongly recommended). There are acrobatic acts, singing, audience participation skits, and even belly dancing. Some of the acts burlesque the concept of variety shows. In one particularly original number the audience watches a provocative striptease under the dancing beam of gaudy neon lights. But when the lights change, they find that they really have been looking at a fully clothed man with dayglow triangles dangling from his chest. The show lasts about two hours; drinks are served at the tables. Seating is on a first-come, first-served basis.

Another show is in the western part of Berlin, just in back of the Freie Volksbühne (Schaperstrasse 24, U-Bahn station Spichernstrasse; Tel: 881-37-42). Called **Bar jeder Vernunft**, this variety show and night salon attracts a host of artists and colorful people.

Yet another variety show has opened, this one the brain-child of European circus creators André Heller and Bernhard Paul. Located at Potsdamer Strasse 96 (U-1 station Kurfürstenstrasse), it's called **Wintergarten-Das Varieté** (Tel: 262-90-16).

In addition to the variety shows, there is *Kabarett:* in Germany, a night spot offering food, drink, and entertainment in the form of a politically and socially satirical floor show. To appreciate the humor you should have a fluent command of German and, in Berlin, of the local dialect.

You might try **Die Stachelschweine**, or The Porcupines (lower level of the Europa-Center), advance ticket sales Monday through Friday 10:30 A.M. to 12:30 P.M., and 4:00 to 7:00 P.M., Tel: 261-47-95; **Die Wühlmäuse**, or The Voles (Nürnberger Strasse 33), box office open daily 10:00 A.M. to 8:00 P.M., Tel: 213-70-47; **Die Distel**, or The Thistle (Friedrichstrasse 101), box-office hours Monday through Friday 10:00 A.M. to 7:00 P.M., Saturdays and Sundays 5:00 to 7:00 P.M., Tel: 200-47-04.

Disco

The dancing scene in Berlin has shifted to the east, into all sorts of spaces, traditional and otherwise.

For disco dancing, the most modern of the modern is in the former no-man's-land between east and west where not so very long ago East German border guards patrolled with their dogs. **Tresor**, on the left-hand side of Potsdamer Platz as you come from the west, means "treasure vault," and it was just that. Before World War II, Jewish-owned Wertheim Department Store used the cavernous safe as a safe-deposit vault. During the war the Nazis took it over as part of a labyrinth of underground bunkers. Now it offers the latest in very, very loud techno disco.

Just across the road, tucked discreetly behind some remaining graffiti-covered slabs of the Berlin Wall, is another disco known as **WMF**. If you happen to know sign language you'll recognize the name spelled out over the entrance, which is a somewhat bedraggled trailer. The underground disco—also part of the bunker complex—is what remains of a famous WMF silverware and shears factory, which moved to West Germany after the Communist takeover. However, WMF objected to the use of its trademark: hence the use of the sketched hand signals.

Neither Tresor nor WMF gets going much before 2:00 A.M. The nearest subway stop is Potsdamer Platz: when you get off, it will look as if you are in the middle of nowhere. Look for parked cars or follow the crowds—there's often a traffic jam here at 4:00 A.M.

Other popular discos in the east are **Praxis Dr. McCoy**, Inselstrasse 9a (U-2 subway to Märkisches Museum); and **Walfisch** (directly at the U-Bahn station Heinrich-Heine-Strasse exit). They're open Thursday through Sunday, from 10:00 P.M. on . . . and on . . . and on.

Back in the western part of the city: The **Big Eden** (Kurfürstendamm 202) and **Big Apple** (Bundesallee 13, near the Spichernstrasse station of the U-2 and U-8 lines) are *the* discos for the younger crowd, with ear-bursting music. The **Metropol** (Nollendorfplatz 5, near the Nollendorfplatz U-Bahn station), a former operetta theater, and the **Coconut** (Joachimsthaler Strasse 1–3, close to Bahnhof Zoo) are similar. The mid-life-crisis and sensitive-ears crowd prefers **Coupé 77** (Kurfürstendamm 177), which is decorated like an Orient Express railway car, and **Annabelle's** (Fasanenstrasse 64). Both are quite expensive.

Lipstick, directly on Richard-Wagner-Platz, is reputed

to be the largest women's disco in Europe. Tuesdays, Thursdays, and Sundays are mixed nights here.

Other Dancing

Disco is not the only kind of dancing that's the rage in Berlin. Ballroom dancing here, especially in the east, where it managed to survive 45 years of Communism—in private hands at that—has a special flavor. The huge ballrooms are a time-machine experience. Two-story **Ballhaus Berlin** (Chausseestrasse 102, U-8 to Bernauer Strasse; Tel: 282-75-75) has telephones at every table, just as in Billy Wilder's film *Foreign Affair*. If you see someone you'd like to dance with, you call him or her up by dialing the appropriate table number. It's fun to watch as table phones ring and callees sweep their eyes across the ballroom to catch a glimpse of their callers. Music ranges from old-fashioned waltzing to some modern rock.

Clärchens Ballhaus tends to more traditional ballroom music. It is popular with foreigners, including some left-over Cuban guest workers from former East Germany who look as if they stepped directly out of the movie *Mambo Kings*. One section of the ballroom (which is at Auguststrasse 24, U-8 to Rosenthaler Platz; Tel: 282-92-95) is also a wine cellar. A third ballroom, **Altdeutsches Ballhaus** (Ackerstrasse 144, U-8 to Rosenthaler Platz; Tel: 282-68-19), is strictly working-class German. The music is traditional, and the atmosphere gives you a flavor of just what social life in East Germany used to be like. Don't expect service, exotic drinks, or sophisticated company, but it's worth a short visit for just a little peep into the past.

Over in the western part of the city, **Café Keese** (Bismarckstrasse 108 (U-1 to Ernst-Reuter-Platz) is a special 700-seat ballroom in which all the asking is done by women (except for an hourly Men's Choice). It opened in 1966, and claims that 95,000 couples have met on their floor and married.

Shows

If dancing's not your thing, then you might want to take in one of Berlin's transvestite shows.

La Vie en Rose, in the Europa-Center, has a show that gets rave reviews. Reservations are essential; Tel: 323-60-06. At the **New Eden** (Kurfürstendamm 71), open daily except Sundays 9:00 P.M. to 4:00 A.M., the emphasis is on striptease. The **Scotch Club** (just south of the Europa-

Center at Marburger Strasse 15) features quieter music and more sophisticated striptease.

Chez Nous (Marburger Strasse 14) has a good transvestite show; Tel: 213-18-10.

Hangouts

Berlin also has an abundance of places for nighttime people-watching and merrymaking. But perhaps more than in other German cities, the borders between cafés and bars and *Kneipen* (a unique German neighborhood bar), wine cellars, beer joints, and restaurants are blurred. Berlin is a city of neighborhoods, and very often what is a café at 9:00 P.M. becomes a swinging bar later on. Or one section of a place is a wine cellar and another a restaurant. It's often best to do your nighttime perusing by geography.

Every tourist is drawn to the **Kurfürstendamm**, or Ku'damm for short, and that includes tourists from Hamburg and Halle as well as from abroad. It's a great place for people-watching, and there are scores of bars, restaurants, and cafés to stop at. On the night of November 9, 1989, when the Wall opened, it was one of the main places newly mobile easterners gathered to stare at the neon lights. The Ku'damm is only a starting place, though; don't make the mistake of thinking it's the only scene in town. The area around **Savignyplatz**, for example, just off Uhlandstrasse on the Ku'Damm, is good for exploring. Try the **Paris Bar**, Kantstrase 152, which doubles as a restaurant and an artists' hangout, or **Café Untreu**, located at Bleibtreustrasse.

But, as in the case of dancing, the major action has shifted to the east. By far the liveliest street in Berlin—east or west—is **Oranienburger Strasse**. Once the center of Berlin's Jewish quarter, the Scheunenviertel, literally "barn quarter," where thousands of immigrant Jews settled in the late 19th and early 20th centuries, the street is now host to dozens of galleries and night spots. The gold-domed newly restored synagogue sits in the shadow of the surreal Communist television tower on Alexanderplatz, and bar-hopping here—in addition to people-watching—is an experience in peeling off layers of German history. **Tacheles**, a cultural-center-cum-movie-theater-cum-bar, almost directly at the Oranienburger U-Bahn station, could easily be mistaken for a building ruin if it weren't for the crowds hanging around. Tacheles, which often has international programs of dancing or theater in English, Spanish, or even Latvian, is a good place to get started, because its programs begin earlier (about 8:00 or 9:00 P.M.) than night-life on the rest of the street.

The later it gets, the livelier Oranienburger Strasse gets, until—in good weather—people are pouring out onto the sidewalks and into the streets. Some of the night spots hark back to the neighborhood's Jewish origins, others provide East German nostalgia, while still others are a new breed of café-bar-*Kneipe* unto themselves. **Silberstein**, an art gallery and bar, is named for a tradi-tional Jewish café, and is directly next to the synagogue. In the early evening it's a quiet café, but by 2:00 A.M., don't expect to hold a conversation. **Café Oren** (Oranienburger 28) has good Jewish food (read Middle Eastern; there's no place in Berlin to get a bagel—although lox and cream cheese are plentiful). It also has an extensive wine list, and as the evening goes on it becomes more of a bar and less of a restaurant. The same goes for **Beth Café**, just around the corner on Tucholskystrasse. In the summer, the courtyard—which used to be part of a Jewish commu-nity center—is turned into a lovely garden café.

These three spots commemorate the neighborhood's Jewish origins, but several other spots here have fun with East German nostalgia. One of the best is also one of the easiest to miss. Called **VEB OZst**, a pun on the East German name for state-owned factories, the basement bar is located at Auguststrasse 90, almost at the corner of Oranienburger Strasse, but out of sight of the casual stroller. The bar has converted seats from Trabis, the little cardboard sputtering cars that became the symbol of East Germany. Pictures of East German leaders and ceremo-nies decorate the walls. Another bar (Oranienburger 49–50) is called **Obst & Gemüse**—fruits and vegetables—and retains the old drab grocery sign of the former tenants. The inside is stark and spare, with hardly any seats at all, but crowds flow out onto the sidewalk.

Other good watering holes along the strip are **Café Orange** (number 32), a bit more upscale, with a wonder-fully ornate high ceiling, and **Insel Kneipe-Galerie** at number 21, a very cozy downstairs bar.

Another neighborhood with an eclectic mix of bars and cafés is in what used to be West Berlin: **Schöneberg**, just a few stops from downtown Berlin (U-Bahn station Eisen-acher Strasse). Schöneberg nightlife gets started consider-ably earlier than its eastern counterparts. A good place to start is **Goltz Strasse**, a block from the subway. At number 33 there's **Café M**, a favorite writers' hangout. Or you can try **Macao**, with its plastic palm trees, billiard tables, and freshly painted wall mural of the ubiquitous Trabi in a tropical setting. The **Lux Café**, with its black-and-white Euro techno decor at number 35, offers excellent mixed drinks and breakfasts at any hour. For a quite different style, try **Franzmann** at the corner of Goltz and Pallas-strasse, a typical German *Kneipe* with solid oak furniture in a flamboyant brick tile turn-of-the-century building. There's also the **Goltz Café** at number 17, which offers soul, jazz, and rhythm and blues.

Off Goltz Strasse, but in the same neighborhood, you can find the trendy **Wohlbold** at Vorbergstrasse 10a. Next door is **Dimelo**, a women's bar and restaurant, a favorite gathering spot for lesbians—but its soft, tranquil atmo-sphere with lush greenery and its excellent and *soft* music (unusual in Berlin) attracts many women who just want a place they can talk and hear their voices easily above the music. Another hangout around here is the **Forum** at Akazienstrasse 19, a café-bar-gallery that bills itself as a gathering spot for unknown authors.

A traditional happening neighborhood in Berlin is **Kreuzberg**. Try the area around Oranienstrasse (not to be confused with Oranienburger) near the Kottbusser Tor U-Bahn station on the U-1 and U-8 lines. The **Rote Harfe** and the **Elefant** are lively bars at Heinrichplatz. Standard dress for Kreuzberg is black, and punks and freaks abound. Some may not find it a comfortable atmosphere.

Jazz

If you'd rather structure your nightlife by theme rather than by neighborhood, well, Berlin is well known for its jazz clubs. The best of these is **Quasi-modo** (Kantstrasse 12, close to Theater des Westens; Kantstrasse runs east to west north of Ku'damm), which often features international talent. **Floz**, at Nassauischestrasse 37, two blocks east of Uhlandstrasse (U-7 to Blisse Strasse), has a cozy atmo-sphere and great music. Directly across Berliner Strasse from Floz is **Badensche Hof**, with equally good jazz and sometimes a dose of reggae or salsa. In Kreuzberg, there's **Huxley's**, Hasenheide 108–114 (U-7 to Südstern).

Over in the eastern part of the city, the jazz scene is also heating up. **Berliner Prater** in Prenzlauer Berg (Kastanienallee 7–9, U-Bahn station Eberswalder Strasse on the U-1 line) has good jazz concerts, as well as non-Western "world music." So does **Franz Club**, Schönhauser Allee 36–39, also in Prenzlauer Berg (U-Bahn station Schönhauser Allee on the U-2 line).

Latin-American and Irish
The decadent 1920s in Berlin might conjure up these jazz clubs, but who would readily think of Berlin's two major multicultural offerings: Latin-American hangouts and Irish pubs? Both have roots in Berlin's history. In the 1970s, when many Latin-American countries were gripped by dictatorships, Chileans and others sought refuge in Berlin. The abundance of Latin night spots is an outgrowth of that tradition, recently reinforced by the presence of guest workers from Latin America in what was East Germany and the rest of the Soviet Bloc.

Salsa (Wielandstrasse 13, just off the Ku'damm) has free music in a lively atmosphere, patronized by a heady mix of Germans and Latin Americans who pulse more intensely to the music as the night goes on. **Nano Club**, at Ku'damm 143 near Adenauerplatz, is the newest of the Latin clubs and one of the liveliest. **El Parron**, a small Chilean-owned bar-restaurant on Carmerstrasse (halfway between Zoo U-Bahn station and Ernst-Reuter-Platz), is a quieter meeting place, but Germans and Latins alike delight in showing off their tango and mambo prowess here after 10:00 on the weekends. **La Batea** is yet another hangout, a cavernous joint with good drinks, great empanadas, but no dancing (Krumme Strasse 42, close to the Deutsche Oper, in Charlottenburg, open until 3:00 A.M.). And there's even a Latin-American *Kneipe,* best on Thursday nights when there's live music. If you're lucky you'll catch Victor, a black Cuban in his eighties who plays a mean bass. (The place is **Latinoamerica**, Droysenstrasse, corner Sybelstrasse, north of the Ku'damm.)

Irish pubs have their roots in another kind of Berlin immigrant: the British soldier. After World War II Berlin was divided into four sectors: American, British, French, and Russian. These pubs, many of which were started by soldiers who married Germans and stayed on, became hangouts for the Brits. The most centrally located of them is the **Irish Pub**, located on the basement level of Europa-Center. The most lively is the **Irish Harp Pub**, Giesebrechtstrasse 15, just off the Ku'damm. The **Irish Pub Halensee** gets a very good mix of people (Ku'damm 129a, at the western end of the boulevard), while the **Irish Folk Pub**, Scharnweberstrasse 16 (near Tegel airport) features a soft band of Irish folk music. The **James Joyce Taverne** at Joachim-Friedrich-Strasse 31 (halfway between Adenauerplatz and S-Bahn Charlottenburg) is a bit more upscale.

The newest of the lot, called **Oscar Wilde**, is located at Friedrichstrasse 112, and features live music and serves Kilkenny Irish beer. It's just a stone's throw from the Oranienburger strip.

Most of the Irish pubs open early (Oscar Wilde, for instance, opens at 11:00 A.M.) but don't really get going until 9:00 or 10:00 P.M. Both the Latin clubs and the Irish pubs are a great way for foreign travellers to meet Germans: Those who go there are obviously interested in other cultures.

Readings

Another good way of meeting people—or just people-watching—are the so-called program-cafés. The program can be a reading, music, or even a theater sketch. **Café EinStein**, the best known, is located in the former town house of actress Henny Porten (Kurfürstenstrasse 58, close to but not to be confused with the Ku'damm). In addition to a comfortable, dark-wood Viennese-style interior, the café has a huge summer garden out back. Readings, often by international writers in Berlin on fellowships, are upstairs in the gallery. Café EinStein is open from 10:00 A.M. to 2:00 A.M.

Literaturhaus, open from 10:00 A.M. to 1:00 A.M., is a stone's throw from the Ku'damm and next to the Käthe Kollwitz Museum (Fasanenstrasse 23). It also features readings in an upstairs room; there is a large garden in summer and an enclosed winter garden.

Blisse Strasse 14 Café (U-7 to Blisse Strasse) often has readings or music programs (including almost always a Sunday morning jazz breakfast). It's about the only café in town with amenities for wheelchairs, and its profits go to a social-therapeutic program for the disabled.

SHOPS AND SHOPPING

By Jennifer Becker

Jennifer Becker began travel writing after many years of teaching German and French language and literature at the Munich International School. British born, she has lived and worked in Germany for over 20 years and is a frequent visitor to Berlin.

If you're looking for Versace or St. Laurent, Louis Vuitton or Cartier, you'll find them all, along with the other major international names you find in every other large city, here in Berlin. All you need to do is stay with the mainstream stores that are mainly to be found on the showcase two-and-one-half mile **Kurfürstendamm**, known to locals as the Ku'damm, and on and around **Tauentzienstrasse** in western Berlin. Both of these streets start at the Kaiser-Wilhelm Memorial Church (Gedächtniskirche).

Serious and enthusiastic shoppers will find the side streets that *intersect* the Ku'damm more rewarding: **Fasanen, Bleibtreu, Uhland, Knesebeck, Schlüter, Wieland,** and **Leibniz.**

Keithstrasse, a small street crossing the Kurfürstenstrasse, between Kleiststrasse and the Landwehrkanal, is well worth exploring, as are **Pestalozzi, Kant, Mommsen,** and **Niebuhr**—all of which run parallel to the Ku'damm—if you're looking for shopping with a difference, be it a piece of old Berlin bric-a-brac, a dress designed in Berlin, original jewelry made by local craftspeople, or an old Berlin etching.

For shoppers there are modest signs of westernization

in eastern Berlin, such as the planned complex—at the moment a gigantic hole in the ground—on Friedrichstrasse that will house the Galeries Lafayette as well as a profusion of other consumer attractions. But, on this same street, the ostentatiously glassed and gilded Escada fashion store only serves to emphasize the depressing drabness of much of the area. (Only recently opened, it may soon close, as the low turnover does not justify the astronomical rent.) But with a few exceptions, your best bet is to shop in the west.

FASHIONS

You will find the clean lines and classic elegance of **Jil Sander** designs at her one boutique in Berlin on Kurfürstendamm 48, and the other leading name on the German fashion scene, Wolfgang Joop, at both **Carin Pfleger**, Kurfürstendamm 192, and **Ralph Setzer**, Kurfürstendamm 46. Joop, though a native of Potsdam with studios in Hamburg, does not yet have his own boutique here. New on the fashion scene is **Anna von Griesheim**, at Pariser Strasse 44, southeast of the Ku'damm. Von Griesheim makes her own designs out of natural fabrics reminiscent of the elegant simplicity of Sander—and at more affordable prices.

Bramigk Design, at Savigny Passage, Bogen 598, just off Savignyplatz, north of Ku'damm, is another small atelier where you can buy not only Nicola Bramigk's own unpretentious clothes, all made in superb-quality Italian fabrics, but also the fabrics themselves. In winter you can buy a pair of her cozy and colorful felt slippers. If your taste runs to folklore with *pfiff* and flair, try **Pupi's Laden** on Schlüterstrasse 54, just off the Ku'damm.

Top-notch second-hand shops as well as those selling unworn designer clothes from previous seasons are mushrooming in Berlin. Perhaps the most prestigious is a store called **First Hand, Last Season** at Kurfürstendamm 56. The entrance is on Wielandstrasse; ring to gain admittance. The clothes all carry top international designer labels and are never more than two seasons old. They sell at between 30 and 50 percent under the original price, so if you're looking for a classic Versace suit for him or her, you'll have a bargain, though it will still cost you upward of DM 1,000. **Seconda Mano**, Schlüterstrasse 63, also carries only designer fashions. Here's your chance to find a Jil Sander or Joop model at a more modest price. **Hannelore Günther**, at Niebuhrstrasse 1 (the street runs parallel to the Ku'damm), is a dynamic woman with her finger firmly on the pulse of the rapidly changing fashion scene in Berlin. She too carries some new last-season clothes, though most of her stock is second-hand designer label.

In Kreuzberg, at Gneisenaustrasse 112, **Molotow's** semi-basement showroom displays the work of no fewer than 35 young Berlin designers, who will even adapt their creations for you on an individual basis; these designs, too, are uncluttered and the prices affordable.

Many young designers who can't afford boutiques sell their work at markets. See below for details.

JEWELRY

If you're interested in rather avant-garde platinum jewelry, try one of Berlin's most prestigious purveyors of pricey bibelots: **Wurzbacher**, Kurfürstendamm 36. **Gobbesso**, on the other side of the avenue at number 201, is less intimidating; you can see this goldsmith working in the back of his small shop, creating classic jewelry in both gold and silver. Not far from Savignyplatz, at Bleibtreustrasse 47, is the small, uncluttered showroom of **Galerie Lalique**, displaying original, high-carat pieces of exquisite workmanship.

Uhlandstrasse 170 (in Uhlandpassage, which runs between Uhlandstrasse and Fasanenstrasse) houses one of the most unusual and exciting jewelry stores in Berlin: **Galeria Cano**, which sells marvelous reproductions of pre-Columbian pieces, originals of which are in the Gold Museum in Bogota. You can spend thousands and have your reproductions in 24-karat gold and diamonds or emeralds, or, for a tenth of the price, choose a piece made of silver alloy that is 24-karat gold-plated. Either way, the jewelry is equally dramatic.

Original jewelry designs are also sold at markets. See below for details.

OFFBEAT

Washi means handmade paper, difficult to find outside Japan. You can buy a wide selection at the shop of the same name at Grolmanstrasse 59, northwest of Savignyplatz. **Kitsume**, at Winterfeldtstrasse 37, south of the Ku'damm, right by the Winterfeldtplatz market square, sells Japanese sandals, meditation rolls, futons, gorgeous fabrics, and marvelous kimonos.

Harry Lehmann, Kantstrasse 106, a stone's throw from the top end of Wilmersdorfer Strasse, has been selling perfumes of his own concoction since 1926. (Kantstrasse runs east-west north of the Ku'damm.) Perfume oils are imported from France, then mixed with eau de Cologne to produce more than 50 different perfumes. You can bring along your own scent bottle or buy an inexpensive vial to be filled with the perfume of your choice. The unusual thing about this shop is that the perfumes are sold by weight; a mere DM 10 for a 13-gram vial of Lambada, for example. Don't be put off by the fake flowers that fill more than half the shop; they are ghastly, but apparently some customers like to make their bouquet of fake roses smell like the real thing.

Konrads Lederaccessoires at Pariser Strasse 59, south of Ku'damm, near the Hohenzollern Damm, is a mine of superb handbags and purses: They are designed and made on the spot, from the swaths of leather you can see hanging on one wall, in wonderfully strong colors and in clear-cut geometric designs. But check before you pay Konrad a call, as there is a 50 percent chance he may have to give up the business in 1993. Tel: 881-94-41.

Italian Ladies Shoes at Sybelstrasse 60 (parallel to the Ku'damm, north of Adenauerplatz) is a useful address for tiny feet; the shop stocks Continental sizes 32 and 34.

At the corner of Probststrasse and Poststrasse in eastern Berlin's Nikolaiviertel you'll find **Salon Plauener Spitze**, just a few yards away from the bank of the Spree, where you can take a break on the terrace of the **Café Spree-blick**. At Plauener Spitze you can buy fine lace, handmade exclusively in Plauen, the lace-making center of the Vogtland in the southwestern tip of Saxony.

Yorckstrasse in Kreuzberg is not only an endlessly long street, it is also dismally drab and somehow typical of this zany part of the city, with trains roaring on elevated tracks across it and graffiti everywhere. However, if you can make it to number 89a your trip will have been worthwhile. **Perlenstrand** surely has one of the largest selections of beads of all shapes and colors: thousands of them. They also sell very fine handcrafted silver jewelry and carry some imported and original pieces from Brazil.

But probably the most unusual store of them all in Berlin is **Knopf-Paul**, at Zossenerstrasse 10, also in the Kreuzberg area. This small, almost Dickensian shop is stacked floor to ceiling with neatly labeled shoe boxes that contain around 1.5 million buttons. (Herr Paul himself isn't sure.) The buttons are made of wood or metal, and there are more than 30 models alone with some type of gold clasp or buckle. If you can resist the temptation to replace half the buttons in your wardrobe, you can change your mind on Saturday when Knopf-Paul has a stand at the Winterfeldt Market (see "Markets," below), though this time the choice is less mind-boggling— "only" 10,000 buttons. Perhaps because of rather special inventory problems, this shop is closed on Wednesday and Thursday mornings and, of course, on Saturdays, when Herr Paul is at the market.

SHOPPING CENTERS

For more conventional shopping there is the **Europa-Center** at Tauentzienstrasse and Budapester Strasse. It is Berlin's largest shopping mall, with about 70 shops on three floors. It also houses more than 20 cafés and restaurants. There are airline offices, a cinema, and a variety of assorted boutiques. On the upper floor a large music shop sells only classical records and CDs. You'll find an interesting jewelry store on the lower floor purveying minerals, fossils, and unusual Finnish silver.

Then there is **Wertheim** at Ku'damm 231, a quality department store with good porcelain and perfume departments. Here you might pick up a bottle of Wolfgang Joop's perfume, Berlin. Germany's leading medium-price department store chains are Hertie, Karstadt, and Kaufhof. You'll find a **Hertie** at Wilmersdorfer Strasse 118–119 (the street runs perpendicular to both the Ku'damm and Kantstrasse) and a **Karstadt** at 109–111, whereas **Kaufhof** is ensconced on Alexanderplatz in the former Communist regime's Centrum, the largest department store chain of the former East Berlin.

ART AND ANTIQUES

The best (and most expensive) antiques shops are in the Ku'damm area, on **Fasanenstrasse** and **Keithstrasse**, with others on Bleibtreustrasse, Schlüterstrasse, and Mommsenstrasse. **Alte Asiatische Kunst**, for example, at Fasanenstrasse 71, offers a wide variety of exquisite porcelain and paintings as well as furniture from all over Southeast Asia.

Serious art buyers and collectors should try to obtain the invaluable *Berlin Arts Guide,* by Irene Blumenfeld, published by Art Guide Publications Ltd., London. Though published in 1986 and thus out of date, and also out of print, it is the only guide in English to the Berlin art scene.

There are close to 200 art galleries in Berlin, and the

city has also become a leading art-auction center, thanks to two energetic art promoters, Bernd Schultz and Peter Graf zu Eltz, who have turned the twice-yearly dispersals (at the end of May and November) at the **Villa Grisebach** (Fasanenstrasse 25) into the most important on the Continent for German art of the modern period—that is, art of the 20th century to around the 1950s.

The most compact little neighborhood for galleries representing modern and contemporary artists is a one-block stretch on **Fasanenstrasse** between Kurfürstendamm and Lietzenburger Strasse.

Rudolf Springer (Fasanenstrasse 13), Berlin's best-known dealer, has been on the scene for more than 40 years. He represented Max Ernst, Joan Miró, and Picasso in the early 1950s, and began showing Georg Baselitz, Jörg Immendorf, Markus Lüppertz, and A. R. Penck in the late 1960s and early 1970s. **Pels-Leusden Galerie**, Fasanenstrasse 25 (in the Villa Grisebach), alternates exhibitions of modern German art and is a good source for works by Lovis Corinth, Käthe Kollwitz, Franz Marc, August Macke, Erich Heckel, as well as other members of the "Brücke" group of Expressionists. **Scan-art**, Fasanenstrasse 41a, shows contemporary Scandinavian art. **Galerie Fahnemann**, Fasanenstrasse 61, is an important dealer of contemporary international painting as well as print art by Penck, Elvira Bach, and Karl Horst Hödicke, the "founder" of the Neue Wilden artists, the Neo-Expressionist painters of the 1970s and 1980s. **Kunsthandel Wolfgang Werner**, Fasanenstrasse 72, is strong on aquarelles and print art by such German Expressionists as Hans-Ludwig Kirchner and Emil Nolde. **Volker Westphal**, Fasanenstrasse 68, carries late–19th- and early–20th-century art, with an emphasis on French and Berlin painting. **Thea Fischer-Reinhardt**, Fasanenstrasse 29, stresses contemporary, politically motivated Neo-Expressionist painting.

On the Ku'damm itself the most important place is **Galerie Brusberg**, at number 213, which features not only René Magritte, Max Ernst, and Francis Picabia but also such contemporaries as George Segal, Fernando Botero, and Dieter Hacker, and established East German painters like Bernd Heisig, Wolfgang Mattheuer, and Werner Tübke. **Galerie Redmann**, Kurfürstendamm 199, represents many American artists, especially from the Northwest. **Blue Point Gallery**, Kurfürstendamm 35, is mainline Classical Modern: Picasso, Dali, Chagall, and Miró among others.

Pariser Strasse, south of the Ku'damm and Lietzen-burger Strasse, also abounds with galleries. **Wewerka & Weiss Galerie**, Pariser Strasse 63, emphasizes abstract painting as well as performance art. **Galerie Carola Mösch**, Pariser Strasse 2, deals in multiples and print editions of young American artists such as Jeff Koons, Ed Ruscha, Cindy Sherman, and Keith Sonnier. **Art Communication**, Pariser Strasse 7, concentrates on the new Expressionism by German and French artists.

Don't pass up other streets intersecting with or near the Ku'damm. **Galerie Ludwig Lange**, Wielandstrasse 26, represents some of the best Berlin abstract and minimal-ist painters, and is especially known for contemporary sculpture. **Galerie Lietzow**, Knesebeckstrasse 32, repre-sents the erstwhile Neue Wilden artist, Salomé. **Natan Fedorowskij**, Leibnizstrasse 60, is committed to showing the Russian avant-garde of the early 20th century, includ-ing works by El Lissitzky, who spent many years in Berlin, and Kasimir Malevich, as well as contemporary Musco-vites such as Ilya Kabakov.

In the Tiergarten district, **Galerie Eva Poll**, Lützowplatz 7, is one of Germany's most important dealerships for figurative painting and sculpture, especially by artists from East Germany who went west *before* the opening of the Wall. **Galerie Raab**, Potsdamer Strasse 7, counts as the discoverer and backer of Berlin's Neue Wilden, and still represents the avant-garde.

Galleries and dealerships are also starting up in eastern Berlin, within walking distance of Unter den Linden. **Galerie Berlin**, Friedrichstrasse 58, has a strong stable of Dresden, Leipzig, and eastern Berlin artists, including Wal-ter Libuda, Hartwig Ebersbach, and Siegfried Klotz. **Gal-erie Leo-Coppi**, Wallstrasse 90, not far from the Ermerler Haus restaurant and the Märkisches Museum, is putting the emphasis on younger eastern German and eastern Berlin artists who dared to be different even before the Wall crumbled, among them Dresden's Angela Hampel.

ART DECO

Decorative Arts, at Niebuhrstrasse 1 (southeast of Savigny-platz), next door to fashion expert Hannelore Günther, specializes in Jugendstil and Art Nouveau objects and has a large range of Murano glass and vases by Loetz. At Bleibtreustrasse 50, off Ku'damm, there's another interest-ing Art-Deco boutique, **Astoria**, with a few reproductions but mostly originals from England, France, and America. The classiest shop, called simply **Art Deco**, is on Leibnizstrasse 64, off the Ku'damm, just south of the Niebuhr intersection; it sells furniture, lamps, jewelry, writing utensils, and cigarette cases, mostly from France and Belgium, and all original.

PORCELAIN

The **Königliche Porzellan-Manufaktur** (KPM) is a Berlin institution, with a history of more than 225 years. In 1763 Frederick the Great took over a private porcelain company and renamed it; it has remained Prussia's answer to Saxony's world-famous Meissen porcelain ever since. KPM porcelain is all handmade and hand painted in the original workshops, which open to visitors, at Wegelystrasse 1 near the Tiergarten; more centrally located is the factory-outlet shop at Ku'damm 26a. Most patterns are 18th and 19th century and the prices are *very* royal. If it's Meissen you're after, visit Unter den Linden 396, where the store always has a few showcases of seconds (marked II or *zweite Sortierung*). The **Rosenthal Studio-Haus** at Ku'damm 226 also sells classic and not inexpensive porcelain.

BRIC-A-BRAC AND COLLECTIBLES

Pestalozzistrasse, north of and parallel to Kantstrasse, is packed solid with bric-a-brac shops for about five blocks between its intersection with Wilmersdorfer Strasse and Schlüterstrasse. You'll find old books, jewelry, silver, glass, and furniture—some of which is definitely more *Trödel* (junk) than antique. By far the largest and one of the best and most varied shops is **Prinz-Dunst**, right on the corner at Schlüterstrasse 16. In addition to silver, glass, and paintings, it specializes in Asian art (one side of the shop veritably teems with Buddhas).

Also on Schlüterstrasse, at number 70, is a splendid shop called **Colonialwaren**, specializing in bags, boxes, sporting equipment, and, best of all, wonderful suitcases from the 1920s and 1930s, in superb condition and gleaming with patina, many of them bearing the initials of long-gone travellers. If you spot one that just happens to sport a set of familiar initials, you'll find the temptation to buy hard to resist. Incidentally, when you're poking around this sort of shop, don't be afraid to bargain: It's fun and quite acceptable, and in most cases it works. The young man who owns this store (he looks a little like Boris Becker) spends vacations in England and Scotland, where he unearths much of the sports equipment he sells. How about a Scots laird's leather golf bag as a souvenir?

On Schlüterstrasse, at number 65, there's a clock specialist (*Uhrenspezialist*) with more than 500 clocks spanning four centuries who will also restore that timepiece you may have brought along. Or, should you have found a piece of delightful but damaged Meissen, all you have to do is go back to Pestalozzistrasse 98, where they will restore it for you.

Helga Ebel Antik at Wilmersdorferstrasse 78, just around the corner from Kantstrasse, has some old jewelry and Meissen china, but the main attraction here is her large collection of antique dolls, including a few from the Biedermeier period.

Ubu, at Bleibtreustrasse 55 (south of Savignyplatz), is worth a visit if you're interested in old Baedeckers. Still on Bleibtreustrasse, at number 53, there's a little shop that restores old Thonet bentwood chairs and sells antique kilims, Oriental rugs with strong geometric designs, which decorate the walls along with a curious display of assorted cheese graters. **Alt Berlin**, at Bleibtreustrasse 48, lives up to its name; this cozy shop only sells antiques and bric-a-brac from old Berlin. Among the glass, silver, and old toys and dolls—even rocking horses—you have a good chance of finding a special souvenir.

Berliner Zinnfiguren at Knesebeckstrasse 88 (east of Bleibtreustrasse) has approximately 10,000 tin figures for sale, including more than 1,000 animals alone. Some are collectors' items; others are appropriate as toys. You can take home Frederick the Great playing the flute, the Potsdamer Soldat (soldier), or a typical Berlin flower vendor. Flat, unpainted figures start at around DM 2.

Still on the hunt for collectibles and souvenirs, like the Egyptian Museum's Queen Nefertiti at Charlottenburg? Then be sure to visit the **Gipsformerei**, Sophie-Charlotten-Strasse 17–18, near Schloss Charlottenburg, a studio of the Berlin State Museums, whose workshop contains more than 7,000 molds of some of Berlin's and the rest of the world's most famous sculptures and bas-reliefs. Many of the smaller items are kept in stock, but you can also have any one of the molds cast to order in plaster (the cheapest), resin, or bronze.

MARKETS

Practically every Berlin neighborhood holds a weekly or twice-weekly market, and one of the largest and liveliest is at **Winterfeldtplatz**, south of Tiergarten, on Wednesdays and Saturdays. In front of the Neo-Gothic church here, you can sit on Postmodern—and rather slippery—stainless-steel benches and listen to the vendors of fresh fruit and vegetables hawking their wares at the top of their lungs. Instead of the usual rather tawdry tee-shirts, etc., often sold at these markets, some young local designers are selling their clothes here because rents have become too high in Berlin for them to afford a boutique.

Well worth a visit also is the **Türkenmarkt** (Turkish Market) in Kreuzberg borough, which starts at Kottbusser Damm and extends for about 400 yards along the Maybachufer on both sides of the street. This area is interesting not only for its superb produce, which reflects the importance of fresh herbs and vegetables in Turkish cuisine, but also for the Oriental feel of the streets and shops. It's a great place to buy a picnic and eat it by the river, watching the occasional tourist boat go by and absorbing the exotic atmosphere above you.

The junk market par excellence is the **Zille-Hof** at Fasanenstrasse 14. Located only a few steps beyond the luxurious Bristol-Hotel Kempinski just off the Ku'damm, it looks like an abandoned junkyard. S-Bahn trains on elevated tracks thunder by overhead as you browse through the piles of old crockery, rusty and often unidentifiable pieces of metal, pots and pans, tarnished door knockers, and dust-ridden books. The large halls on your right as you enter the courtyard often contain the contents of whole households, though the one farthest down sells better-quality bric-a-brac. This market is open every day of the week except Sundays.

The "market of markets," held every Saturday and Sunday beginning at 8:00 A.M. on **Strasse des 17. Juni**, is a treasure trove of collectible junk, bric-a-brac, and antiques. You can easily pick up a book bargain here and there, old records and CDs, and myriad things you absolutely don't need. Be sure to bargain. It is also a good idea to get here early, as the place is fairly crowded by noon.

When you have exhausted the possibilities of the four packed shopping aisles, turn your back on the Brandenburger Tor at the far end of the boulevard, go through the stone portals, and cross the bridge just west of the Tiergarten S-Bahn station. This is where the arts and crafts section of the market, called **Berliner Kunstmarkt**, is held. It's a great place to see a wide variety of local crafts in one place and to buy something to take home. Stall holders lease their space from weekend to weekend on the condition that their merchandise is handcrafted. With a few exceptions, this ruling is strictly adhered to, which means you are not confronted at every turn with cheap Far Eastern imports. Some stalls sell kitschy things— rather tinny jewelry and crude ceramics—but, for the rest, the quality of the goods for sale is astonishingly high.

Many young designers who work at home or in a small studio use this and other markets as the only place to sell their work. Most of them design in natural fabrics—wool, linen, silk, etc.—and produce clothes for which you would pay much more in a boutique. Susann Scheer is a designer who has had a stall here for six years and has a clientele of regular local customers. Her designs are distinctive and prices very reasonable. (There is even a makeshift changing room.)

Jewelry offerings range from extravagant costume pieces to beautiful and original designs in high-quality gold, silver, and even brass. Hand-blown glass—candlesticks and lamps for perfumed oil in abstract designs— are probably too fragile to be taken home, though the young man who makes them will certainly wrap them well for you. Colorful clocks and reliefs in china clay, all done by one young woman, from design through hand painting, make attractive gifts—particularly the reliefs of open toy cupboards: perhaps a little kitschy, but nice to decorate a child's room. Last, an original souvenir to beat them all: How about a lamp or sculpture made from a piece of an old Trabi? (The Trabant is the infamous East German car made of a virtually indestructible synthetic called Toroplast).

BOOKS OLD AND NEW

You will find many of the more than 200 bookshops in Berlin concentrated on **Knesebeckstrasse**, which intersects Ku'damm. **Galerie 2000**, at 56–58, is Berlin's oldest art bookshop, with a large selection in all the fine arts as well as fashion, design, and film. **Marga Schoeller's Bücherstube** at number 33 specializes in theater, music, and ballet, and is *the* shop for books in English. On Savignyplatz, (north of Ku'damm and west of Europa-Center) at Stadtbahnbogen 593, is the **Bücherbogen**, specializing in architecture as well as art, design, film, international catalogues, and art magazines. You will find specialist books in English here too.

For its huge selection of antique books—the shop is packed floor to ceiling—it's hard to beat **Düwal** at Schlüterstrasse 17. (Schlüterstrasse intersects Ku'damm and is west of Savignyplatz.) If you're looking for first editions, this is the place. They're open Monday through Friday from 3:00 to 6:30 P.M. and on Saturdays from 11:00 A.M. to 2:00 P.M.

In the Tiergarten borough, **Jeschke und Richter Antiquariat** at Winterfeldtstrasse 51, which faces the Winterfeldtplatz market square, covers a wide range of subjects, but tends to specialize in old books on travel, geography, and literature.

ETCHINGS AND ENGRAVINGS

Berlin-Grafik, Spandauer Damm 1, located across from Schloss Charlottenburg, sells original drawings and reproductions, many of Berlin architecture. You can buy engravings of Berlin for as little as DM 20. Another good place to find a small souvenir of Berlin is **Kunsthandlung Bandoly** at Brandenburgische Strasse 27, a three-minute walk south from Adenauerplatz off the Ku'damm. They stock reproductions of famous paintings as well as etchings and copperplate prints.

COMESTIBLES

Berlin's—some say Europe's if not the world's—greatest food emporium is on the sixth floor of the huge **KaDeWe** department store, Tauentzienstrasse 21, not far from the Kaiser Wilhelm Memorial Church. Some 25,000 different comestibles are sold in more than 50,000 square feet of sales and display space here. Among the delicacies are 1,800 varieties of cheese and 500 kinds of bread, baked fresh daily. Sixty different salads are prepared hourly, and there is a weekly turnover of 40 tons of fruit and vegetables imported from every continent. The meat counter seems as long as a football field, and 18 huge tanks contain live seafood that is flown in three times a week. It is a gourmet's and a gourmand's dream.

At **Der Teeladen** in the Nikolaiviertel in eastern Berlin you can choose from among more than 200 different types of tea and also buy tea sets and all the paraphernalia connected with tea-making at this friendly, tiny shop located on Probststrasse, right opposite the Nikolaikirche.

(There are two other branches: at Ku'damm 209 and in the Europa-Center.)

For lovers of sweets, candies, and, in particular, marzipan, a visit to the **Marzipankonditorei** at Pestalozzistrasse 54a is a must. The proprietors, Herr und Frau Wald, have been making their goodies from local, East Prussian recipes since 1947. Note: this shop is only open in the afternoon from 2:30 to 6:30 P.M.

USEFUL FACTS ON SHOPPING

Business Hours

Department stores and most major shops are open Monday through Friday from 9:00 or 10:00 A.M. to 6:00 or 6:30 P.M. and on Saturdays from 9:00 A.M. to 2:00 P.M. On the first Saturday of the month shops remain open until 6:00 P.M. October through April, and until 4:00 P.M. May through September. On Thursdays you can shop at most places until 8:30 P.M.

Many of the smaller side-street shops and boutiques do not open until 11:00 A.M. or even noon, and some galleries and antiques shops are open only in the afternoon. Major stores accept credit cards, though most of the smaller boutiques do not.

When you set out on a shopping exhibition, be sure to check your map for the location of street numbers; many Berlin streets are incredibly long and the rather exotic system of street numbering causes even taxi drivers problems. At each intersection the numbers of that particular block are given below the street sign—odd and even numbers run on the same side of the street.

Tax Refund

If you are resident in a country outside the European Community (EC) you are entitled to a full refund of the value-added tax (*Mehrwertsteuer*), which at the time of going to press 15 percent or 7½ percent depending on the type of merchandise.

The procedure for obtaining this refund is as follows: All department stores and most major shops will issue a tax-free shopping check (and fill it out for you) at the time of your purchase; smaller shops and boutiques do not usually have these available, so you need to acquire a form called, tongue-twistingly, an *Ausfuhr-und Abnehmer-bescheinigung* (certificate of export) and have it filled in for each purchase you make. Be sure to have and keep a receipt as well. You can buy these forms at most larger shops selling office supplies (*Bürobedarf*), but if you have a problem obtaining them, check with the tourist information office.

When you leave Germany present the tax-free shopping check or the export certificate *with* the receipt from the store *and* the *unused* goods themselves to the German customs (*Zoll*), which will stamp your check. If you are leaving from Berlin's Tegel or Schönefeld airport, you can receive your discount immediately at the Berliner Bank in the main hall. At major border crossings you get your stamp at customs and obtain your refund at the *Verkehrsbank* or at other refund points listed on the tax-free shopping check envelope. As a last resort, you can fill in the reverse side of the envelope (explanations in English) and thus apply for your refund.

Export of Artworks

If you buy a work of art of substantial value, you need confirmation (*Bestätigung*) from the auction house, gallery, or antiques shop that your purchase is not on the list of national treasures. (A problem is highly unlikely, because only four objects in the whole of Berlin are on the list at present.)

DAY TRIPS FROM BERLIN

*By John Dornberg
with Phyllis Méras*

Just as Berlin itself is a city of villages, forests, rivers, lakes, and large areas of agricultural land, so is the region around it—the erstwhile March of Brandenburg, or *Altmark* (Old March), as it came to be known in the 14th century when German colonists and the Knights of the Teutonic Order, having conquered what had been Slavic territories, began pushing the frontiers of the Holy Roman Empire even farther eastward into what today is again Poland.

The *Altmark* is a land of plateaus laced by dozens of verdant river valleys, such as those of the Spree, Havel, Dahme, Dosse, and Panke; canals; countless little lakes; here and there some rolling hill country; and patches of dark forests. It is bordered on the east by the Oder river, which forms Germany's frontier with Poland, on the south and west by the Elbe, and on the north by the lake country of Mecklenburg and Pommerania.

Next to Mecklenburg-Pommerania, the modern state of Brandenburg is Germany's least densely populated region, with hamlets, villages where storks still nest on chimneys and medieval turrets, small towns in which life seems to have stood still since the 1930s—and only a few urban centers that can be called cities, of which only one within an 80-mile radius of Berlin—Potsdam—has more than 100,000 population. And Potsdam is in effect a suburb of Berlin, reachable by S-Bahn from the Friedrich-strasse station in about 40 minutes.

With its 3.5 million people, Berlin (a city as well as one of Germany's 16 federal states) has more inhabitants than all of surrounding Brandenburg (also a state, with Pots-dam its capital), which is somewhat larger than Maryland or Wales and has a population of only 2.6 million. So Berlin sits there like an urban giant among rural dwarfs amidst the wide-open spaces of what used to be the heartland of Prussia.

Until the Wall crumbled and the German Democratic Republic disintegrated as a sovereign political entity, this region around Berlin was virtually forbidden territory. To citizens of West Berlin it was almost entirely closed; West Germans could go there only with difficulty, after sur-mounting bureaucratic hurdles. Other Western travellers required GDR visas that often restricted them to a single district or even county. Even Potsdam, the city of Freder-ick the Great's most dazzling summer palaces and some of Europe's most splendid 18th-century dwellings, was accessible to Westerners from West Berlin, which it ad-joins, only through East Berlin aboard tour buses or by applying for a visa. These difficulties of access, exacer-bated by the paucity of hotels, touristic amenities, and travel information, made the surroundings of Berlin a blank spot on the map of Germany and Europe.

Yet it is an area rich in scenery, history, art, architecture, and culture, and now that it has opened up it is once again a worthwhile travel area, with a growing number of vaca-tion pleasures, good restaurants, and cozy inns. Though it will remain economically depressed, and thus socially volatile, for a number of years to come, there is much to see and do here.

This is one reason we have limited our day-trip propos-als from Berlin to destinations within this region, to a radius of no more than 100 kilometers (62 miles) from Kurfürstendamm or Unter den Linden.

Another reason is that although definitely improving, and in some areas faster than hoped or predicted, road and rail conditions in eastern Germany are far below western German standards. The problems are compounded by the rapid motorization of eastern Germany (which started when East Germans dumped their antiquated Trabants, half-lovingly, half-hatingly called "Trabbies," and bought flashier Western cars) and by the construction and repair work being done on highways. The result is traffic jams and inordinate delays. Therefore, destinations farther afield are simply unmanageable if a day trip is to remain that: starting off from Berlin in the morning and returning in the evening.

The itineraries we propose start with Potsdam, at the southwest corner of Berlin, and go in a clockwise direction around Berlin: west to the city of Brandenburg; northwest to the town of Neuruppin and nearby Rheinsberg; northeast to Eberswalde-Finow, Chorin, Niederfinow, and Bad Freienwalde; east into Brandenburg's "Little Switzerland," the Märkische Schweiz, Müncheberg, Neu-Hardenberg, and Frankfurt on the Oder; southeast to Lübben, Lübbenau, and the Spreewald; and southwest to Wittenberg.

There are a number of package riverboat and bus–boat tours from Berlin to some of these towns, and train connections to most of them, though our descriptions are intended for drivers. At the end of each section we discuss the logistics of getting to each destination, as well as the approximate travel time.

Some of the trips could be combined. For example, Eberswalde–Chorin–Niederfinow–Bad Freienwalde could be done along with the Märkische Schweiz–Müncheberg–Neu Hardenberg, for a more rushed day out of Berlin or an overnight stay at one of the locations. Thus we also suggest one or two overnight accommodations in many of these destinations. For booking details see the Accommodations Reference section at the end of this chapter.

MAJOR INTEREST

Potsdam
Sanssouci Park with its palaces
Neuer Garten with Schloss Cecilienhof
Holländisches Viertel
Brandenburger Tor
Nikolaikirche
The Marstall (Royal Stables) with the Filmmuseum
The Einsteinturm
The Havel and the lakes

Brandenburg
Dom (Cathedral)
Katharinenkirche
The Altstadt

Neuruppin and Rheinsberg
Klosterkirche
Fontane birthplace
Schinkel birthplace
Heimatmuseum
Schloss Rheinsberg

Eberswalde Area
Eberswalde-Finow Stadt und Kreismuseum
The monastery at Chorin
Schiffshebewerk (ship elevator) at Niederfinow
Schloss Bad Freienwalde

Märkische Schweiz to Frankfurt-an-der-Oder
Naturpark Märkische Schweiz
Buckow with Schermützel lake
Müncheberg with medieval walls
Schloss Neuhardenberg
Kleist Museum in Frankfurt
Museum Viadrina in Frankfurt

Spreewald
The château in Lübben
Spreewald bayou and punt rides

Wittenberg
Lutherhaus
Melanchthonhaus
Schlosskirche
Stadtkirsche St. Marien
Cranach Houses

POTSDAM

Although it is almost 250 years older than Berlin itself and will be celebrating its 1,000th anniversary from May through October 1993 with a spate of cultural activities and festivities, Potsdam has always been in Berlin's shadow. Its eastern city limits adjoin the western ones of Berlin, and its center is a scant 18 miles from Unter den Linden. In prewar days Berliners thought of Potsdam largely as a place for Sunday outings. To compensate for the patronizing attitude of their arrogant neighbors, Potsdamers cultivated a kind of deliberate reserve and understatement while discreetly fancying their town as being the "Prussian Versailles." In many respects it is, though it had taken a while to make it that.

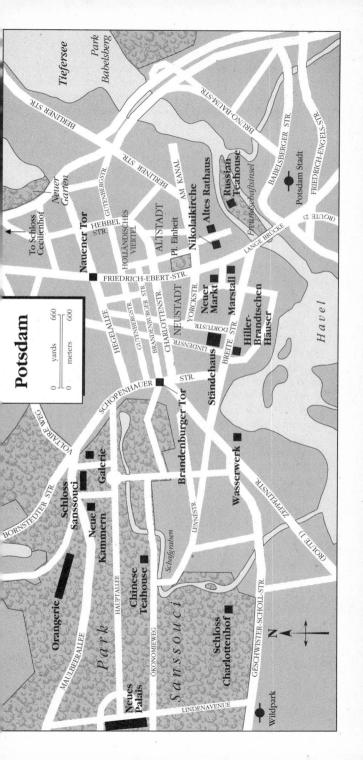

Potsdam began as a fortified Slavic settlement, called Poztupimi, that Holy Roman Emperor Otto I deeded to the convent of Quedlingburg (founded by his mother) on July 3, 993. The gift was largely a gesture, as Germans exercised no real control over the area, and another 200 years were to pass before the Margraves of Brandenburg could claim unchallenged suzerainty and get title to Poztupimi. Though Potsdam was granted the status of a city in 1345, it was off the main trade routes; fishing was its main industry in the Middle Ages. Brandenburg's Elector Joachim I started using the walled town as a base for his hunting expeditions in the 16th century, but it remained a backwater for another 100 years until Frederick William, the Great Elector, decided to develop it.

He liked the countryside—a landscape of peaceful lakes and small tributaries of the Havel river—and in 1664 commissioned the building of a palace in the center of the *Altstadt* (Old Quarter), not far from the harbor and the Havel embankment, of which only the Marstall, the royal stables, now used as a cinema museum, survived World War II. He made Potsdam his summer residence. No less significant, he also encouraged many of the persecuted French Huguenots, whom he had invited to Brandenburg, to settle in Potsdam. They were highly skilled artisans—faïence creators and fine glassmakers and silk weavers—who gave the town its first industries.

The Great Elector's grandson, Frederick William I, known as the Soldier King, had different tastes. He turned Potsdam into Prussia's biggest military garrison, a project continued by the son he hated and who hated him, Frederick the Great. Under Frederick the Great's reign Potsdam literally turned into an army with a town: By 1774 there were 139 military barracks and other army buildings in the little city. But it was also Frederick the Great who turned it into the "Prussian Versailles" and gave Potsdam its greatest and most beautiful attraction: the park and palace of Sanssouci, northwest of the Altstadt and about a half hour's walk, or a 15-minute bus ride, from the S-Bahn station and the excursion-boat landing.

Sanssouci and Other Châteaux

Sanssouci Park covers an area of 741 acres, and besides Schloss Sanssouci itself has several other palaces and important buildings that you will want to visit. With miles of paths and lanes to walk as well, Sanssouci could easily occupy you the entire day. The rooms in Schloss Sanssouci can be seen only on guided 40-minute, German-language tours that start daily every 20 minutes between 9:00 A.M. and 12 noon and 1:00 to 5:00 P.M. Only 1,800 people are allowed in each day and the number on each tour is limited, so you are assigned your tour time when you buy a ticket. The start of your tour may be later than you wanted or planned, so either arrive early in the day or use the waiting time to explore the park and other buildings that can be visited on your own.

SCHLOSS SANSSOUCI

Small by the standards of its day—Sanssouci was built between 1745 and 1747—Frederick the Great's golden summer palace of ten rooms, plus a vestibule and a marble hall, is an architectural and decorative gem. It seems to bring the outdoors indoors in a near-miraculous way.

Frederick was a writer, artist, and musician. He wrote poetry and prose and played the flute, for which he composed concertos. J. S. Bach wrote his "Musical Offering" for Frederick in 1747. Though often curt to people, he was devoted to animals and to nature. Indeed, he asked to be buried in the garden here beside his beloved greyhounds. Instead, he was buried first in the Garnisonskirche (Garrison Church) in Potsdam (destroyed in World War II) where his father, Frederick William I, was also buried. Then he was moved to Württemburg. But at last, in 1991, Frederick was brought here.

Frederick drew the plans for Sanssouci himself, setting his palace at the top of a terraced vineyard. He wanted a single-story structure so he could open his doors and step out into the garden. To make his design a reality he selected an old friend, Georg von Knobelsdorff, an army officer turned architect. From the garden entrance, guests entered a long, low, narrow building with a center dome and mounted a graceful flight of stairs. There, between the long windows of the façade, 36 caryatids lean outward.

At the north entrance, where today's guests enter, Frederick's visitors who came by coach would, stepping out, look through a semicircular colonnade of Corinthian pillars to a view of artificial Roman ruins in the distance. The palace was constructed in what has come to be called "Potsdam Rococo."

Bacchus and nymphs dance in relief above the doors in its cheerful entrance hall. Flora, goddess of flowers, looks down from the painted ceiling. In the art gallery, paintings of the school of Jean-Antoine Watteau and sculpture and busts (including a bust of Frederick made from his death mask) line the walls. Off Frederick's library—filled in his day with more than 2,000 books in French, for he admired everything Gallic—are his study and bedroom. Though the furniture is Rococo, the rooms themselves have since been rebuilt in Neoclassical style. It was in the alcove here, sitting in his wing chair, that Frederick died in 1786, at the age of 74. The French clock that he always took great care to wind himself is said to have stopped at the moment he died.

The ceiling in the bright music room, which especially seems to bring nature indoors, is gaily painted with spiders and birds, baskets of flowers, and dogs chasing rabbits. Murals inspired by Ovid's *Metamorphoses,* done by the French painter Antoine Pesne, seem somehow to expand the walls.

In the reception room, with its painted ceiling of Flora, goddess of flowers, and Zephyr, god of wind, the king thoughtfully hung French paintings that he liked, so that those awaiting an audience could while away their time fruitfully.

Frederick had the central hall of his palace fashioned after the Pantheon in Rome, with Carrara marble columns. Off the central hall are the guest rooms—one in Chinese style, based on the paintings on Chinese porcelain; a second done in blue; a third in red. Finally, there is the Voltaire room, with a bust of the French philosopher scrutinizing the parrots flying on its lemon-yellow walls.

A great admirer of Voltaire, Frederick corresponded with him for years and invited him to move to his court so they could talk together of matters the king considered important: philosophy and literature. Voltaire came and stayed for a while, but the pair quarreled and the philosopher left. "He is like a lemon," Frederick remarked afterward. "You can press out the juice and throw the rest away."

SANSSOUCI'S GROUNDS AND PARK

A stroll over the extensive grounds of the palace is as important a part of a visit to Sanssouci as seeing its buildings. At the foot of the stairs to the garden, the great fountain plays. Down the Hauptallee from the fountain is the obelisk portal entrance to the park, with two goddesses—Flora of flowers and Pomona of fruit—standing on a wall beside sets of Corinthian columns. In the Neptune grotto, the god of the sea brandishes his trident over a Baroque arch set against a backdrop of trees.

North of the grotto rises the **Bildergalerie** (Picture Gallery), said to be the first building ever constructed solely for the purpose of exhibiting works of art. Here (open daily except the fourth Wednesday of each month, 9:00 A.M. to noon, 12:45 to 5:00 P.M.) are paintings by Peter Paul Rubens, Lucas Cranach the Elder, Guido Reni, Caravaggio, and Anthony Van Dyck.

The **Neue Kammern**, just southwest of the main palace, was the original orangerie, built by Knobelsdorff, but converted into a guest house in 1774. Open daily except Fridays 9:00 A.M. to noon and 12:30 to 5:00 P.M.

West of the Neue Kammern and the palace is the **Orangerie**, built in the 1850s in Italian Renaissance style by King Frederick William IV. Inside the decoration is French Regency and Empire, and copies of 47 Raphael paintings hang on the walls. It is used for rotating art exhibitions. Open daily except the fourth Thursday of each month, 9:00 A.M. to noon, 1:00 to 5:00 P.M.

About 2 km (1½ miles) west of Sanssouci, along the park's main walkway, the Hauptallee, is the extensive **Neues Palais** (New Palace), whose construction at great expense, just after the Seven Years' War with France, Austria, Russia, Saxony, and Sweden had exhausted the nation, dismayed Frederick's subjects considerably. The king, who himself called this enormous brick palace ostentatious (with a marble concert hall 100 feet long and a Grotto Hall decorated in marble and glittering quartz), seemed to think it important to build it in order to show off the powers of his state. Open daily except the second and fourth Monday of each month, 9:00 A.M. to 12:45 P.M. and 1:15 to 5:00 P.M. The **Schlosscafé**, attached to the palace theater, is a delightfully ornate spot for a coffee break, snack, or even light lunch.

South of the Hauptallee, about halfway between Sanssouci and the Neues Palais, is the gay little **Chinesisches Teehaus** (Chinese Teahouse), with a tent-shaped roof, treelike columns, gilded sculptures, and, on the roof, a statue of a mandarin sitting beneath a parasol. This was a period of great admiration for things Chinese all across Europe, for China seemed to Europeans, from the little they were learning of it, a paradise on earth. This teahouse, designed by John Büring in 1757, is one of the finest examples of chinoiserie. It is due to reopen in

1993, after being closed two years for renovation and restoration work, as a museum of European and Asian porcelain.

Near the southern boundary of the park, about 2 km (1½ miles) southeast of Sanssouci itself, is another of King Frederick William IV's 19th-century additions, **Charlottenhof**, a little palace designed by Karl Friedrich Schinkel in the 1820s in villa style. Its wide lawns, maples, copper beeches, lindens, and extensive flower beds were largely laid out in their present form by master landscape architect Peter Joseph Lenné. Among other late additions are the Römische Bäder (Roman Baths), the Fasanerie (Pheasantry), the Friedenskirche (Peace Church), and a number of gardens. Charlottenhof Palace is open daily except the fourth Monday of each month, 9:00 A.M. to noon and 12:30 to 5:00 P.M.

There is a separate admission charge, ranging from DM 2 to DM 6, for each palace and building on the grounds of Sanssouci.

SCHLOSS CECILIENHOF

The **Neuer Garten** is a park area about a 2-km (1½-mile) walk northeast of Sanssouci, hugging the shore of Heiliger See, a picturesque little lake at the edge of the city. It was here, in Schloss Cecilienhof, that modern history was made: the 1945 Potsdam Conference when Harry S Truman, Joseph Stalin, and Winston Churchill (and his successor as British prime minister, Clement Attlee) met to decide the postwar fate of Germany and set up the occupation zones.

Schloss Cecilienhof, now part hotel, part historical museum, is a 1913 copy of an English country house. It was built on the palace grounds for Kaiser Wilhelm II's son, Crown Prince William, and his wife, Cecilia. Thirty-six rooms of the palace were renovated and used for the Potsdam Conference. Today, only a few are open to the public as a museum of the conference (daily except the second and fourth Monday of each month, 9:00 A.M. to 4:00 P.M.). The Soviet delegation to the conference met in the former study of the crown princess. The paneled smoking room of the crown prince became the working room of the American delegation. (It was here, reportedly, that Truman learned of the successful completion of the atomic bomb with a telegram declaring cryptically, "A baby is born.") At the writing desk in the crown prince's blue study, Winston Churchill worked for a few days before Clement Attlee's Labour Party came into power and Attlee succeeded him.

Most of Schloss Cecilienhof today is a first-class hotel with 42 rooms, all exquisitely appointed, a good spot to stay if you want to spend a night in Potsdam and also if you do not want or cannot find accommodations in Berlin itself. The hotel's **Schlossrestaurant** serving German cuisine and known for game dishes in season, is ideal for lunch or dinner in Potsdam.

SCHLOSS BABELSBERG

Yet another château with surrounding park in Potsdam is Schloss Babelsberg, in the suburb of Babelsberg at the southeastern edge of the city, adjacent to the Berlin city limits and near the DEFA Film Studios (which are discussed in our section on Berlin's lakes, above). Babelsberg was built by Schinkel between 1833 and 1835 in Neo-Gothic style as a summer and weekend palace for Wilhelm I, Germany's first kaiser. (Then a young man and second in line to the Prussian throne after his brother, Frederick William IV, Wilhelm succeeded his brother in 1861 at age 64, and went on to reign as Prussia's king and Germany's emperor for 27 years.) Like Cecilienhof, Babelsberg is modeled after an English estate. It is now used as the **Museum of Brandenburg's Pre- and Early History**, open daily except Mondays 9:00 A.M. to 5:00 P.M. The lovely park and gardens surrounding the château were landscaped by Peter Joseph Lenné in the 1830s.

The City of Potsdam

Though Potsdam was heavily damaged during World War II and sadly neglected during the years of Communist rule, it has been undergoing accelerated renovation and restoration since German reunification and now, as capital of the state of Brandenburg, has plenty to offer the visitor besides its famous palaces and parks. Much of the inner city has been turned into pedestrians-only zones and is closed to private motor vehicles, so count on walking.

A good starting point, after coming from Sanssouci, is the **Brandenburger Tor** (Brandenburg Gate; not to be confused with the one in Berlin), at the corner of Schopenhauerstrasse and Brandenburger Strasse, near the eastern tip of Sanssouci Park. This Baroque city gate was built in 1770, using Rome's Trajan Arch as a model. Brandenburger Strasse, the main shopping street, is a pedestrian mall lined by recently spruced-up Neoclassical houses that were once the homes of Prussian officers. For a lunch break here you might consider the **Gaststätte Börse**, Brandenburger Strasse 35–36. This cozy, moderately priced inn has a pedigree going back to the 18th century, and, being close to Potsdam's stock exchange, used to be the favorite of local bankers and merchants.

Brandenburger Strasse intersects with Friedrich-Ebert-Allee, where you should take a left turn toward the **Nauener Tor** (Nauen Gate), the northern entry to the inner city, leading toward the Neuer Garten and Schloss Cecilienhof. The gate is an ocher-colored Neo-Gothic structure designed to look like a medieval castle, but built in 1755 according to plans and sketches by Frederick the Great.

Der Klosterkeller, Friedrich-Ebert-Allee 94, is a 250-year-old tavern now doing multiple duty as a café, with sidewalk tables in summer, beer garden, restaurant, and late-night bar, where you can have either a light lunch, afternoon coffee with creamy, calorific pastries, or a substantial dinner. There are prix-fixe three-course menus (for example, clear oxtail soup, medallions of veal in a cream-and-fresh-mushroom sauce, and chocolate sundae for dessert) at around DM 40, and four-course dinners at DM 55 to DM 60. Evenings it is advisable to reserve; Tel: (0331) 212-18.

A short stroll up Friedrich-Ebert-Allee toward the Nauener Tor, to the intersection with Mittelstrasse, will take you to the **Holländisches Viertel** (Dutch Quarter), a neighborhood of 134 virtually identical gabled, three-story brick houses that look as if they had been transplanted straight from Holland. In fact, they were built between 1734 and 1742 by Dutch masons under the direction of the Prussian architect Johann Boumann, and were intended as housing for Dutch immigrants whom the Soldier King and Frederick the Great wanted to attract to Potsdam the way the Great Elector had brought in the Huguenots. But few came, and after a few years local artists and artisans began moving into the cozy single-family dwellings. The much-neglected district has been undergoing restoration since the 1980s, and chic boutiques and art galleries are now setting up shop here.

Going back down Friedrich-Ebert-Allee toward the Havel river and the S-Bahn station will lead you to Potsdam's original **Altstadt**. Though much changed in the 17th and 18th centuries by the Great Elector, the Soldier King, and Frederick the Great, then ravaged in World War II and by the Communist era's "urban renewal," it still offers a few gems alluding to the past. One is the huge **Nikolaikirche** (St. Nicholas Church), which towers over the area and is visible from afar. The most distinguishing feature of the church, for which Schinkel drew the original plans but which was built by the architect Ludwig Persius between 1830 and 1837, is its enormous dome, reminiscent of that on the Capitol Building in Washington, D.C.—but in fact patterned after the one on London's St. Paul's Cathedral. Just across from the church, on Alter Markt, is the **Altes Rathaus** (Old Town Hall), built by John Boumann in Neoclassical style in the 1750s. Nowadays it is a cultural center and art gallery for visiting exhibitions. Atop its tower, and looking a bit incongruous, is a statue of Atlas holding aloft the world.

The area west of Friedrich-Ebert-Allee is the **Neustadt**, the new city that originated with the Great Elector's development of the town in the 17th century. All that remains of the former Elector's Palace, badly damaged during the war and then razed in 1960, is the **Marstall** (Royal Stables) at the corner of Friedrich-Ebert-Allee and Breite Strasse. Built in the 1740s by Knobelsdorff, the elaborate Baroque structure is now the **Filmmuseum Potsdam**, a collection of equipment and documents recounting the history of German cinema until 1945. Classic old movies are also shown. Open daily except Mondays 10:00 A.M. to 5:00 P.M.

Be sure to stroll around the **Neuer Markt** and the district between Friedrich-Ebert-Allee, Breite Strasse, Dortustrasse, and Yorckstrasse. A number of the 17th- to 19th-century burgher and patrician houses, all in elaborate Baroque or Neoclassical style, survived the war or were carefully reconstructed, among them the **Hiller-Brandtschen Häuser**, two adjacent town houses on Breite Strasse modeled on Whitehall in London.

And in case you're wondering about the mosque-like structure with dome and minaret visible across the Neustädter Havelbucht, the bay-like inlet of the Havel, be assured it is not a mosque at all but the **Wasserwerk**, the waterworks, built that way between 1840 and 1842; the "minaret" disguises the smokestack.

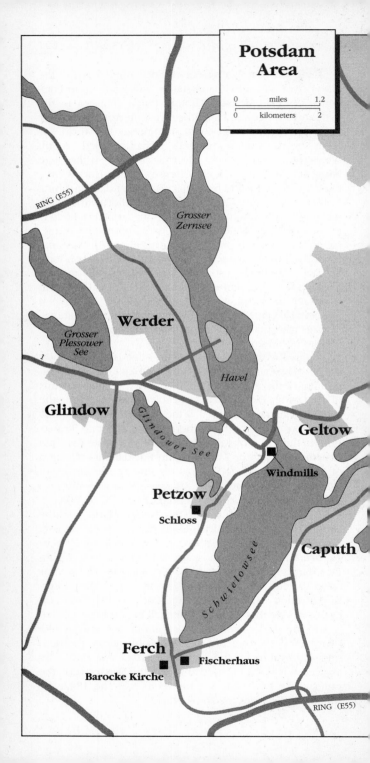

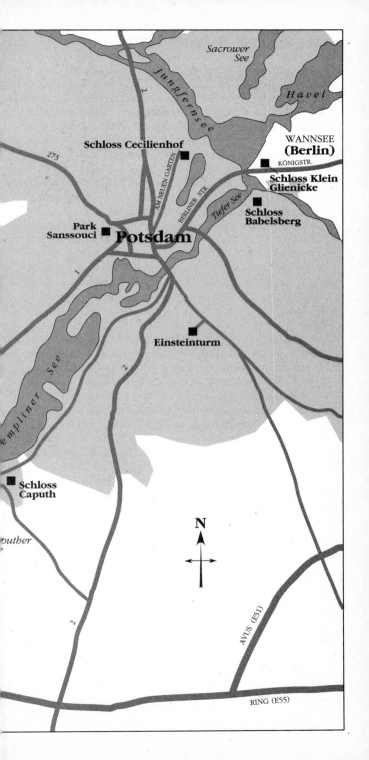

Along the Havel River

For a completely different aspect of Potsdam, drive or take the A-3 municipal sightseeing bus line south from the S-Bahn station along the Havel embankment, around Templiner and Schielow lakes, to the suburbs of Caputh, Ferch, Petzow, and Werder. It's a round-trip drive or ride of about 35 km (22 miles).

About a kilometer (half a mile) south of the S-Bahn station, along Albert-Einstein-Strasse, is the *Telegrafenberg* (Telegraph Hill), topped by the **Einsteinturm** (Einstein Tower), a solar-physics observatory built by the Expressionist architect Eric Mendelsohn in 1921. The unique, sculpturelike structure, a precursor for those he built later—like the Hadassah University Medical Center in Jerusalem, the Maimonides Medical Center in San Francisco, and the Atomic Energy Commission buildings in Berkeley, California—is Mendelsohn's most famous work. Though Einstein never worked here, the solar observatory, still one of the most important in the world, was built to test and prove his relativity theory by measuring and observing spectroanalytical phenomena. Mendelsohn, who liked to design while listening to the music of Bach, originally wanted to make the entire building of concrete, a new material at the time, to which he attributed "flowing architectural" qualities. It didn't quite work out, and the steel-concrete shell had to be covered with bricks, which were then plastered over to give the observatory its curvaceous appearance. But when Mendelsohn showed Einstein the finished building and asked for his opinion, the scientist took a long, deep breath, then said almost in a whisper: "Organic, very organic."

The road, along the Havel, here so wide that it looks like a lake—this stretch is called the Templiner See—leads south from the area around Telegraph Hill for about 5 km (3 miles) to **Caputh,** the little town where Einstein lived (at Am Waldrand 3) during his last four years as director of Berlin's Kaiser Wilhelm Physical Institute before emigrating to the United States in 1934. **Schloss Caputh,** commissioned by the Great Elector in 1662, was a much-loved summer residence of his wife Dorothea, and later the property of King Frederick I's wife Sophie-Charlotte. It is a Baroque château in a blend of Italian and Dutch design, surrounded by a lovely park that was landscaped by Peter Joseph Lenné. Until recently it was a school, but it is now being renovated and reconstructed; there are no definite plans for its future use. It is not open to the public at present.

Following the road around the "lake," which farther on changes its name to Schwielowsee, will take you first to the village of Ferch (about 10 km—6 miles—south of Caputh), where the main attractions are a thatch-roofed fisherman's house and an unusual 17th-century half-timbered Baroque church.

The route then continues north along the lakeshore to Petzow, notable for its château, **Schloss Petzow**, erstwhile home of the Kähne family, a local dynasty that became rich making what were reputed to be the best bricks in and around Berlin and Potsdam. The manor, a blend of English countryhouse and Italian castello, was designed by Schinkel, and the park around it landscaped by Lenné. In GDR times it was an institute of economics and business administration; now it is a hotel with café and restaurant, perfect for lunch or a coffee break. If you happen to be here on a summer Saturday afternoon, you can enjoy a concert of brass and woodwind music.

Just north of the château, where the Schwielowsee narrows to again become the Havel river, is the first of several windmills that you will see on the road farther along (now north) to **Werder**, an island town that has preserved much of its medieval architecture and atmosphere. Just south of the town center is the main highway, on which it is a 15-minute drive back to the center of Potsdam, and from there by car or S-Bahn 45 minutes back to Berlin.

GETTING AROUND POTSDAM

By S-Bahn. Take the S-3 from Alexanderplatz, Friedrichstrasse, or Bahnhof Zoo (and S-Bahn stations in between) or the S-1 from Friedrichstrasse to Wannsee station and from there continue on the S-3 for two stops to Potsdam Stadt station.

By car. The most convenient route from central Berlin is to drive out of town (direction Nürnberg/Munich) on the Avus, the municipal Autobahn, to the Zehlendorf/Wannsee exit, then toward Potsdam on the Potsdamer Chaussee, which becomes Königstrasse (Bundesstrasse, or federal highway, B-1) across the bridge, the Glienicker Brücke, into central Potsdam.

By bus. Take the number 116 from Wannsee S-Bahn station to Glienicker Brücke (last stop), walk across the bridge and board the number 93 or A-2 streetcar in

Potsdam, which takes you into the center. The DM 12 Berlin 24-hour ticket is valid in Potsdam.

Within Potsdam. The local transit authority, Stadtwerke Potsdam Verkehrsbetrieb, offers three sightseeing street-car and bus tours on its regular routes (bus line A-1, streetcars A-2 and A-4) from the S-Bahn station to Sans-souci Park, Neuer Garten with Schloss Cecilienhof, and along Friedrich-Ebert-Allee. You can get off at the regular stops and board the next vehicle when it arrives to continue the journey. There is a similar sightseeing line—the A-3 bus—that follows the route around the river and lake to Caputh, Ferch, Petzow, and Werder, ending at the Werder train station where you can catch the S-Bahn for a three-stop ride back to central Potsdam.

By boat. Besides the various Berlin-based steamer lines that make excursions to Potsdam, Potsdam's own Weisse Flotte has several two-hour city round-trips daily, operating from the Tegel landing in Berlin direct to Postdam's Lange Brücke landing in the middle of town, with intermediate stops (and boarding opportunities) at Spandau and the Wannsee S-Bahn station. There are also once-daily excursions to Caputh and Werder Island, as well as river trips to the city of Brandenburg. Ticket office and information: An der Langen Brücke, D(0)-1560 Potsdam; Tel: (0331) 215-27.

Tourist information. Potsdam Information, Touristen-zentrale am Alten Markt, D(0)-1560 Potsdam, Tel: (0331) 211-00 or 233-85, Fax: 23012, open Monday through Friday 9:00 A.M. to 8:00 P.M., Saturdays and Sundays to 6:00 P.M.

Sanssouci, Neuer Garten, Babelsberg information: Abteilung Besucherbetreuung, Stiftung Schlösser und Gärten Potsdam, Am Grünen Gitter 2, D(0)-1561 Potsdam, Tel: (0331) 238-19.

BRANDENBURG

Berliners who want to see written proof of their city's founding have to travel about 70 km (43 miles) westward to the town of Brandenburg and visit its magnificent cathedral, the Dom St. Peter and Paul. There in the museum of the treasury are two pieces of parchment, each about 22 by 18 inches, weighted with huge seals, dated in 1237 and 1244, on which, in italic script, are the first mentions of Cölln and Berlin. The documents deal with disputes over their tribute payments to the margrave of Brandenburg, who then had his capital in this town on the banks of (and laced by) the Havel river. No other place played so important a role in the centuries-long struggle between the Germans and the Slavic Wends over the March as this ancient city in the marsh and lake country of the Havelland.

Archaeological finds prove that "Brennabor," as it was called in Slavic, was settled in the Stone and Bronze ages. Whatever role early Germanic tribes may have played, they left and moved southward in the Dark Ages, to be replaced in the sixth or seventh century by Slavic groups, notably the Hevelians, for whom, presumably, the Havel is named. By the late ninth century Brennabor was their major center, with a strong fortress on the hill overlooking the river and the surrounding lakes, bogs, and marshes that provided natural defenses.

But the defenses were not strong enough to ward off Henry the Fowler, duke of Saxony and king of an incipient German feudal confederation, who conquered and subjugated Brennabor in 928. Twenty years later Henry's son, Holy Roman Emperor Otto I, established a church and diocese here, probably on the fortress island and close to where the present cathedral is situated. In 983 the Hevelians overthrew German rule, recaptured the citadel, destroyed the Ottonian church, and reestablished their suzerainty over the territory. For nearly 200 years Brennabor, along with the surrounding March of Brandenburg, was the scene of frequent battles and power struggles between Germans and Slavs.

Finally the last Hevelian ruler, Prince Pribislaw, who had converted to Christianity, promised the stronghold and surrounding lands to Margrave Albrecht the Bear. After Pribislaw's death some of his heirs and nobles refused to honor the legacy, but Albrecht finally defeated them in 1157 and made Brennabor, soon renamed Brandenburg, one of his residences and the de facto capital of his margraviate. The cornerstone for St. Peter and Paul Cathedral was laid in 1165. Two new settlements soon developed near the cathedral and fortress island: the Altstadt to the west, the Neustadt to the south on an island of its own. Like Berlin and Cölln they remained rivals for a long time—indeed did not unite into one city until 1715.

But by then Brandenburg was the provincial backwater that, in a sense, it still is today. For shortly after the

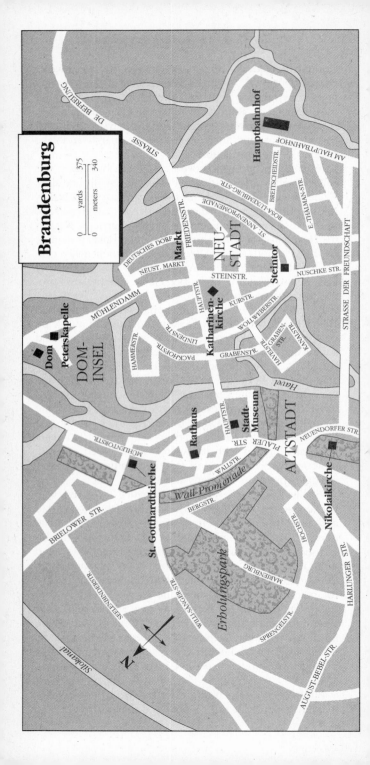

Hohenzollern family became the margraves and electors of the March, in the 15th century, they began construction of a palace in Berlin-Cölln and made it their capital and chief residence. The city of Brandenburg went into 400 years of decline, from which it made only a slight recovery as a garrison town in the 18th century and as an industrial center in the 19th. In more recent times it was noteworthy only for its grim penitentiary, in which the ex-GDR's former leader, Erich Honecker, was incarcerated from 1935 to 1945 for his underground anti-Nazi activities, and as the site of one of the Third Reich's first concentration camps.

Though administratively one city, Brandenburg is still divided into three parts—the Dom-Insel (Dom Island), Neustadt, and Alstadt—clearly demarcated by branches and canals of the Havel. Though the main road from Berlin and Potsdam (Bundesstrasse, or federal highway, B-1) will automatically lead you first to the Neustadt if you are driving here, it is on the Dom-Insel, just north of the Neustadt, and with **Dom St. Peter and Paul** that you should start your visit.

DOM-INSEL

The Dom, surrounded by ancillary buildings, a park, and stands of old linden, chestnut, and sycamore trees, is a stunning example of 12th- to 13th-century Romanesque architecture with 14th- to 15th-century Gothic alterations, all in cinammon-red brick. There were some additions made to the basilica in 1670, and Karl Friedrich Schinkel designed the 1837 spire that crowns the northern belfry tower. The interior is a remarkable study in contrasts: the brick walls stuccoed and painted off-white, the Romanesque archways and Gothic rib-vaulting left in the original red brick. Be sure not to miss the **Krypta** (crypt), whose pillar capitals are intricately carved with 13th-century legends, myths, and allegorical scenes, and the **Bunte Kapelle** (Painted Chapel) with its floral design frescoes on the vaulted ceilings.

The most important works of art in the Dom are the 13th-century stained-glass windows; a Romanesque crucifix; the gilded, intricately carved **Böhmischer Altar**, a work by an unknown Bohemian master from the late 14th century; a panel-painting crucifixion altarpiece from around 1500; and the organ by Joachim Wagner, one of the best organ builders of the early 18th century.

The **Dommuseum** (Cathedral Museum) in the east wing of the adjacent canons' cloister includes an archive and library among whose treasures are important medieval documents, including those parchments about Cölln and Berlin, beautifully illustrated and printed bibles going back more than 500 years, fine pieces of ecclesiastical art, and the illuminated **Brandenburg Book of Hours**, dating from the early 13th century. The cathedral is normally open from 10:00 A.M. to 2:00 P.M. daily, starting 11:00 A.M. on Sundays, until 5:00 P.M. in July and August. The museum is open Tuesday through Saturday from 10:30 A.M. to 2:30 P.M. and only after 2:30 P.M. on Sundays. Organ concerts are given almost daily during the summer months, starting at 7:30 P.M.

On your walk toward the Neustadt, down Domlinden, stop off at the little **Peterskapelle** (St. Peter's Chapel), at the corner of Burgweg. The parish church, dating from 1320, is on the site of an earlier chapel where, allegedly, the Hevelian Prince Pribislaw was buried in 1150. From here the way leads down Mühlendamm, lined by old mills, across the Havel to the Neustädter Markt, and the Katharinenkirche.

NEUSTADT

The **Katharinenkirche** (St. Catherine's Church) on Katharinenkirchplatz was built between 1395 and 1401 by the medieval architect Hinrich Brunsberg and ranks as one of Germany's finest examples of elaborate Gothic brick construction. It is remarkable for the degree of exterior decoration that Brunsberg achieved with the use of both normal red bricks and glazed ones, and for the brick tracery in the window arches and on the gables. Among the interior treasures of ecclesiastical art are a number of 15th-century altarpieces, including one by Gerhard Weger; a richly sculpted brass baptismal font by Dietrich Molnar, a 15th-century Erfurt master; a Renaissance pulpit; and a Baroque organ. As in the Dom, there are frequent organ concerts, indeed every Monday night during July and August, starting at 7:30 P.M.

A long walk—or a less strenuous streetcar ride—down the Hauptstrasse, Brandenburg's main street, which is closed to private motor vehicles, will take you across the Havel again, from the Neustadt into the Alstadt and the Rathaus at Altstädter Markt.

ALTSTADT

With its gables and high spire the **Altstädtisches Rathaus** (Old City Hall) looks like another church. The illusion was deliberate—a show of burgher power in defiance of ecclesiastical might. Brandenburg's city hall, completed in 1470 just as the city's importance as capital of the margraviate started to decline, is as notable for its elaborate brickwork as is Katharinenkirche, and astonishing for the tracery work in rosette windows and for the vaulted arches that medieval craftsmen were able to achieve with bricks. The 16-foot-high statue of Roland, the sword-bearing knight in front of the building, symbolizes the city's independence and dates from 1474. The mayor still has his office here, and the city council also meets in the building.

Their preference for lunch is the ground floor and basement **Ratskeller**, and it should also be yours. In fact, it's about the only eatery in town one can recommend. Forty years of Communist rule left Brandenburg rather a culinary wasteland. The cuisine in the Ratskeller is largely stick-to-the-ribs German, but prices are moderate, with main courses averaging DM 25. Open daily from 11:00 A.M. to 11:00 P.M.

Some of Brandenburg's oldest houses, many dating from the Middle Ages, line the narrow streets, such as Bäckerstrasse and Fischerstrasse, leading south from the Rathaus and the market square in which it is located. You will find what is Brandenburg's oldest church and older even than the cathedral, St. Gotthardtkirche, about 250 yards northeast of the Rathaus by walking along Pardium and Mühlentor streets.

St. Gotthardtkirche (St. Gotthardt's Church) at St. Gotthardtkirchplatz traces its origins to an abbey founded by Pribislaw, the Slavic prince, in 1138. It became the seat of Brandenburg's diocese in 1161, before the start of the Dom's construction. A few elements of that Romanesque fieldstone church and monastery are incorporated in the foundations and walls of St. Gotthardt's, which is a late-15th–century Gothic hall church, with a Baroque cupola topping its belfry. It, too, is a gem of brick construction in which the architect blended sandstone elements with an array of glazed bricks to create decorative effects.

Among its interior treasures are an intricately sculpted cast-bronze baptismal font dating from around 1300, a three-by-sixteen-foot tapestry from the 1470s depicting the unicorn legend, a 16th-century altarpiece by the

Leipzig painter Wilhelm Gulden, a triumphal crucifix carved in the late 15th century, and some intricately sculpted epitaphs. The organ, installed only in 1986, is a fine example of East German instrument making and can be heard, like the much older ones in the Dom and St. Catherine's, in a series of summer concerts.

To be sure, there's more to be seen in Brandenburg: remnants of the city's medieval defensive walls and some of the turrets and towers; 18th-century burgher houses in the Neustadt along Steinstrasse, Neustädtischer Markt, Gorrenberg, Kleine Münzstrasse, and Kurstrasse; and also the **Stadtmuseum** of local history in the Baroque Frey-haus at Hauptstrasse 96, one block south of the Altstädter Rathaus. But what is striking is that this city, which suffered comparatively little wartime destruction, decayed and crumbled so abjectly during the 40 years of Communist rule. Granted, something is being done to stop the rot and inject new life into an old city: A preservation, conservation, restoration, and reconstruction project with the name of "Brand-Neu"—Brand New—is under way. To see what has already been accomplished and what is planned, visit the exhibition center for Stadterneuerung (urban renewal) Brandenburg in the old mill, Heidrische Mühle, Mühlendamm 16–18 (between the Dom-Insel and the Neustadt), open daily except Mondays 12 noon to 6:00 P.M., Saturdays and Sundays from 10:00 A.M. to 5:00 P.M. But the plans are going to take decades to carry out and will cost millions.

GETTING AROUND BRANDENBURG
By car. Drive from Berlin as you would to Potsdam, then along Bundesstrasse (federal highway) B-1 westward for about 40 km (25 miles). Depending on local traffic, figure 1 to 1½ hours driving time.

By train. There are a number of fast daily connections from (eastern) Berlin Hauptbahnhof, Friedrichstrasse, and/or Bahnhof Zoo to Brandenburg and back. Here are a few: Departure Berlin Hauptbahnhof 8:00 A.M., Friedrich-strasse 8:12, Zoo 8:22, arrival Brandenburg 9:17 A.M.; de-parture Hauptbahnhof 10:04 A.M., Friedrichstrasse 10:15, Zoo 10:24, arrival Brandenburg 11:12 A.M. For return: departure Brandenburg 2:47 P.M., arrival Berlin Zoo 3:56, Friedrichstrasse 4:20, Hauptbahnhof in eastern Berlin 4:34 P.M.; departure Brandenburg 4:48 P.M., arrival Berlin Zoo 5:56, Friedrichstrasse 6:20, Hauptbahnhof 6:34 P.M.

By boat. Some Berlin and Potsdam operators offer excursions to Brandenburg. *Berlin:* Reederei Riedel, Planufer 78, D(W)-1000 Berlin 61; Tel: 691-37-82 or 693-46-46. *Potsdam:* Weisse Flotte Potsdam, An der Langen Brücke, D(0)-1560 Potsdam; Tel: (0331) 215-27.

In Brandenburg. Streetcars number 1, 2, and 9 stop at the Bahnhof and run through the Neustadt and Altstadt along Friedensstrasse and Hauptstrasse. Bus number A-2, to which you can transfer at Neustädter Markt, will take you to the Dom.

Information. Brandenburg-Information, Plauer Strasse 4, D(0)-1800 Brandenburg; Tel: (03381) 237-43.

NEURUPPIN AND RHEINSBERG
Neuruppin

No matter how lovely, idyllic, and romantic the surrounding countryside—a land of lakes, gently rolling hills, and lush green forests that justify its description as the Ruppiner Schweiz (Ruppin's Little Switzerland)—Neuruppin, present population 27,000, some 45 miles northwest of Berlin, might be just a pinpoint on the map had this sleepy provincial town on the shore of the Ruppiner See not been the birthplace of two of Prussia's most famous native sons: the architect and artist Karl Friedrich Schinkel and the essayist and novelist Theodor Fontane.

Less important, though certainly not insignificant, is that Frederick the Great, while crown prince, was commandant of its military garrison, and that for most of the 19th century and the first few decades of the 20th the Neuruppin printing and publishing houses of Gustav Kühn and Oehmigke and Riemenschneider supplied much of Europe with what could be called a precursor to television: the "Neuruppiner Bilderbogen." The Bilderbogen were a periodical series of colored illustrations depicting life's oddities, incidentals, and famous people as well as great, dramatic, and tragic events, such as battles of the Crimean War, the 1860 massacre of Christians in Damascus, the funeral of King Frederick William IV in 1861, and Prussia's victory over Austria in the 1866 Battle of Königgrätz. Like TV today, the Bilderbogen were widely criticized then for pandering to viewers' lust for violence and sensation.

Moreover, Neuruppin is just 10 miles from the resort

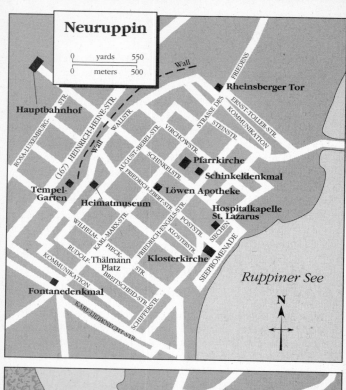

Neuruppin

| 0 | yards | 550 |
| 0 | meters | 500 |

Wall

Rheinsberger Tor

FRIEDENS

ERNST-TOLLER-STR.

KOMMUNIKATION

STRASSE DES

STEINSTR.

Hauptbahnhof

ROSA-LUXEMBURG-STR.

HEINRICH-HEINE-STR.

WALLSTR.

Wall

(167)

VIRCHOWSTR.

AUGUST-BEBEL-STR.

SCHINKELSTR.

Pfarrkirche

Schinkeldenkmal

FRIEDRICH-EBERT-STR.

Löwen Apotheke

Tempel-Garten

Heimatmuseum

Hospitalkapelle St. Lazarus

WILHELM-

KARL-MARX-STR.

RUDOLF-

PIECK-

POSTSTR.

KLOSTERSTR.

SIECHEN

FRIEDRICH-ENGELS-STR.

Thälmann-Platz

STR.

BREITSCHEIDSTR.

Klosterkirche

SEEPROMENADE

KOMMUNIKATION

Ruppiner See

Fontanedenkmal

KARL-LIEBKNECHT-STR.

SCHIFFERSTR.

N

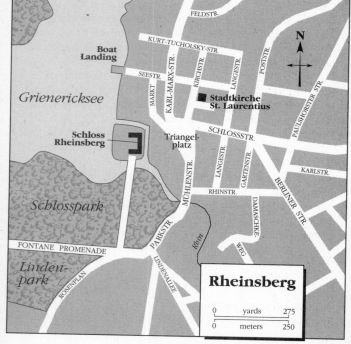

FELDSTR.

Boat Landing

KURT-TUCHOLSKY-STR.

N

POSTSTR.

Grienericksee

SEESTR.

MARKT

KARL-MARX-STR.

KIRCHSTR.

LANGESTR.

PAULSHORSTER STR.

Stadtkirche St. Laurentius

Schloss Rheinsberg

Triangel-platz

SCHLOSSSTR.

KARLSTR.

Schlosspark

MÜHLENSTR.

LANGESTR.

GARTENSTR.

BERLINER STR.

RHINSTR.

Rhin

DAMASCHKE-

WEG

FONTANE PROMENADE

PARKSTR.

Linden-park

ROSENPLAN

LINDENALLEE

Rheinsberg

| 0 | yards | 275 |
| 0 | meters | 250 |

town of Rheinsberg, site of one of the favorite palaces of
Prussian princes and kings, immortalized in stories by
Fontane and Kurt Tucholsky—and covered here follow-
ing Neuruppin.

Like most of the March of Brandenburg, Neuruppin
and its environs were Slavic territory until the late 12th
century and did not enter written Germany history until
the early 13th—but then with a distinct difference. Ruppin, called Rapin in the Slavic Wendish dialect, was an
independent fief and county, ruled from a castle in what
is now the village of Alt Ruppin, which preserved its
independence until 1524 when its last ruler died and
Brandenburg's Elector Joachim I inherited the territory.
During the Middle Ages Neuruppin was an important
beer-brewing and cloth-making center. In the early 18th
century it became a military garrison and civil-service
town. A fire in August 1787 wiped it off the map: 401
burgher houses, three churches, a school, and 425 barns,
stables, and other commercial buildings were destroyed,
and more than 4,000 of the then 6,500 inhabitants were
left homeless. King Frederick William II, Frederick the
Great's nephew and successor, ordered the town reconstructed as a totally planned city with rectangular blocks
of housing and straight intersecting streets, very much
like an American one. And that is what you will see today:
It has not changed in 200 years.

Nonetheless, there is something akin to an "old quarter" around the Klosterkirche, the monastery church,
where Neuruppin had its beginnings, and where you may
want to start your tour.

The **Klosterkirche**, on Niemöllerplatz, adjacent to the
Seepromenade along the Ruppiner See (Ruppin Lake), is
not only the town's oldest surviving structure but also one
of the oldest churches in Brandenburg. Its origins go back
to the founding of a Dominican monastery here in 1246.
The early-Gothic brick basilica was completely renovated,
restored, and partly reconstructed by Karl Friedrich Schinkel in 1836 as a gesture to his home town and a tribute to
his father, who had been superintendent of Lutheran
churches in Neuruppin. The spires to the two towers were
added in 1907. Though the church is starkly austere in
appearance, there are some interesting pieces of ecclesiastical art inside, including a Romanesque baptismal font, a
late-Gothic Pieta, and some fine 15th-century sandstone
sculptures on the main altar. The church is open to visitors
daily 10:00 A.M. to 6:00 P.M. April through October.

Near it, on the grassy lakeside grounds, still partly surrounded by remnants of the medieval city wall, stands the *Wichmannlinde,* a 650-year-old linden tree named for Abbot Wichmann. A good spot from which to contemplate it, get a panoramic view of the lake, and have a coffee or a snack is the terrace of the **Gaststätte zur Wichmannlinde**, Poststrasse 17, the street adjacent to the church, which also leads down to the excursion-boat landing, if you want to take a one- or two-hour trip around the lake.

A short walk up Poststrasse leads to its intersection with Siechenstrasse, where you should turn right for a stroll through one of Neuruppin's oldest and most picturesque districts—narrow, cobblestoned streets, lined by two-story half-timbered houses that have been the target of renovation and restoration since 1990. The **Hospital-kapelle St. Lazarus** is a small 15th-century brick chapel that was part of the medieval *Siechenhaus* (hospital for incurable diseases) on Siechenstrasse. Right behind it is the **Uphus**, one of the few half-timbered houses that survived the 1787 conflagration. A left turn at the next intersection takes you into Fischbänkenstrasse and the **Predigerwit-wenhaus**, literally the "Preacher's Widow's House," where Schinkel spent the decisive years of his childhood.

The famous architect was born in 1781 the son of Johann Cuno Christoph Schinkel, superintendent of Protestant churches and schools in Ruppin county. On the day of the great fire the superintendent was out on an inspection trip, and when he heard of the conflagration he rushed back the ten kilometers with horse and wagon to aid his wife and five children and to help the firefighters. The physical and emotional strain brought him down with pneumonia, of which he died a few weeks later. His wife, three daughters, and two sons moved into one of the few surviving houses, now known as the Prediger-witwenhaus, Fischbänkenstrasse 8. Karl Friedrich was then six years old. There is nothing to see except a dusty plaque on the wall of what is now the shop of a venetian blinds and shutters supplier, but it is a place to stop and think about Schinkel.

He lived and grew up in this small house, for seven years, until 1794, when his mother moved the whole family to Berlin, where she had relatives. But during that time the boy lived in an environment that focused on architecture and building. All of fire-ravaged Neuruppin was one vast construction site, with the sights, sounds, and smells of new houses going up, masons working, surveyors measuring, and architects and engineers poring over plans and sketches. Though he had shown an intense interest in and considerable aptitude for art even before his father's death, it must have been this experience that tipped the scales and persuaded him to become a builder and enter Berlin's newly founded Bauakademie in 1799.

Schinkel had many other interests and talents. He was a painter and illustrator, designed furniture and china, made theater sets, and staged opera productions. But above all he was a master architect who changed the face of Berlin and Potsdam and left a legacy of hundreds of innovative, beautiful, and enduring structures all over the March of Brandenburg and what used to be Prussia. If the tablet on the Fischbänkenstrasse house seems rather paltry for a native son of such stature, then continue up the street, which changes its name to Schinkelstrasse, to its intersection with Friedrich-Engels Strasse and the square dominated by the Pfarrkirche St. Marien (St. Mary's Parish Church), a Neoclassical building designed in 1801. Right behind it is a more fitting monument to Schinkel: a bronze statue of him sculpted in 1883.

The church faces on Neuruppin's main street, Karl-Marx-Strasse (the name may be changed). Along it, just south of St. Mary's and the square with the Schinkel monument, is the **Löwen Apotheke** (Lion Pharmacy), Karl-Marx-Strasse 84, where Theodor Fontane spent his childhood and part of his youth, and which he visited frequently in later years. Fontane was born in the house in 1819 as the son of the pharmacy owner, lived with his parents here until 1827, was then sent to a boarding school, and returned in 1832 to attend the Neuruppin *Gymnasium*. A tablet on the building marks the spot (the Löwen Apotheke is still Neuruppin's biggest and busiest pharmacy).

Like his father, Fontane studied and initially practiced pharmacy, making and dispensing medicines in the family shop in Neuruppin, but then he turned to journalism and writing. He was a foreign correspondent for a Berlin paper in London, a war correspondent covering the Franco-Prussian War, and a theater critic, travel writer, essayist, and composer of ballads strongly influenced by his stays in England and Scotland. During the last 20 years of his life he turned to writing the novels—15 of them— that established his fame. Fontane's greatest tribute to his homeland is the four-volume collection of essays and travel stories, *Wanderungen durch die Mark Brandenburg,* published in German between 1862 and 1882, but never translated into English.

But Fontane is best known for his fiction, to which he turned at age 59, becoming a master of the realistic social novel and of dialogue whose influence is felt strongly in the works of Thomas Mann. Many of his books deal with the decline of the Prussian nobility and rise of the mercantile-industrial bourgeoisie and are peopled with characters who either live in the past or cannot cope with the present. Among the best that have been translated into English are *Trials and Tribulations, The Adulteress, Frau Jenny Treibel,* and *Effi Briest,* which the late Rainer Werner Fassbinder made into a television miniseries and feature movie in 1974. Fontane is honored in a little park at the southern end of Karl-Marx-Strasse by a fine bronze monument, showing him sitting—hat, cane, and satchel nearby—gazing out distantly over the landscape of the March.

Diagonally across from his birthplace and the pharmacy is the **Hotel und Restaurant Märkischer Hof**, Karl-Marx-Strasse 51–52, where you can have lunch, or, if you do want to make more than a day trip, spend the night in moderately priced comfort. The restaurant, which has a terrace for use on sunny days, serves specialties of the March, particularly fresh fish from Ruppin Lake.

Continuing west on Schinkelstrasse to its intersection with August-Bebel-Strasse, then turning left, will take you to the **Heimatmuseum**, August-Bebel-Strasse 14–15, located in a fine Neoclassical mansion built just after the great fire. It is many cuts above the usual German "local history museum," and worlds apart from those you would find in other towns the size of Neuruppin. Most important are the memorial rooms devoted to Schinkel and Fontane, full of pictures, photographs, original documents, personal effects, and furnishings of their times. There is a section devoted to Frederick the Great's stay in Rheinsberg as crown prince and his command of the Neuruppin garrison, with busts of Voltaire and of Frederick's brother Prince Henry. A whole section is devoted to the *Neuruppiner Bilderbogen,* those illustrated colored sheets sold by the thousands to entertain and inform the masses, especially in rural areas. Some 5,000 originals are in the collection, dating from some of the first, published in 1810, to the last in 1937. Directly across the street from the museum is the printing plant where they were published from 1865 to 1937. The museum is open daily except Mondays from 10:00 A.M. to 5:00 P.M., Saturdays and Sundays until 4:00 P.M.

Just behind the museum, in the park area along Neuruppin's former defensive wall, between Heinrich-Heine-Strasse and August-Bebel-Strasse, is the Tempelgarten with the columned, circular **Greek Temple** that Georg Wenzeslaus von Knobelsdorff built for Frederick the Great, then crown prince, in 1735. Knobelsdorff, born in 1699, was a Prussian aristocrat who left military service in 1729 to train as a painter. He was a friend of Frederick, who encouraged him to turn to architecture. The little Neuruppin temple, which Frederick co-designed, was his first effort and the beginning of a stellar career, for it was Knobelsdorff who subsequently designed and built the finest structures associated with Frederick the Great's reign: extensions of Schloss Charlottenburg, the Staatsoper on Unter den Linden in Berlin, Sanssouci in Potsdam, and the enlargement of Schloss Rheinsberg.

Rheinsberg

From spring to autumn the drive north from Neuruppin to Rheinsberg—a distance of 16 to 26 km (10 to 16 miles), depending on which route you choose—is a journey through a wonderland of nature with lakes, dense forests, here and there a farming hamlet, and narrow, winding, sometimes cobblestone roads lined by venerable linden, chestnut, oak, beech, and sycamore trees whose bending branches give you the feeling of motoring through a series of lush, leafy green tunnels.

Situated at the southern tip of the Grienericksee, one of more than 100 lakes that the last Ice Age left in this area, Rheinsberg, present population 5,000, has a tumultuous history going back into the Dark Ages, when it was a Slavic settlement. German colonists drove out the Slavs in the early 13th century and built a moated, strongly fortified frontier castle here. The fortress provided protection for the farmers, craftsmen, and fishermen who settled here, presumably after 1250. It is believed that many of them were colonists from the Rhineland, and that this explains the subsequent name, Rheinsberg. The first mention of it is in a document relating to one Gerhardus von Rhynesberge, dated 1291, and the first documentary evidence of a town is from 1335, referring to a Pastor von

Freyenstein who had been appointed parish priest in "Rhynesperg" by the margrave of Brandenburg. It was a time when the March was plagued by robber barons and feudal lords battling each other ruthlessly for territory, and toward the end of the 14th century Rheinsbergers built a thick, 30-foot-high wall with towers, turrets, fortified gates, and a moat around their town to protect themselves. Remnants of it can still be seen.

Countless calamities and catastrophes ravaged the town in the Middle Ages: a peasant uprising in 1527; fires in 1566, 1675, and 1740; and devastation and plunder in 1635 during the Thirty Years' War. It was the 1566 fire that resulted in reconstruction of the castle that was a precursor to the splendid Baroque palace Schloss Rheinsberg is today, and the conflagration of 1740 that led to the little city's planned rebuilding, similar to that of Neuruppin, with long, straight streets and rectangular blocks. Frederick the Great and his budding architect friend Knobbelsdorff had pivotal roles in both Baroque endeavors. What they created in the 18th century was the basis for Rheinsberg's popularity as a weekend and vacation resort, a retreat for princes, princesses, commoner lovers, artists, and writers in the 19th and 20th centuries. Best known among the latter was Kurt Tucholsky, the journalist and political satirist, whose first book, *Rheinsberg, Ein Bilderbuch für Verliebte* (Rheinsberg, A Picture Book for Lovers), became an immediate best-seller upon publication in 1912 and—80 years later—still draws people in droves to the town.

That it has remained idyllic is due as much to geography as to historical vicissitudes. It is off the beaten path—so far so that in 1861 Theodor Fontane wrote: "To get to Rheinsberg is not easy." There was no direct train (only postal stages), and there still isn't. The *Postmeilensäule* (postal mileage pillar) on Triangelplatz (Triangle Place), a tree-shaded common just east of the château, makes the point graphically. The stone, dating from the 1760s, spells out precisely how far it is by stagecoach from Rheinsberg to the most important destinations on the European continent: Berlin, Moscow, St. Petersburg, Riga, Frankfurt am Main, Paris, Munich, Rome, Vienna, Prague, Dresden, Leipzig, *and* Neuruppin. Coaches left every Monday and Friday.

That kind of isolation also protected Rheinsberg from the turbulence of the Industrial Revolution. Most of its burghers remained small-holding farmers who had their homesteads within the city limits. The only industry of note was a porcelain, faïence, and stoneware manufacturer launched in 1762. Its most famous products to this day, trademarked with a flamboyantly scrawled "R" on the underside, are tea services (cups, saucers, pots, sugar bowls, and creamers) of red clay with black or spangled brown glaze and ocher-yellow decor, available in gift shops around town, such as Monika Wille, Schlossstrasse 7, or the Rheinsberg Keramik factory store on Rhinstrasse. East German authorities tried to change all that by erecting the GDR's first atomic power plant 6 miles east of Rheinsberg in 1957; mercifully it was shut down in 1991 for safety reasons and to forestall a potential German Chernobyl. Thus, aside from the lovely landscape and the recreational opportunities on the lake—from fishing to water skiing—Schloss Rheinsberg, now the scene of summer music festivals and opera performances in the palace garden, is the town's main attraction.

SCHLOSS RHEINSBERG

Schloss Rheinsberg, situated on an artificial island that juts into Grienerick see (Grienerick Lake), joined to the mainland only by a stone bridge, has foundations going back to the Middle Ages, when it was the moated 13th-century fortress around which the town evolved. It was often destroyed and rebuilt and also changed owners numerous times. In the early 18th century its proprietor was a French Huguenot immigrant, Benjamin Chenevix de Beville, who reconstructed the old digs, had its defensive walls torn down, and turned it into a manor house and moved in. In 1734 Frederick William I, the Soldier King, bought it from de Beville, along with most of the town of Rheinsberg, surrounding villages, forests, and 22 lakes, and gave it to the son and heir he despised, Crown Prince Frederick, subsequently aka Frederick the Great.

This was hardly a boorish, despotic father's belated act of benevolence. Rather the contrary. In all likelihood the king thought that it was a good way to get Frederick out of Berlin and far from the court. After all, just a few years earlier Frederick, then 18, had been tried for desertion and treason for attempting to flee to England with his friend and lover, Lieutenant Katte, and in 1733 had reluctantly married, only to separate from his wife shortly after the wedding. Nor was he showing much enthusiasm for his latest official job, commanding the regiment at Neuruppin. The king probably figured that if Frederick in-

sisted on pursuing the fine arts rather than the martial
ones, instead of helping to make Prussia into an army
with a state, then let him do so in a backwater like
Rheinsberg. And Frederick grabbed at the chance. But he
refused to accept his father's choice of an architect—
Johann von Kemmeter—to turn Rheinsberg manor into a
utilitarian princely château. Instead, he commissioned his
friend Knobelsdorff to make it into a splendid residence.

And Knobelsdorff, eager to try his hand at architecture
on a grand scale, plunged into the job with verve. He chose
as collaborators his own painting teacher, Antoine Pesne,
the Frenchman who was the official portraitist at the Prussian royal court; the sculptor Christian Glume; and the
stucco artist and muralist Augustin Dubuisson. Within four
years, using parts of the original fortress, notably its keep,
and some of Kemmeter's components, they turned Rheinsberg into the dazzling palace it is today: a three-winged
structure, joined by a colonnade that encloses the lakeside
courtyard, in which elements of late-Rococo and early
Neoclassicism blend in unusual harmony. A lovely park
adjoins it on the south side.

Inside, its 70 rooms are a blinding splash of French
Rococo ornamentation, the grandest being the ballroom
with gilded mirrors on the marble walls and Pesne's ceiling fresco depicting Minerva surrounded by the symbols
of the arts and sciences and looking into an opened book
in which the names Homer and Voltaire are inscribed.
Knobelsdorff later was to use many of the architectural
ideas he had first tested in Rheinsberg at Sanssouci in
Potsdam, with Frederick's enthusiastic support. In fact, on
one of the original sketches for Sanssouci there is a hand-
written comment by Frederick: "like in Rheinsberg."

Frederick spent some of the happiest years of his life
here. In Rheinsberg he composed some of his best flute
and chamber music, played in chamber groups with the
composers Karl Heinrich Graun and Johann Quantz, studied philosophy and physics, wrote his provocative anony-
mous treatise "Anti-Machiavelli," and started his correspondence with Voltaire, who also visited him in Rheinsberg.
But it was a brief interlude. In 1740, upon the death of his
father, Frederick was crowned king and established his
residences in Berlin and Potsdam. In 1744 he deeded
Rheinsberg to his youngest brother, Henry.

Henry made the palace his permanent residence in
1752 and during the 50 years he lived here changed the

interior decoration and appointments and turned Rheinsberg into a center of the arts, music, and theater. But after
his death in 1802 the château went into gradual decline.
Few Hohenzollerns visited or spent time in it, and by
1843 its upkeep was simply left to the court administration, which turned it into a museum.

A son of Kaiser Wilhelm II, August Wilhelm, later infamous as a Nazi storm-trooper general, stayed here briefly
in 1918, 1922, and 1923, and also sold off most of the
furniture, so that by the end of World War II, when the state
of Prussia itself was dissolved, Rheinsberg was a lovely but
empty shell.

In 1951 East German authorities turned it into a sanitar-
ium for diabetics, which it remained—with considerable
damage caused to the priceless decoration, such as by
installation of central steam heating, replacement of the
crystal chandeliers with neon lights, and transformation
of princely bedrooms into hospital wards—until June
1991. Since then it has been undergoing extensive restoration and renovation, which you can see in progress on
weekdays. There are plans to use the ballroom for concerts and to refurnish other rooms with original objects
now in storage at Sanssouci and Charlottenburg to make
it a proper castle museum. Completed rooms, though
empty except for a spate of Knobelsdorff and Pesne paintings, as well as those on which work continues, can
already be seen. It is open daily except Mondays 9:30 A.M.
to 12:30 P.M. and 1:00 to 5:00 P.M. in the summer months,
until 4:00 P.M. November through April.

RHEINSBERG TOWN

Be sure to stroll around the town of Rheinsberg itself, for
it is as much Knobelsdorff's doing as the palace. When
the 1740 fire devastated the little city, Frederick gave him
the job of rebuilding, and he laid it out as a planned city
with rectangular blocks of housing and straight intersecting streets, all paved with rounded rocks and stones that
might have been fine for sturdy coaches and wagons with
their huge wheels but shake up modern cars mercilessly.

Most of the houses, which adjoin one another in long
rows, are single story, and belonged to Rheinsberg farmers and artisans. Wealthier burghers added a floor or two,
but the completeness of the architectural ensemble is
unique. Worth a visit too is the **Stadtkirche St. Laurentius**
(St. Lawrence Municipal Church) on Kirchstrasse, a 16th-

century Renaissance structure that incorporates some of the elements of the original 13th-century church, destroyed in the 1566 fire.

STAYING AND DINING IN RHEINSBERG

Being a resort town, Rheinsberg does not want for eateries or places to stay. The **Ratskeller**, Markt 1, is fine for lunch if you're looking for rustic interiors or a large garden. **Zum Alten Fritz**, Schlosstrasse 11, is good for a coffee break, snacks, or lunch, with main courses moderately priced at DM 12 to DM 25. The **Goldener Anker**, Karl-Marx-Strasse 25, closed Wednesdays and Thursdays, specializes in game dishes and lake fish and offers Rheinsberg Fischtopf, a fish stew, as a starter.

If you do decide to spend a night, the best bet, right in the center of town and five minutes walk from the château and the lake, is the **Deutsches Haus** on Seestrasse, the street leading to the boat landing where you can board an excursion steamer for a trip around the lake.

GETTING AROUND NEURUPPIN AND RHEINSBERG

By car. The fastest and most convenient way to Neuruppin is to take the Autobahn from Berlin-Charlottenburg or Berlin-Pankow in the direction of Hamburg and Rostock, getting off at the Neuruppin exit, which is about 3 km (2 miles) from the center of town. There are alternative routes, all on unnumbered country roads, to Rheinsberg, but all well marked. The prettiest is by way of Alt-Ruppin and Köpernitz. The best return route to Berlin is via Gransee, where the country road intersects with federal highway B-96 in the direction of Oranienburg; from there to the Berliner Ring Autobahn circling the city; and then the *Avus,* or inner Berlin Autobahn.

By train. There are no direct train connections from Berlin to Neuruppin, and the indirect ones require so many transfers that you would be en route for three to four hours. Rheinsberg, too, is hard to reach by train, with several train changes making it a two- to three-hour trip. We do not advise either.

By boat. There are excursion boats that make trips on the lakes in both Neuruppin and Rheinsberg. Fahrgast-schiffahrt-Stadt Neuruppin, Seeufer 9, Tel: (03391) 24-43; Weisse Flotte Rheinsberg, Markt 3, Tel: (033931) 20-88.

Information. Fremdenverkehrsamt (Tourist Office) Neuruppin, August-Bebel-Strasse 15, D(0)-1950 *Neuruppin,* Tel: (03391) 23-45, open Monday through Thursday 8:00 A.M. to 4:00 P.M., Fridays to 3:00 P.M., Saturdays 9:00 A.M. to 1:00 P.M. Fremdenverkehrsamt Rheinsberg, Im Kavaliershaus am Markt, D(0)-1955 *Rheinsberg,* Tel: (033931) 20-59, open daily 9:00 A.M. to 5:00 P.M.

THE EBERSWALDE AREA

The lake country northeast of Berlin, stretching to the Oder River valley and the border with Poland, has an archaeologically documented history going back to the Bronze Age. That is the most important message given to us by the spectacular *Goldschatz von Eberswalde*—the Eberswalde Gold Treasure—found in 1913 in the Finow district of this industrial city of 55,000, some 40 km (25 miles) by car from Alexanderplatz. The treasure, consisting of 81 beautifully crafted solid-gold objects, including bracelets, neckrings, and eight embossed bowls, was judged to date from around 900 B.C. The objects had been placed in a lidded earthenware container, found during excavation work for the foundations of a brass foundry in Finow. Like many other art treasures belonging to Berlin and Brandenburg museums, they have been missing since the end of World War II, but evidence is mounting that they survived and are in a deposit of confiscated art in Russia.

Eberswalde

You can see replicas of the treasure in the **Eberswalde-Finow Stadt und Kreismuseum**, Kirchstrasse 8, which is one reason for starting this journey in Eberswalde. Another is to visit the **Stadtkirche St. Maria Magdalena** (St. Mary Magdalene Church) on Kirchstrasse, just opposite the museum. This 14th-century brick church is notable especially for the red-clay terra-cotta figures on its main portal depicting scenes from the life of Mary and Jesus.

Beyond that there is little to see in this small city astride the Finow Canal and just south of the Oder–Havel Canal. Whatever charms it might have had before the electors of Brandenburg and kings of Prussia began promoting iron and steel making in Eberswalde–Finow in the 17th and 18th centuries were either wiped out during World War II or were razed by East German authorities to

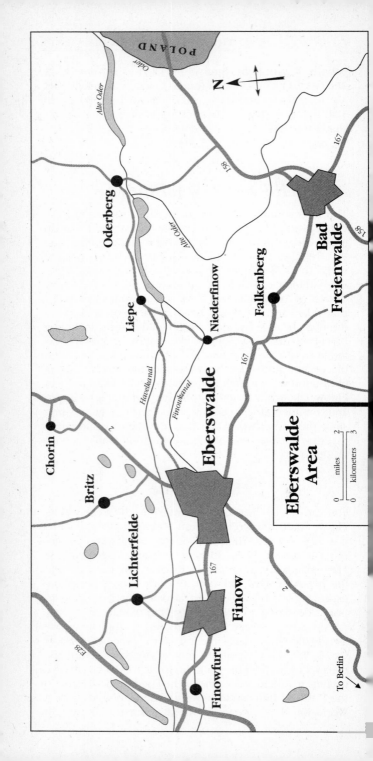

make room for yet more factories. But it is a convenient starting point for travelling along the old canals and through the lush, hilly woodlands of this region to more rewarding destinations, notably Chorin, Niederfinow, and Bad Freienwalde.

Chorin

Chorin, 8 km (5 miles) north of central Eberswalde along federal highway B-2, was, during its golden age, one of the largest Cistercian monastery complexes in Europe, encompassing three towns and 60 villages that belonged to the abbey. The monastery was disbanded in 1542, after Elector Joachim II had converted to Protestantism and introduced the Reformation in Brandenburg, and it has been a ruin since being sacked and burned during the Thirty Years' War.

But it is a *deliberate* ruin, one of the finest examples of Gothic brick architecture in the March, preserved as such by Karl Friedrich Schinkel when, in addition to all his other architectural activities, he was Prussia's royal conservator of old monuments; his collaborator Peter Joseph Lenné landscaped the grounds surrounding it.

Though the monastery buildings and the huge abbey church contain no interior furnishings or great pieces of ecclesiastical art, as a work of Gothic brick architecture Chorin has no equal for medieval craftsmanship, which may explain why an average of 150,000 people now visit each year.

All structural elements—the huge single-naved basilica itself, the cloisters, refectory, sacristy, and library—have been preserved and restored, but with only the bare brick walls and decorative masonry showing. There is a small museum of architecture showing surviving artifacts of abbey life in what used to be some of the friars' cells. Each summer there are weekly symphony concerts in the shell of the church. The complex and museum are open daily from 9:00 A.M. to 6:00 P.M. April through October, until 4:00 P.M. November through March.

Just adjacent to the complex is a perfect spot for lunch: the **Alte Kloster Schänke**. This tavern, which had its origins as a smithy, was turned into an inn shortly after the Thirty Years' War. The fare is as rustic as the ambience, and moderately priced.

From Chorin back toward Eberswalde and then along

the 300-year-old Finow Canal, on an unnumbered road, is the Schiffshebewerk Niederfinow.

Niederfinow

The **Schiffshebewerk**, just 2 km (1.2 miles) north of the village of Niederfinow, is a monument to technology: the largest ship elevator in Europe. Completed in 1934 after seven years of construction, it was designed to overcome the 120-foot difference in altitude between the Oder and Havel rivers on the Oder–Havel Canal. What had previously required 17 locks could be done with a single lift operation. As an engineering marvel this movable lock has few equals. The steel tower construction with all its complex machinery is almost 200 feet tall, over 300 feet long, and some 90 feet wide. It can lift a 230-foot-long barge with 1,000 tons displacement in five minutes, and the whole operation—allowing for ship maneuvering, tying up, and moving out of the lock again—takes 20 minutes.

But it is more than just a technological monument. With trade and barge traffic between Poland and Germany as well as between Eastern Europe and Western Europe in general increasing, the canal lift is in operation around the clock, and on an average day, if you were to stand around long enough to watch, you would see 60 to 70 vessels, private yachts and excursion boats included, going up or down. You can watch the activity any time from below, and from the observation platform at the top between 9:00 A.M. and 6:00 P.M. in the summer months, until 4:00 P.M. in winter. On a Saturday, Sunday, or public holiday the parking lot at the site may be full, so that you may have to queue to get in. A number of Berlin fleets offer trips through the canal and lift lock (see Getting Around, below).

From Niederfinow it is about 2 km (1.2 miles) south along a narrow cobblestone road to the intersection with federal highway B-167, where you should turn left for the remaining 8 km (5 miles) to Bad Freienwalde.

Bad Freienwalde

Bad Freienwalde, population 13,000, situated idyllically in wooded hill country overlooking the Oder and almost within shouting distance of Poland, has been a popular spa since the discovery of its iron-rich mineral springs in

1683. None less than the Great Elector and his son, King Frederick I, took the waters here to cure whatever they felt ailed them.

In fact, it became a kind of royal residence when Queen Friederike Luise, the widow of Frederick William II, commissioned the architect David Gilly (Schinkel's teacher and mentor) to build a small Neoclassical château on one of the highest hills around the town, into which she moved upon her husband's death in 1797. The **Schloss** on Apothekerberg is surroundeed by a 30-acre park that was landscaped by Lenné. The house became a footnote to history more than a century later when Walther Rathenau, the electrotechnician and industrialist who became Germany's foreign minister during the Weimar Republic, bought the mansion from the Hohenzollern family in 1909 as a weekend and vacation retreat. He used it until his assassination by radical rightists in 1922. Today it serves as a cultural center with rotating art exhibitions. Open Wednesday through Friday 9:00 A.M. to noon and 2:00 to 5:00 P.M., Saturdays and Sundays from 1:00 to 5:00 P.M.

The **Stadtkirche St. Nikolai** (St. Nicholas Church), on Uchtenhagenstrasse in the center of town, is a 15th-century brick Gothic structure built on the foundations of an older fieldstone church. Among its interesting works of ecclesiastical art are a Romanesque baptismal font, an elaborate Renaissance pulpit, and two 17th-century paintings depicting Martin Luther and Philipp Melanchthon. Restoration work in the 1970s brought to light some fine 15th-century murals that had been painted or plastered over in later times. Visiting hours for a look around are brief: Tuesdays and Thursdays from noon to 1:00 P.M., Saturdays and Sundays from 1:00 to 2:00 P.M.

Almost adjacent to the church is the Neoclassical Rathaus, and directly opposite, the **Oderland Museum**, Uchtenhagenstrasse 2. The museum, in a 16th-century building, shows archaeological finds of early Germanic settlement in the area, craftsmen's tools, and objects of local folk art and applied art. Open Tuesday through Friday 9:00 A.M. to noon, 2:00 to 5:00 P.M., and Sundays from 10:00 A.M. to noon and 1:00 to 4:30 P.M. from March through October.

For an unusual example of how old architecture can be put to contemporary uses, walk up the Hauptstrasse to Georgenkirchstrasse for a look at the **St. Georgskirche** (St. George's Church). The 17th-century half-timbered church has been turned into Bad Freienwalde's concert hall, with a modern organ and stage. There is an art gallery attached to it.

The **Ratsstüberl**, Karl-Marx-Strasse 3, adjacent to the Rathaus, is a good place for lunch, if you like rustic interiors and solid Berlin and Brandenburg dishes, with prices ranging from DM 10 to DM 20 for main courses. And if you wish to spend the night here, the best bet is the **Gasthaus zum Löwen**, right on the Hauptstrasse in a picturesque, recently renovated early-18th–century town house.

GETTING AROUND THE EBERSWALDE AREA

By car. From central Berlin take Bundesstrasse 2 (B-2) north by way of Bernau to Eberswalde–Finow, approximately 40 km (25 miles) or, alternatively, get on the Berliner Ring Autobahn at the junction with B-2, head 1 km east toward the Prenzlau junction, and there drive north in the direction of Szczecin (Stettin), getting off at the Finow–Eberswalde exit. From Eberswalde center to Chorin it is 8 km (5 miles) north along B-2 to Chorin. From Chorin, return toward Eberswalde and take the marked cutoff (left turn) to Schiffshebewerk Niederfinow (about 8 km/5 miles) east along the canal. From Niederfinow, it is 2 km (1¼ miles) to the junction with B-167, which leads into Bad Freienwalde. From Bad Freienwalde federal highway B-158 takes you southwest for the 50-km (31-mile) drive back to Berlin.

By train. There are a number of morning connections from Berlin–Lichtenberg station to Eberswalde: 8:17 A.M. departure, arrival 9:03 A.M.; 10:17 A.M. departure, arrival 11:03 A.M., with return to Berlin–Lichtenberg station departing at 4:53 P.M., arrival 5:40 P.M. A local train runs from Eberswalde main station to the Chorin Kloster station, departure 11:59 A.M., arrival at 12:06 P.M., and return to Eberswalde with departure at 1:30 P.M., arrival 1:42 P.M.

You can get by train from Eberswalde to Niederfinow and Bad Freienwalde on several trains that stop at Niederfinow and continue on to Bad Freienwalde. Departures are 11:24 A.M., 1:25 P.M., 3:08 P.M. It's a 12-minute ride to Niederfinow, and 12 minutes again from there to Bad Freienwalde. But there are no direct train connections from Bad Freienwalde to Berlin, meaning you must return to Eberswalde.

By boat. The Weisse Flotte Potsdam offers two-day trips, with an overnight hotel stop, from Potsdam along the Havel, Oder–Havel Canal, through the Schiffshebe-werk at Niederfinow, and back, eight times during the summer months. Departure is at 7:00 A.M. and return 9:00 P.M. the following day. Weiss Flotte Potsdam, An der Langen Brücke, D(0)-1560 Potsdam; Tel: (0331) 215-27, Fax: 21090.

Information. Verkehrsamt Eberswalde–Finow, Pavillon am Markt, D(0)-1300 *Eberswalde-Finow,* Tel: (03334) 231-68, open Monday through Friday 9:00 A.M. to 5:00 P.M. winters, 10:00 A.M. to 6:00 P.M. summer. Klosterverwaltung Chorin, Amt 11, D(0)-1301 *Chorin,* Tel: (033366) 206, open daily 9:00 A.M. to 6:00 P.M. April through October, until 4:00 P.M. November through March. Oberbarnim Information, Karl-Marx-Strasse 25, D(0)-1310 *Bad Freienwalde,* Tel: (03344) 34-02, Monday through Thursday 9:00 A.M. to 5:00 P.M., Friday to 2:00 P.M., Saturdays 10:00 A.M. to 12 noon, from May through October only.

IN AND AROUND
THE MARKISCHE SCHWEIZ

There is, it seems, a German fascination with Switzerland. From the Dutch border in the west to the one with Poland in the east, from the North Sea and the Baltic down as far south as Nürnberg, whenever and wherever there is a patch of land that is hilly and wooded and dotted with lakes and laced with small streams, it has been dubbed a *Schweiz*—a "Switzerland."

The Märkische Schweiz—"Switzerland of the March"—which starts about 12 miles east of Berlin's city limits and extends almost to the Oderbruch, the marshy lowlands on the left bank of the Oder river, can at least claim a long history, for the label even predates Theodor Fontane, who mentioned it more than 120 years ago in his *Wanderungen durch die Mark Brandenburg.* "The name," he wrote, "conjures up friendly landscapes: mountains and lakes, slopes covered with pines and ravines filled with leafy trees, little brooks that trickle over rocky, pebbly beds, and birch trees that seem half uprooted by the wind, their branches hanging into a forest brook."

Well, there are lots of little lakes and streams, and also plenty of tree-covered slopes, but you have to allow for poetic license in the mention of mountains. The highest one is the Krugberg, whose summit is a mere 430 feet

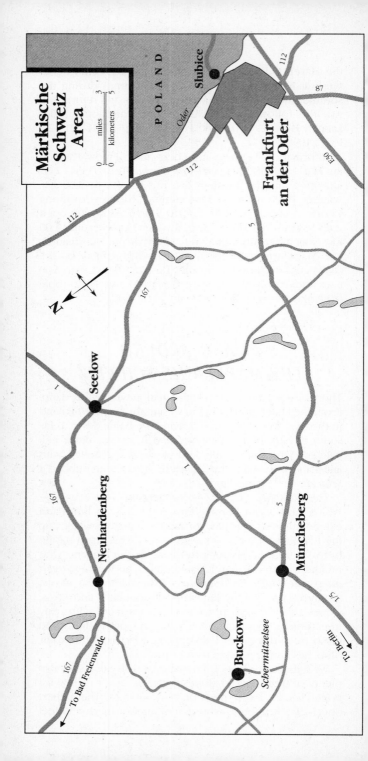

above sea level, which makes it rather a hillock. Berlin's television tower on Alexanderplatz, the "Speared Onion," is nearly three times as high. But the Switzerland of the March *is* a distinct geographical area, the **Naturpark Märkische Schweiz**, a nature preserve some 80 square miles in area with 24 little towns and villages and 15,000 inhabitants who busy themselves with farming, forestry, fishing, gardening, and tourism. Characteristic of the hamlets are cobblestone streets, fieldstone village churches, and, in the case of some of the larger ones, remnants of medieval fortifications and watchtowers on which stork nests perch. The nature park, according to its administration, is home for 229 different species of birds, 49 kinds of butterflies, 31 varieties of dragonflies, and 129 types of snails and conches. And it is lovely.

Buckow

The center is Buckow, a picture-book village of 2,500, which you reach by driving east out of Berlin on Bundestrasse (federal highway) B-1. Situated idyllically on the **Schermützelsee**, the largest and deepest (150 feet) of the Märkische Schweiz lakes, the town was first mentioned in 1249, as Castrum Bucove. It was the property and fief of the diocese of Lebus in the Middle Ages, when Buckow gained importance as a hop-growing and beer-brewing center. In the 17th century some Buckowers started raising roses, and became suppliers for the electoral and royal gardens of the Hohenzollern palaces in Berlin and Potsdam. Tourism started around 1860, and Berliners began building summer houses and villas around the **Pfarrkirche**, a medieval fieldstone church embellished in Baroque style in the 17th century, and the colorful **Marktplatz** with its artfully crafted wrought-iron fountain. Bertolt Brecht and Helene Weigel bought one of the 19th-century houses as a vacation retreat after returning to Berlin and starting their Berliner Ensemble theater in 1949. Brecht wrote his cycle of poems *The Buckow Elegies* here. Since 1977 the **Brecht-Weigel-Haus**, Bertolt-Brecht-Strasse 27, close to the lake, has been a museum showing documents, manuscripts, some of the original furnishings, and, most interesting of all, the original covered wagon from the premiere performance of *Mother Courage* in December 1949.

You can swim in Schermützel lake—there's a popular beach area near the Brecht-Weigel-Haus—rent a rowboat or canoe, or just sit on the terrace of one of the cafés along the shore, have coffee, and take in the lovely landscape. For snacks and ice cream try the **Seeterrassen**, Wriezener Strasse 28, near the swimming area. The **Buchenfried**, Am Fischerberg on the west side of the lake, with a view of the town from its terrace, is a good spot for lunch.

Müncheberg

A narrow country road south from Buckow passes through lush forests and the hamlets of Waldsieversdorf and Schlagenthin to Müncheberg, a 750-year-old market town still encircled by its medieval defensive wall and some of the gate towers, such as the Berliner Tor and the Küstriner Tor. Atop the latter is a stork's nest to which the same pair of birds return each year to raise a new brood. Though the 1.8-km- (1.1-mile-) long wall is still standing, it apparently did little to protect Müncheberg (the name derives from the monks of Lebus Abbey who founded the town) in centuries and decades past. The form was devastated in the Thirty Years' War and Frederick the Great's Silesian and Seven Years' War, and Napoléon turned the 13th-century parish church on the Monakeberg into a munitions depot. To top it off, in late April 1945 the local SS commander, Colonel Kleinheisterkamp, a fanatical Nazi, declared the town a last-ditch fortress and coldly rejected burgher entreaties to surrender, with the result that a Soviet army storm attack turned it into a rubble heap. All that remains of medieval Müncheberg, besides its defensive wall and gate towers, is the gutted shell of St. Mary's, a 13th-century Gothic brick church.

Neuhardenberg

Until early 1991 maps showed a town 16 km (10 miles) northeast of Müncheberg with the name of Marxwalde. That was what Neuhardenberg was called during more than 40 years of Communist rule. For more than 150 years prior to that, since its purchase in 1814 by Prince Karl August von Hardenberg, Prussia's prime minister and chancellor under King Frederick William III, the town and fields around it had been the estate of the Hardenberg family. As they did with all other big landholders, East German authorities expropriated the Hardenbergs' possessions, charging that they had been junk-ers, exploiters of the peasant masses, militarists, and Nazi sympathizers, and after collectivizing the properties renamed the town in honor of Karl Marx.

But in the case of the Hardenbergs they got their history and facts all wrong. Karl August von Hardenberg had been one of the key players in the early 19th century to reform and improve Prussia's government system, and it was to him that Prussia owed such advances as abolition of serfdom and privileges of the nobles, more home rule for municipalities, and the reform of education. More than that, one of his descendants, Count Carl Hans von Hardenberg, the last lord of Neuhardenberg, had been one of the key conspirators with Count Claus Schenck von Stauffenberg to assassinate Hitler, attempted to commit suicide to avoid arrest after the plot failed, and then spent the remaining nine months of the Third Reich as a prisoner at Sachsenhausen concentration camp.

The story is told graphically in the family's ancestral château, **Schloss Neuhardenberg**, now a museum, hotel, and restaurant in the center of the town. Though its origins go back to the mid-18th century, when Lieutenant Colonel Joachim von Prittwitz, an aide to Frederick the Great, built it as a single-story Baroque country mansion, Schloss Neuhardenberg and the town are largely the work of Karl Friedrich Schinkel and represent one of his finest architectural achievements in the Neoclassical style. It was Schinkel who, on Prince von Hardenberg's commission, turned the house into the three-wing two-story castle you see today. It was also Schinkel who, after a fire, made Neuhardenberg into a planned town with ruler-straight streets and neat little farmers' and artisans' houses and who then designed the Neoclassical **Dorfkirche** on the village green.

In the early postwar years the château was first used as an apartment house, then as a school, as a youth center, and as a hostel for construction workers. In 1978 East German officials decided to make it into a cultural and advanced-education center and started restoring and renovating, a job completed in 1988. The ground floor of the main tract and one wing have been beautifully restored with original furnishings in the public rooms.

The ballroom/banquet hall is used for chamber concerts. The ornate library again looks as it did in the 19th century. In the east wing there are rooms with a documentary exhibition on the Hardenberg family and on the anti-Nazi resistance circle in which Carl Hans von Hardenberg, who died in western Germany in 1958, was involved. The 42-acre park that spreads behind the mansion has been restored to the way Peter Joseph Lenné planned it in 1821.

Schloss Neuhardenberg and its museum are open Wednesday through Friday 11:00 A.M. to 5:00 P.M., Saturdays and Sundays to 6:00 P.M. The café and restaurant in the west wing are a perfect spot for a light lunch, and in case you want to stay overnight, the hotel has 17 pleasantly furnished rooms, all however, without private bath.

SEELOW

World War II, especially its closing phase, seems omnipresent in this part of the March of Brandenburg, and it is virtually inescapable in the town of Seelow, 14 km (8½ miles) southeast of Neuhardenberg. The plateau above it, the Seelöwer Höhen, was the scene of one of the bloodiest battles of the war, the start—on April 16, 1945—of the Soviet offensive against Berlin; it then became Marshal Georgy Zhukov's command post. The **Gedenkstätte Seelöwer Höhen** (Seelöwer Höhen Memorial), Clara Zetkin Strasse, on the site is not only a Soviet war memorial and military cemetery, but also an important museum with a strong antiwar slant, despite its exhibits of tanks and guns. There is a reconstruction of Zhukov's command post and a diorama depicting the nighttime Soviet attack on the hill, and you can watch a 12-minute slide show in 13 languages as well as the 1991 movie *Requiem for Millions*. Open daily except Mondays 9:00 A.M. to 4:30 P.M.

Frankfurt-an-der-Oder

Still hanging over Frankfurt-an-der-Oder, 26 km (16 miles) southeast of Seelow and directly across the river from its Polish sister town of Slubice, is the question of who actually destroyed the city. Was it, as the common German version goes, an April 22, 1945, aerial bombardment? Or was it a fire in May 1945, after the war was already over, triggered by a confrontation between Polish forces and a Nazi resistance group, that ravaged nearly all of the remaining 80 percent of the city that had survived the air raid and fighting relatively undamaged?

Whatever the truth, the fact is that one of Germany's most beautiful and important cities was almost totally destroyed and that its rebuilding by East German authorities resulted in an architectural nightmare of faceless, utilitarian functionalism. There are only a few sights and sites, although those few are of considerable importance.

Like most of the cities and towns in the March of Brandenburg, its documented history goes back only to the early 13th century when it was a frontier trading post, but by 1253 it had municipal rights and began booming, thanks to its location on the principal east–west trade route, on the banks of the navigable Oder, which gave it access to the Baltic Sea and which led to its early membership in the Hanseatic League. In the Middle Ages its markets and fairs were every bit as important as those of Leipzig and Frankfurt am Main, and the founding of its University Viadrina in 1506 also made it a center of learning and culture. Among the university's most famous students over a period of 300 years were Ulrich von Hutten, the 16th-century humanist and collaborator with Luther in the Reformation; the poet and dramatist Heinrich von Kleist, who was born in Frankfurt-an-der-Oder; Wilhelm von Humboldt, the statesman and educator; and his younger brother Alexander, the naturalist and geographer. But the shift of Baltic Sea trade farther north on the Oder to Szcecin (Stettin) in 1571, the Thirty Years' War, the decline of the importance of its fairs in the 18th century, and the transfer of its university to Wroclaw (Breslau) in 1811 all contributed to the city's growing irrelevance and provincialism in the 19th and 20th centuries.

What remains of its erstwhile greatness is all in a four-block area at its easternmost periphery, right on the banks of the Oder (from which you have a view of Slubice and Poland), and can be seen in very quick time.

The **Marienkirche** (St. Mary's Church) on Scharrnstrasse, a huge 12th-century Gothic brick basilica with a central nave 250 feet long, is a ruin, but is presently being reconstructed as a cultural center and concert hall. The sections of it that have been restored are already being used for summer theater stagings.

A walk up Scharrnstrasse to Rathausplatz leads to the **Rathaus**. The City Hall, portions of which date from the 13th and 14th centuries, is one of the few structures in the Old Quarter that survived the 1945 devastation relatively undamaged. It is notable especially for its richly ornamented Gothic brick and Renaissance gabled façades. In it, in addition to the mayor's offices and council chambers, is the **Galerie Junge Kunst** (Gallery of Young Art), a museum of contemporary works that shows primarily paintings, graphics, and sculptures by East German artists.

Open Tuesday through Saturday 10:00 A.M. to 6:00 P.M., Sundays 11:00 A.M. to 5:00 P.M. .

East of the Rathaus is **Museum Viadrina**, Carl-Philipp-Emanuel-Bach-Strasse 11, a beautifully restored Renaissance-style house from the early 16th century that served university students and teachers as a dormitory. Besides being a museum of local and regional history it has an important collection of 18th- to 20th-century fine and decorative art, and a treasure trove of 180 musical instruments, dating from as far back as the 16th century—some of which are used in concerts every first and third Sunday morning of the month. C. P. E. Bach, Johann Sebastian's third son, for whom the street is named, studied at Frankfurt's Viadrina University from 1734 to 1738 and was then cantor and music director of the Marienkirche. Open Tuesday through Friday 10:00 A.M. to 6:00 P.M., Saturdays and Sundays 10:00 A.M. to noon and 1:00 to 5:00 P.M.

Right by the river, south of the Museum Viadrina, is a finely restored Baroque mansion that houses the **Kleist Museum** (Faberstrasse 7). A dramatist and novella writer who is considered by many the greatest of all German authors in both genres, Kleist was a contemporary of Goethe and Schiller and ranks with them as one of the great figures of German literature, though he lived only 34 years, committing suicide in 1811. Among his best and most performed works are *The Broken Jug, Michael Kohlhaas, Das Käthchen von Heilbronn,* and *Prinz Friedrich von Homburg.* Kleist was born in 1777 just a block away on Grosse Oder Strasse in a very similar town house, the son of Prussian aristocrats, and served briefly in the army as an officer, but resigned his commission in 1799 to study mathematics and philosophy. In 1801 he turned to writing. In addition to creating his novellas and plays he worked journalistically, and in 1810 began editing the *Berlin Evening News,* a paper in which he took a firm stand against Napoléon. The paper was shut down by the censors in 1811 and Kleist, having given up hope of a German insurrection against Bonaparte and in despair about the lack of literary recognition, killed himself. The museum documents his life, and among its exhibits are the original manuscripts of *The Broken Jug* and *Das Käthchen von Heilbronn.* Open daily except Mondays 10:00 A.M. to 5:00 P.M., Tuesdays until 6:00 P.M.

Your best bet for a lunch or coffee break, close to the Altstadt and museums, is the restaurant or café of the

Kongresshotel, Logenstrasse 2, a functionally modern high-rise establishment, just a block south of the Marienkirche. From the terrace there's a great view of the Oder.

The easiest and fastest way back to Berlin is by way of the Autobahn.

GETTING AROUND IN THE MARKISCHE SCHWEIZ

By car. Drive east from Alexanderplatz (following signs to Frankfurt) on Karl-Marx and Frankfurter Allee. This is also Bundestrasse (federal highway) B-1. Continue approximately 20 km (12 miles) past the Berlin city limits to the town of Hoppegarten, there turn left on an unnumbered country road, following signs to Buckow and Märkische Schweiz for another 9 km (5½ miles). From Buckow drive south to Waldsieversdorf, Schlagenthin, and Müncheberg, total about 12 km (7½ miles). From Müncheberg continue east again on B-1 for about 7 km (4½ miles) to the village of Jahnsfelde where there is an unnumbered country road leading, after a left turn—and for a 10-km (6-mile) drive—to Neuhardenberg. From Neuhardenberg drive southeast on federal highway B-167 approximately 15 km (9 miles) to Seelow. From Seelow it is 26 km (16 miles) southeast along B-167, which is joined by B-112 to Frankfurt-an-der-Oder. From Frankfurt the Autobahn distance back to Berlin is approximately 90 km (54 miles).

By train. There are no train connections at all to Neuhardenberg, none from Berlin to Seelow. But you can get to Buckow and Müncheberg from eastern Berlin's Lichtenberg station, and to Frankfurt-an-der-Oder and from Frankfurt to Seelow. Morning departures into the Märkische Schweiz are: departure Berlin Lichtenberg 8:00 A.M., arrival Müncheberg 8:44, departure Müncheberg 8:50, arrival Buckow 9:00 A.M.; or departure Berlin Lichtenberg 9:08 A.M., arrival Müncheberg 9:32, departure Müncheberg 9:48, arrival Buckow 9:58 A.M. There are returning trains from Buckow, connecting with Müncheberg and returning to Berlin, leaving Buckow at 10:53 A.M., 11:58 A.M., 12:50 P.M., 2:38 P.M., 3:47 P.M., and 5:33 P.M.

There is a fast morning train to Frankfurt-an-der-Oder from Berlin: departure Berlin Bahnhof Zoo 8:55 A.M., Friedrichstrasse 9:05, Hauptbahnhof 9:24, arrival Frankfurt 10:22 A.M. Afternoons back from Frankfurt: 3:00 P.M. arrival Hauptbahnhof 3:58, Friedrichstrasse 4:22, and Zoo at 4:32 P.M.; Frankfurt departure 5:00 P.M., arrival Hauptbahnhof 5:58, Friedrichstrasse 6:22, and Zoo 6:32 P.M. From Frankfurt to Seelow, a 28-minute ride, there are trains at 10:30 A.M., 11:07 A.M., 2:34 P.M., and 3:07 P.M., with returns from Seelow to Frankfurt at 12:56 P.M., 1:03 P.M., 12:56 P.M. 4:50 P.M., and 6:05 P.M.

Information. *Buckow:* Fremdenverkehrsverein, Karl-Marx-Strasse 12, D(0)-1276, Buckow, Tel: (033433) 558; *Müncheberg:* Stadtverwaltung, Rathausstrasse 1, D(0)-1278 Müncheberg, Tel: (033432) 892-80; *Seelow:* Stadtverwaltung, Fremdenverkehrsverein, Puschkinplatz 12, D(0)-1210 Seelow, Tel: (03346) 73-78-50; *Frankfurt-an-der-Oder,* Fremdenverkehrsverein, Karl-Marx-Strasse 8a, D(0)-1200 Frankfurt-an-der-Oder, Tel: (0335) 32-52-16, open Monday through Friday 9:00 A.M. to 6:00 P.M., Saturdays 10:00 A.M. to noon.

THE SPREEWALD

According to the legend they'll tell you here, one day long, long ago, the Devil was out plowing with a team of oxen, drawing the furrow that was to become the Spree river. About halfway between the hill country of the Ober-Lausitz (Upper Lusatia), where the river rises, and Berlin, where it joins the Havel, the oxen got tired and lay down. The Devil was furious. He screamed and cursed and threw rocks at them. This so frightened the animals that they ran away wild, first in this direction, then that, and back again in confusion, all the time pulling the plow after them. And that, the story goes, is how the labyrinth of the river's 330 branches, rivulets, byways, streams, and canals in the Spreewald came into being.

The scientific geological explanation is that after the last ice age, when the glaciers receded and the rivers started cutting their way through the masses of rock deposit left behind, the Spree reached an area about 60 miles southeast of Berlin where, because of the flat terrain and gentle downgrade of only 20 feet in more than 20 miles, it began spreading out in a lacework of channels.

The result is a region so singular in Europe that it is under special UNESCO protection: more than 67 square miles of bayou country with fauna and flora found nowhere else in Germany; 194 navigable waterways connecting small villages, hamlets, and individual farmsteads that you can negotiate either by rented rowboat or pedal-boat if you want to explore on your own, or aboard a punt

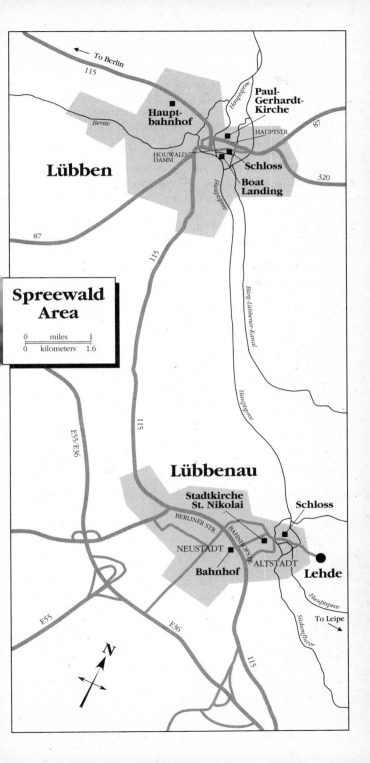

seating up to 35, steered by a poleman who stands at the rear like a gondolier. Moreover, the Spreewald is homeland of the Sorbs, the modern Slavic descendants of the Wends over whom the Knights of the Teutonic Order and the margraves of Brandenburg triumphed in the 12th and 13th centuries. Over the hundreds of years since then, though often discriminated against but at other times coddled and protected like an exotic species threatened with extinction, this ethnic and linguistic minority of 80,000 to 100,000 has managed to preserve its customs and culture—to such a degree that in Spreewald towns like Lübben and Lübbenau (called Lubin and Lubnjow in Sorbic) street, road, and shop signs are in two languages.

Small wonder then that the Spreewald has long been touristic turf. Even in GDR times, when only East Germans and East Berliners came here, everyone else needing visas or special permits, it drew on average one million visitors annually. Nowadays, when the area with its many recreational facilities and picturesque villages and towns is accessible to everyone, those numbers are much higher, especially during the summer school vacation periods and on weekends. The time from May to October is best, and to avoid the crowds try making this trip on a weekday. By car or train the starting point—Lübben—is about one hour's travelling time from Berlin.

Lübben

Like other towns and villages in the Spreewald, Lübben (Lubin in Sorbic) was a site of rivalry and conflict between Gemans and Slavs. After Germanic tribes moved out in the fifth century, Slavic ones began filling the void in the sixth. Near the corner of Steinkirchner Dorfstrasse and Spreestrasse in the southern part of town there are still remnants of the outer defenses of a Wendish castle. Later, in the 17th and 18th centuries, the conflict was between Saxony and Prussia. Prussia finally triumphed in 1815 when the German mini-kingdoms, principalities, and duchies realigned their borders at the Congress of Vienna. Although Lübben was almost 80 percent destroyed during World War II, a section of its 15th-century defenses, including a Gothic watchtower, remain standing and have been well restored.

The **Paul-Gerhardt-Kirche**, a three-naved, late-Gothic hall church, just off the Hauptstrasse, is named for its 17th-century pastor, Paul Gerhardt, considered one of the greatest German Lutheran hymn writers. Its fine interior furnishings include a Renaissance pulpit and baptismal font dating from around 1610 and a triumphal crucifix from around 1550.

Just south of the church, near the punt landing, is the **Schloss** (Ernst-von-Houwald-Damm 14), a Renaissance-style castle from the 17th century, incorporating a 14th-century residential keep, which served the bailiffs and administrators of the Saxonian dukes as their local residence. Though the building now houses municipal offices and an adult education center, it incorporates a small museum of local history where you should be sure to see the *Wappensaal,* the former knights' hall now used as a concert hall, whose walls and ceilings are richly ornamented with murals depicting the coats of arms of a succession of Saxonian rulers and lords of Lübben. For dining in equally historic surroundings, albeit evenings only, consider the **Historischer Weinkeller** in the tower of the castle, Ernst-von-Houwald-Damm 14.

EXPLORING THE BAYOUS

About 200 yards west of the Schloss, along Ernst-von-Houwald-Damm, is the **Kahnabfahrtsstelle**, the landing for punt rides and also for renting rowboats and pedalboats for do-it-yourself exploring of the Unterer (lower) Spreewald bayous. (Though if you do, be sure to stop at one of the kiosks near the landing and buy a map with English supplement, and also the *Wanderführer Unterer Spreewald,* a hiking-biking-boating guide to the waterways and canals—they are a maze in which you can easily get lost on your own.)

The punts, some of which can seat up to 35 passengers, are all privately owned and operated by their *Fährmänner,* "ferrymen," as the gondoliers are called in German. They work in cooperatives, some of which were founded 80 years ago. Although there are other departure points in and around Lübben, this is the largest and most centrally located, with 30 punts. You can choose between a number of excursions lasting from an hour and a half to four hours as well as all-day trips with several stops that take seven to eight hours.

Though beverages—coffee, beer, wine, soft drinks— are available on the punt, meals are usually not, and on longer trips there are stops at inns and cafés along the route. But you are more than welcome to bring your own food—a picnic lunch or snacks; the big stand at the landing, selling anything from candy bars to sausages and sandwiches, even reminds you with a big sign that reads: *"Essen nicht Vergessen"*—Don't Forget Food.

If you want to postpone your ride until you reach Lübbenau in the Oberer (upper) Spreewald (see below), you can have a coffee break to watch the busy scene around you, or a more substantial lunch, at the **Spreewald-gaststätte Strandcafé**, Ernst-von-Houwald-Damm 16, right on the pier of the landing. A rustically appointed gasthaus inside, with a large terrace facing the the departure lagoon with its weeping willows, this is a good spot to sample Spreewald specialties such as Sorbic solyanka soup, onion soup, or cold cucumber soup; *quark* (a kind of cottage cheese) with linseed oil, chopped onion, pickles (which Spreewalders claim are the world's best), and boiled potatoes; steamed carp, pike, or zander with creamed horseradish or herb butter and boiled potatoes, or eel in a wonderful green herb sauce with boiled potatoes. Top price for a main course is about DM 25.

From Lübben it is a 15-minute drive or eight-minute train ride south to Lübbenau, the chief center of the Oberspreewald, an even more charming town with an even lovelier environment, whose appeal is diminished occasionally—when the wind blows—by the penetrating and acrid odor of burning brown coal. The smell—endemic to eastern Germany and eastern Europe in the cold months when people heat their homes—emanates from the *Schwarze Pumpe* (black pump) lignite-burning power and coal gasification plant that the East German regime built near Hoyerswerda (Wojerecy in Sorbic), 45 miles southeast of Lübbenau. Not only is the plant with its emissions an irritating legacy of 40 years of GDR socialism, but even worse is the environmental and ecological damage caused to Lower Lusatia (the Niederlausitz) by the unconscionable, and still ongoing, strip-mining for brown coal in a 100-square-mile area between Schwarze Pumpe and the Oder River valley.

Lübbenau

Lübbenau (Lubnjow in Sorbic), population 22,000, had its known beginnings in the ninth century as a fortified settlement of the Lusizi, a West-Slavic tribe. Remnants of this have been excavated on the grounds of Schloss Lübbenau, the castle (now château) that was built on the site of the

Slavic settlement in the early 14th century. Despite constant strife with the ruling counts, Lübbenau blossomed into an important linen-weaving, cloth-making, and beer-brewing center in the Middle Ages. It declined in importance during the early Industrial Revolution but soon regained prominence and prosperity in the late 19th century when it became accessible by railway. Berliners in droves began arriving as vacationers and weekend tourists to enjoy the bayous, the rural surroundings, and Sorbic folk customs, such as the annual horseback processions at Easter time. And they're still coming: an astonishing 600,000 in 1989, the last season before the Berlin Wall crumbled and the GDR began imploding, with an upsurge since Germany's reunification.

On a weekday it's an inviting town with a picturesque old quarter of winding, narrow cobblestone streets, lined by half-timbered houses surrounding a shady Marktplatz, whose dominating feature is the **Stadtkirche St. Nikolai** (St. Nicholas Church), a Baroque structure dating from the mid-18th century.

SCHLOSS LÜBBENAU

About 500 yards east of the Marktplatz is Schloss Lübbenau, now a hotel. This magnificent Neoclassical château has a turbulent history dating from the 14th century, when a feudal castle was erected on the foundations of the erstwhile Slavic settlement. Over the centuries it had many owners, among them—from 1505 until 1621—the counts von der Schulenburg, an old aristocratic family of the March of Brandenburg, one of whose descendants, Friedrich von der Schulenburg, was Nazi Germany's ambassador to the Soviet Union, helped draft the Hitler–Stalin pact, and then was executed in August 1944 for his pivotal part in the plot to kill Hitler. In 1621 the Schulenburgs sold the castle, grounds, estate, and lands surrounding Lübbenau to Count Johann Siegmund zu Lynar, scion of a noble Tuscan family, closely linked to the Medicis in Florence, that had come to Germany in the 16th century through trade in flax. (The flax blossom in their coat of arms attests to this.) And, except for the 46 years during which their holdings were expropriated, first by the Nazis, then by the Communists, the Lynars still own it, and that is part of the château's story.

The father of the present count and proprietor, Count Wilhelm Friedrich zu Lynar was a Wehrmacht major and adjutant to Field Marshal Erwin von Witzleben, and, like

Schulenberg, one of the key members of the conspiracy around Stauffenberg to assassinate Hitler. Like hundreds of others in on the plot, he was executed by strangulation at Berlin's Plötzensee prison in September 1944. And, as with many of the other aristocratic and land-holding officers in the conspiracy, his family's possessions were expropriated. The East German authorities upheld the confiscation, turned the castle into a training school, but allowed his widow and their son, Christian, to continue living in three of its rooms. In 1953 they fled to West Germany.

Christian zu Lynar, now living near Hannover, successfully reclaimed his property after German reunification in 1990 and has turned the château into a first-class hotel, with renovation and expansion expected to continue through 1993, to promote tourism to Lübbenau. If you want to spend the night at Lübbenau instead of returning to Berlin, the **Hotel Schloss Lübbenau** is the best spot. And the **Schloss Hotel Restaurant** on the ground floor is good for lunch, especially if you're interested in trying Spreewald specialties. Its terrace, overlooking the surrounding park and ancillary buildings, is a delightful place for a coffee break on a warm summer day.

In one of these buildings, the former chancellory, you will find the **Spreewaldmuseum**, a fine collection of local Sorbic folk art, costumes, handicrafts, and artifacts, as well as porcelain, faïence, earthenware, and paintings, including pictures by Antoine Pesne and F. A. Tischbein that used to hang in the château. In an adjacent hall there are a locomotive and passenger and freight cars from the early 20th-century narrow-gauge railroad that used to run between Lübbenau and Cottbus to the east. Open daily except Tuesdays 9:00 A.M. to 5:00 P.M. May through mid-October.

EXPLORING THE BAYOUS

From the museum and the castle grounds it is just a 300-yard walk to the **Kahnfährthafen**, where you can rent rowboats and canoes and, most important, board one of the punts for a trip through the bayous. Prices approximate those in Lübben—about DM 5 per hour—and the most rewarding round-trip to take, which you can reduce by about an hour by walking back along clearly marked trails, is the three-hour excursion that includes a stop in the village of Lehde, a "Little Venice of the Spreewald." (See below.)

It is a journey through an aquatic wonderland of nature and rural life. The 200 waterways with a navigable length of more than 320 miles in the Oberspreewald are densely lined by weeping willows, silver poplars, ashes, birch, and alder trees, many with trunks five feet in diameter and nearly a century old. Patches of water lilies and reeds narrow the channels to little more than six or eight feet in width in places. The usually voluble boatman will tell you that the whole area is a unique biological reservation with plants, animals, birds, fish, and insects virtually extinct elsewhere in Germany and Europe, and that no fewer than 80 pairs of storks come back here to roost every year. Among the fish in the three- to five-foot-deep channels, canals, and streams you will find carp, pike, burbots, zanders, tenches, perch, sheathfish, and numerous varieties of eel.

The bayous are also very much inhabited by farmers, craftspeople, gondoliers, and vacationers, who live in the scores of wooden, thatch-roofed houses that you'll see along the way. Although there are paths, bicycle lanes, a few roads, and bridges that connect the various islets now, most people who live and work here still travel by boat. The mailcarrier comes in a rowboat and so does, in an emergency, the fire department. And there is commerce, as you will discover when your punt pulls up to a stand on the shore where a Sorb farmer will offer you the region's greatest specialties—linseed oil, horseradishes, pumpkins, and pickles in a jar.

Lehde, where your punt will make a stop and where you can decide whether to continue or walk back to Lübbenau, is the first of a series of colorful villages, such as Leipe, Dupkow, and Wotschotska, that you can see on the longer excursions, but it is also the most picturesque and rewarding, a city of lagoons in vest-pocket size. Its greatest attraction is the **Spreewald Freiland Museum**, an open-air museum of three fully furnished and equipped Sorbic farmyards with 200-year-old log and thatch-roofed houses that were brought from other areas and set up here to give visitors a three-dimensional picture of what life for the Sorbs was like in the Spreewald. You will see not only farming tools, displays of costumes, and arrays of domestic artifacts, but also a folk art that expresses itself in the colorfully painted wardrobes and plate racks of the living rooms. Open daily except Mondays, 9:00 A.M. to 5:00 P.M. May through mid-October.

And if you're in the mood for coffee and cakes, stop in

at the **Café Venedig** right across from the punt landing and the museum entrance.

Good little restaurants serving local specialties, particularly fish, abound in Lübbenau. One of the pleasantest and most moderately priced, with a view of the lagoon and the harbor, is the **Café zum Nussbaum**, Dammstrasse 76. Two can dine royally on local fish, a couple of glasses of wine, and perhaps a soup to start with for less than DM 70. On a balmy summer evening, when it stays light in this part of the world until almost 10:00 P.M., this is the perfect place to have supper before returning to Berlin.

GETTING AROUND THE SPREEWALD

By car. Estimate about 1½ hours from Berlin, and take the Autobahn in the direction of Dresden, exiting at Freiwalde/Lübben, from where it is 10 km (6 miles) into Lübben. From Lübben it is 13 km (8 miles) south on federal highway B-115 to Lübbenau. To return, you can get back on the Autobahn to Berlin at Lübbenau. The ramp is 3 km (1½ miles) west of the center of town.

By train. There are good connections from eastern Berlin's Lichtenberg station to Lübben and Lübbenau. Morning departures: 7:46 A.M., arrival Lübben 8:51 and Lübbenau 8:59 A.M.; 9:46 A.M., arrival Lübben 10:51 and Lübbenau 10:59 A.M.; 11:46 A.M., arrival Lübben 12:51 and Lübbenau 12:59 P.M. Afternoon and evening returns: departure Lübbenau at 4:13 P.M., Lübben 4:21, arrival Berlin Lichtenberg 5:28 P.M.; departure Lübbenau 6:13 P.M., Lübben 6:21, arrival Berlin Lichtenberg 7:28 P.M.; departure Lübbenau 8:13 P.M., Lübben 8:21, arrival Berlin Lichtenberg 9:28 P.M.

By boat. The *Kahnfährthafen* in Lübben is at Ernst-von-Houwald-Damm 16, Tel: (03546) 71-22, open from 9:00 A.M. daily April through October. The *Kahnfährthafen* in Lübbenau is at Dammstrasse, Tel: (03542) 22-25, open from 9:00 A.M. daily April through October.

By bicycle. Bikes can be rented in Lübben at K. H. Oswald, Am Frauenberg 6, D(0)-7550 Lübben, Tel: (03546) 40-62; rates are DM 1.50 per hour up to 7 hours, DM 15 for entire day. In Lübbenau, bicycle rental is provided by Erich Goyn, Bahnhofstrasse 30, D(0)-7543 Lübbenau, Tel: (03542) 22-71, open Monday through Friday 9:00 A.M. to 6:00 P.M., and Kowalsky Fahrradservice, Ernst-Thälmann-Strasse 6, D(0)-7543 Lübbenau, Tel: (03542) 28-35, open Monday through Friday 9:00

A.M. to noon, 2:00 P.M. to 7:00 P.M., Saturdays 9:00 A.M. to 1:00 P.M., Sundays by appointment. Rates for both, DM 15 per day.

Information. Fremdenverkehrsverein Spreewaldkreis Lübben, Lindenstrasse 14, D(0)-7750 *Lübben,* Tel: (03546) 30-90; Fremdenverkehrsamt Lübbenau, Poststrasse 25, D(0)-7543 *Lübbenau,* Tel: (03542) 22-36.

WITTENBERG

Few other towns have had as lasting an impact on world history and religion as this picturesque little city of 50,000 people an hour's drive or an hour and a half train ride southwest of Berlin. It was in Lutherstadt Wittenberg, as it is officially named, where Martin Luther started the Reformation more than 475 years ago and laid the foundations for the Protestant faith.

Small wonder then that wherever you turn here there are reminders of Luther, his friends and collaborators, fellow Reformers, and their times in the early 16th century: the castle church, on whose portal he posted his 95 theses in 1517; the parish church, where he often preached; the houses, apothecary, and studios of his painter-printer-politician friend Lucas Cranach the Elder; the home of his closest adviser and friend Philipp Melanchthon; the Augusteum, where Luther was first a monk and, as it was part of the university, where he taught and then lived as a married man.

And all are meticulously preserved. Although Wittenberg, which will be celebrating its 700th anniversary in 1993, suffered considerable damage in 1760 during the Seven Years' War and again in 1814 when it was occupied by Napoléon, it emerged from World War II with just a few scratches. And East Germany's Communist authorities, reluctant to alienate the influential Evangelical Lutheran Church in the GDR (indeed, they tried to court it in the 1970s and 1980s) did more to preserve historical architecture in Wittenberg than in most other towns of East Germany.

But there is more to Wittenberg than Luther and his legacy; it predates the Reformation by hundreds of years. The town's first mention as a fortification on the Elbe river, the "Witteburg," was in 1180 during the reign of Frederick Barbarossa as Holy Roman Emperor. But a stronghold, manned by feudal knights and barons, was all it was. That changed during the next century when traders and merchants, artisans and money changers settled around the castle, behind whose walls they could retreat for protection in case of attack. By 1293 the settlement, thriving because of its location on a major trade route and on the Elbe, was important enough to gain a charter as a city. By then it was also part of the Duchy and Electorate of Saxony, which was ruled by the same dynasty—the Askanians—who were margraves of Brandenburg. When the Askanian dynasty died out in the early 14th century the duchy and electorate passed to the Wettin family, whose ruler, Frederick the Quarrelsome, decided to make Wittenberg his capital and occasionally came to reside in its old 12th-century castle. His grandson Frederick III, known as the Wise, decided in 1486 to turn the old fortress into a grand palace, replete with palace church—the Schlosskirche—and settled in Wittenberg for his residence. He was called "a prince among scholars and a scholar among the princes," and after building the palace established Wittenberg's university, which opened its gates in 1502 adjacent to an Augustinian monastery, whose friars worked as teachers and lecturers at the new school's departments of theology and philosophy.

Martin Luther was soon to become one of the university's most outspoken and influential professors. Luther was born in Eisleben, about 60 miles southwest of Wittenberg, and in 1501, at age 18, entered the University of Erfurt. After getting his master of arts degree in 1505 he intended to go for a law degree, but several months after starting in the law department he had a sudden religious experience—surviving a nearby lightning bolt during a thunderstorm—that persuaded him to become a monk. He entered Erfurt's Augustinian abbey, began an intensive study of theology, and was ordained a priest in Erfurt in 1507. The following year his abbot sent him to Wittenberg's monastery to continue his studies toward a doctorate in theology, and at the same time to help the new university by teaching philosophy and lecturing on Aristotle. He soon became one of Wittenberg University's most popular teachers and helped spread its reputation as a center of humanist learning far and wide.

In 1510 he was sent for a year to Rome on business for his order and, once there, was shocked by the spiritual laxity apparent in high ecclesiastical circles. Upon returning to Wittenberg in 1511 he completed work on his theological doctorate and was appointed a full professor at the university while simultaneously working as a priest and, in 1515, becoming district vicar and pastor of the Marienkirche (St. Mary's), the parish church. But all along Luther was becoming increasingly disenchanted with church policies and practices, particularly the selling of indulgences, or as he viewed it, buying pardon for sin through contributions to the Church. In 1517 he was so incensed that he posted his 95 theses, condemning this and other practices, on the door of the Schlosskirche (castle church), starting the long rebellion against papal authority that culminated in his formal excommunication in 1521 and the turbulence of the Reformation. Through it all, Saxony's Frederick the Wise protected and supported him, making the duchy and Wittenberg the font from which Protestantism spread through central and northern Germany and much of northern Europe. It was Wittenberg's golden age: an era when the town was the spiritual, cultural, and political center of much of Europe. But it was brief, ending with both the Wettin dynasty's move to Dresden after Frederick the Wise's death in 1525, and with Luther's death in 1546.

LUTHER'S WITTENBERG

To see where it all happened you need only walk the length of Wittenberg's main street, closed to motor vehicles, which is called Schlosstrasse at its western end, Collegienstrasse on its eastern half—a distance of only little more than 1 km (slightly over half a mile). If you are driving to Wittenberg, you will find parking areas just south of it near the Altstadt wall. If you are taking a train: The main station is just ten minutes' walk from the eastern end of Collegienstrasse. A good place to start your tour is at the halfway point, on the **Markt**, Wittenberg's marketplace.

In the Markt, monuments to both Luther and Philipp Melanchthon stand in front of the High Renaissance **Rathaus**, with its striking two-story portico. From the town hall balcony sentences for malfeasance were issued, and in the marketplace itself executions were carried out. Modern-day strollers often sit for a while on park benches in the Marktplatz to watch the passersby.

The Rathaus is still Wittenberg's city hall, where the mayor has his offices and the town council meets. And you could well meet them in one of their favorite water-

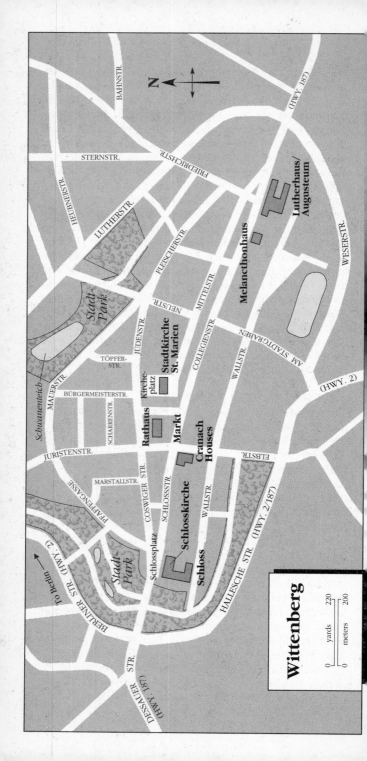

ing spots, the **Ratsschänke**, Markt 14, a popular old tavern, good for lunch, especially if you like game dishes and trout.

Just east of the market square, on Kirchplatz, is the **Stadtkirche St. Marien** (St. Mary's parish church), where Luther often preached and, in 1525, married Katharina von Bora, one of nine Wittenberg nuns who had withdrawn from convent life. The three-naved church is Wittenberg's oldest building, dating from the 13th century with additions and alterations, such as the two helmeted spires, from the early 15th century.

If you visit that Gothic church today you will see Luther preaching on a panel of the altar triptych that his friend and fellow resident of Wittenberg, Lucas Cranach the Elder, painted in 1547. He is also there as Junker Jörg—the knight he was disguised as in Wartburg Castle, in Eisenach, west of Erfurt, where he hid in 1521 after his excommunication, spending the time completing his translation of the Bible into German. His wife, Katharina; his protector, Frederick the Wise; and his friend, adviser, and professor of Greek, Philipp Melanchthon, are also depicted on the altarpiece. Among the church's other art treasures are a 15th-century brass baptismal font, sculpted and cast by the Nürnberg master sculptor Hermann Vischer, and a very beautiful-sounding organ.

From the Stadtkirche and the Markt westward is Wittenberg's main street, **Schlossstrasse**, which leads to the Schlosskirche and the erstwhile castle of Frederick the Wise. It is lined on both sides by elegant Renaissance and Baroque houses, most of them under "monuments protection" and many with tablets of the famous who once lived or stayed there. The list includes Russia's Tsar Peter the Great, Sweden's King Carl XII, and the revolutionary Anabaptist preacher Thomas Münzer, who played an important role in the 1524–1525 Peasants' War. But you will also find plaques commemorating Johann Böttger, the alchemist whom Saxony's King August the Strong briefly imprisoned in Wittenberg and then brought to Meissen to start the famous porcelain manufactory there; Werner von Siemens, the 19th-century Prussian army officer and electrical engineer who started the Siemens electrical and electronics company, now Germany's second-largest industrial corporation; and Wilhelm Weber, the inventor of the electrodynamometer and one of the earliest telegraphs.

The most important of these houses, subject to a massive restoration effort that will continue through 1993, are the **Cranach Houses** at Markt 4 and Schlossstrasse 1. Lucas Cranach, born in 1472 in the Franconian town of Kronach, from which he drew his name, came to Wittenberg in 1505 as the highly paid court painter to Frederick the Wise and soon became one of the richest men in town. He built and bought houses all over the Altstadt, took over an apothecary in the house at Markt 4, where the Cranach Apotheke is still in business, and opened a wine tavern and printing shop in the house at Schlossstrasse 1, where his son Lucas the Younger, an equally talented painter, was born in 1515. But Cranach was more than just one of the greatest artists of the 16th century. He was a mover and shaker of Wittenberg who served eight terms as a town councillor and three as mayor, was one of Luther's closest friends and supporters, and used his printing plant to publish many of the Reformer's most important treatises and dissertations.

Of Frederick's **Schloss** itself little remains. It went into decline after the Saxonian rulers moved their capital to Dresden and was almost totally destroyed during the Seven Years' War. Some of the rooms of the structure, partly rebuilt during the 19th century, are now the home of Wittenberg's Museum of Natural History and Ethnography (Natur und Völkerkundemuseum).

But the **Schlosskirche**, the castle church on whose portal Luther posted his 95 theses in 1517, still stands. One of its remarkable features is the round belfry tower, capped with a spiked-helmet dome and encircled by a huge mosaic, visible from far away, that spells out the opening words of one of Luther's most famous psalms: "A mighty fortress is our God, A bulwark never failing. . . ."

In its present form the Schlosskirche, which has been destroyed and restored many times, is largely 19th century. Frederick the Wise is buried here beneath an early German Renaissance bronze plaque by the Nürnberg sculptor Peter Vischer the Younger. On one side of the church are Philipp Melanchthon's remains; on the other, under the late-Gothic altar, are those of Martin Luther.

The original door on which Luther posted his theses was destroyed in a 16th-century fire. A bronze 19th-century door engraved with the 95 points of protest has replaced it. The church is open for sightseeing Tuesday through Saturday 9:00 A.M. to 11:45 A.M., 2:00 P.M. to 4:45 P.M., Sundays 10:30 A.M. to 11:45 A.M., and 2:00 P.M. to 4:45 P.M. May through October; starting and closing one hour later from November through April. Organ recitals are given every Tuesday from 2:30 to 3:00 P.M.

A walk eastward from the Markt along the main street, here called Collegienstrasse, will take you first to the Melanchthonhaus and then to the Lutherhaus in the Augusteum. But if you feel it's time for lunch or a snack, stop off first at the **Hotel Goldener Adler**, Markt 7, diagonally across from the market square and the Rathaus. It has good German food, carefully prepared, at moderate prices. The hotel is also a place to stay if you decide to spend an extra day in Wittenberg. It has been an inn since 1524 and has been undergoing renovation and modernization since reverting to private ownership in 1990.

The **Melanchthonhaus**, Collegienstrasse 60, has stood here since Philipp Melanchthon built it in 1536. Melanchthon—the word is Greek and means "black earth" and was the pseudonym he used for his family name Schwarzerd—was born in southwestern Germany, not far from Heidelberg, in 1497 and came to Wittenberg in 1516 as professor of Greek at the university. A man of towering intellect and great learning, he soon became not only Luther's closest friend and adviser, but also his most important associate in the Reformation, representing him at many conferences and propagating the Protestant concepts with eloquent writing. The house is now a museum devoted to Melanchthon and his life and work as one of the most influential educators and intellectuals of the 16th century. The furnishings are from his time and some pieces, like the desk at which he worked and the benches along the walls of his study, are original. The documents and exhibits include the original first editions of many of his books and provide insight into what life was like for a highly paid, well-to-do professor at the time. Be sure to go out into the garden at the back. Started and used by Melanchthon's wife, it is still tended in the manner of medieval gardens. The yew tree here was planted by Melanchthon himself.

A few steps farther up the street will take you to the **Augusteum**, the 16th-century university buildings, in whose courtyard is the entrance to the **Lutherhaus**, in which Luther lived from 1508 until his death in 1546. When he moved in it was part of the Augustinian monastery, which also included the theology department of the university. As his fame as a professor grew, Luther had not just a cell but the entire second floor for his use. The abbey was dissolved as part of the Reformation in

1522, but Luther continued to live here, along with his wife. In 1532 he was given the entire house as a present by Frederick the Wise's successor, Elector Johann the Steadfast. The Renaissance entrance portal was a gift from Katharina von Bora for Luther's 57th birthday in 1540. The building is now a museum of the Reformation showing richly colored Bibles, prints, coins, medals, paintings by Cranach, and, in the Luther Room itself, his lectern from the university lecture hall and the pulpit from the Stadtkirche from which he preached. It is open daily except Mondays 9:00 A.M. to 5:00 P.M.

A walk to the right when you come out of the Augusteum (used today, incidentally, as a Protestant seminary and graduate theological school) will take you to the triangle intersection of Collegienstrasse with Lutherstrasse and Weserstrasse. In the little park just across the intersection is the **Luthereiche** (Luther oak tree). The tree itself is only little more than 160 years old, planted here in 1830, but the spot is historic, for it is here, allegedly, that Luther publicly burned the Papal Bull threatening his excommunication in 1520. The nearby terrace of the **Haus des Handwerks**, Collegienstrasse 53a, the café and restaurant of Wittenberg's chamber of trade, is a good spot to rest your feet, have a coffee, and contemplate it all.

GETTING AROUND WITTENBERG

By car. From around the Kurfürstendamm area, take the Avus, the city Autobahn, out in the direction of Nürnberg/Leipzig, get onto the Berliner Ring, direction Nürnberg/Leipzig/Magdeburg, at the Drewitz entrance, and get off again immediately at the next exit, Potsdam Süd/Beelitz. Then drive south on Bundestrasse (federal highway) B-2, via the towns of Beelitz and Treuenbrietzen to Lutherstadt Wittenberg. From the exit it is 56 km (about 35 miles) to Wittenberg. Under normal traffic conditions it should take about one hour from central Berlin.

By train. There are two good morning connections from eastern Berlin's Lichtenberg station. Departure Berlin Lichtenberg at 8:53 A.M., arrival in Lutherstadt Wittenberg 10:37 A.M., or departure at 9:53 A.M. and arrival in Wittenberg at 11:23 A.M. Afternoon and early evening return schedules from Wittenberg to Berlin Lichtenberg station are departure at 3:53 P.M., arrival Berlin Lichtenberg 5:24 P.M.; departure at 4:41 P.M., arrival at 6:12 P.M., departure at 5:53 P.M., arrival at 7:24 P.M., and departure at 6:41

P.M., arrival at 8:12 P.M. There are also later trains, the last at 9:53 P.M., arrival Berlin Lichtenberg 11:24 P.M. The Wittenberg Hauptbahnhof is about 10 to 15 minutes' walk from the Luther oak and the eastern end of Collegienstrasse.

Information. Fremdenverkehrsbüro Wittenberg Information, Collegienstrasse 29, D(0)-4600 Lutherstadt Wittenberg, Tel: (03491) 22-39. Open Monday through Friday 9:00 A.M. to 6:00 P.M., Saturdays and Sundays 10:00 A.M. to 2:00 P.M. April through October; until 5:00 P.M. weekdays, same hours Saturdays and Sundays November through March.

ACCOMMODATIONS REFERENCE
When telephoning from outside Germany, the country code is 49 and the "0" in front of each city code given below should be deleted. When calling or faxing from Berlin or anywhere else in Germany, you should use the zero, as indicated on the listings. The city code numbers are in parentheses.

Room prices given are projections for 1993 for double occupancy and include service, taxes, and breakfast.

Bad Freienwalde
▶ **Gasthaus zum Löwen**, Hauptstrasse 41, D(0)-1310 **Bad Freienwalde**. Tel: (03344) 52-15. DM 130.

Frankfurt-an-der-Oder
▶ **Kongresshotel Frankfurter Hof**, Logenstrasse 2, D(0)-1200 **Frankfurt an der Oder**. Tel: (0335) 38-70; Fax: 387587. DM 200–220.

Lübbenau
▶ **Hotel Schloss Lübbenau**, Schlossbezirk 6, D(0)-7543 **Lübbenau**. Tel: (03542) 81-26; Fax: 3327. DM 175–270.

Neuhardenberg
▶ **Hotel Schloss Neuhardenberg**, Schloss, D(0)-1214 **Neuhardenberg**. Tel: (033476) 223; Fax: 224. DM 110–130.

Neuruppin
▶ **Hotel Märkischer Hof**, Karl-Marx-Strasse 51–52, D(0)-1950 **Neuruppin**. Tel: (03391) 28-01; Fax: 2556. DM 160.

Petzow
► Hotel Schloss Petzow, Zelterstrasse 5, D(0)-1512 **Werder (Havel)**. Tel: (03352) 31-53 or 26-78. DM 100.

Potsdam
► **Hotel Schloss Cecilienhof**, Neuer Garten, D(0)-1561 **Potsdam**. Tel: (0331) 231-41; Fax: 22498. DM 275–360.

Rheinsberg
► **Hotel Deutsches Haus**, Seestrasse 13, D(0)-1955 **Rheinsberg**. Tel: (033931) 27-77 or 25-66. DM 120.

Wittenberg
► **Hotel Goldener Adler**, Markt 7, D(0)-4600 **Wittenberg**. Tel: (03491) 20-53 or 20-54; Fax: 2054. DM 130–180.

CHRONOLOGY OF THE HISTORY OF BERLIN AND BRANDENBURG

Pre- and Early Historic Origins

Although present-day Germany was the scene of human activity some 500,000 years ago, with the fossil of "Heidelberg Man" as the best evidence, the earliest archaeological finds in and around Berlin and in the state of Brandenburg date only from around 8000 B.C. Some of them can be seen in Berlin's Märkisches Museum and in the Museum for Pre- and Early History. Settlement intensified in the Bronze Age and reached its zenith between 1200 and 800 B.C. The most important evidence of this can be found in the Buch district of Pankow borough and in Steglitz borough's Lichterfelde district, where remnants of Bronze-Age villages have been excavated. The most dazzling find was the discovery in 1913 of 81 embossed and engraved gold objects, stashed in an earthenware bowl, near Eberswalde, about 30 miles north of central Berlin. The "Gold Treasure of Eberswalde," dating from the 11th to 10th centuries B.C., belonged to the Museum for Pre- and Early History but has been missing since the end of World War II. Recent investigations hint that it may be in Russia.

- **c. 700 B.C.:** Early Germanic tribes, notably the Swebians, settle in and around Berlin and in Brandenburg.
- **c. 600 A.D.:** As the Germanic groups migrate south and southwest, they are replaced by Slavic peoples, notably the Wends, who start to establish the rudiments of a feudal state in the region.

The Wendish Period

Throughout the Dark Ages there were frequent tussles between Wends and Germans, with one or the other gaining the upper hand for a while. The eighth-century Burgwallanlage south of present-day central Spandau, known in Slavonic as Spandovo, is the remnant of a Wendish fortress, and old walls in Köpenick, which the Wends called Copnice, are what remain of a ninth-century Slavic prince's castle here. Charlemagne, in his wars against the Saxons, made brief and successful incursions into Wendish territory in the 780s, but a coalition of Slavic tribes regained the territory and rebuffed various attempts at eastward expansion in the late 11th and early 12th century. The region was the Holy Roman Empire's "wild east," and the Wends were its "Indians."

- **1134–1170**: German colonization of this eastern frontier region, the March of Brandenburg, begins in earnest.
- **1147**: Holy Roman Emperor Conrad III, Duke Henry the Lion of Saxony, and Count Albrecht the Bear, margrave of the Northern March, join forces to launch another offensive against the Wends and their leader, Prince Jaczso, and defeat them conclusively.
- **1150**: Albrecht the Bear titles himself margrave of Brandenburg.
- **1197**: The first mention of Spandau, one of Jaczso's last citadels, in documents.
- **1210**: The crusader Knights Templar establish churches and estates on what is today Tempelhof airport, and in the villages, now districts, of Marienfelde and Mariendorf as part of the German colonization of eastern Europe.

The Beginnings of Berlin

Germans began settling around and reinforcing some of the Wendish forts, such as Spandau and Köpenick, and established towns. Around 1230 two more towns, then little more than frontier trading posts, were founded about halfway between Spandau and Köpenick, directly facing each other: one, called Cölln, on an island in the Spree river; the other, called Berlin, on the Spree's northeastern bank. The origins of both names remain in doubt.

For almost a century they were bitter rivals, each with its own town hall and surrounded by its own protective walls, though only a few yards of water divided them.

- **1237**: The first mention of Cölln in documents.
- **1244**: Berlin is first mentioned in a document.
- **1307**: Berlin and Cölln are both flourishing from commerce because the margraves had relocated a major east–west trade route so that it crossed the Spree here; they agree on an alliance to defend themselves against marauding robber barons, form a confederate union, and build a third city hall, in which councillors of both towns can meet, on the Long Bridge (*Lange Brücke*) spanning the Spree between them.
- **1319**: Margrave Waldemar the Great dies.
- **1320**: Title to the March of Brandenburg reverts to the Holy Roman emperor, Ludwig the Bavarian, who deeds it to his son Ludwig as an imperial fief.
- **1359**: Berlin-Cölln, with a combined population of about 5,000, joins the Hanseatic League of trading cities.
- **1375**: Holy Roman Emperor Charles IV, a Hapsburg, forces the Bavarian Wittelsbach family to surrender the March and confers the territory on his own son, Wenceslaus.

Advent of the Hohenzollerns

Though Berlin-Cölln itself prospered from trade and commerce during the 14th and early 15th century, the March was in turmoil because of the dynastic struggles of its lords and incessant feuds between its nobles. On several occasions Brandenburg was pawned to various money-lenders in order to finance the wars of the Holy Roman emperors and those of their relatives who had title to the March. When Wenceslaus was elected emperor he gave Brandenburg to his brother Sigismund who, in 1411, after having become Holy Roman Emperor himself, transferred ownership to one of his most loyal supporters and lieutenants, the burgrave of Nürnberg, Frederick von Hohenzollern.

- **1411**: Frederick von Hohenzollern becomes margrave of Brandenburg. It is the start of more than 400 years of Hohenzollern rule, first over Berlin-Cölln and the March, then over Prussia and eventually all of Germany by this South German family whose ancestral castle is near Stuttgart.

- **1415**: Frederick is named as one of the seven electors (*Kurfürsten*) of the Holy Roman Empire, who are authorized and entitled to choose the emperor. The hereditary position makes Brandenburg one of the key players in subsequent German politics. With the help of the cities, notably Berlin-Cölln, he routs the robber barons and subjugates the Brandenburg gentry.
- **1432**: Berlin and Cölln finally turn their confederation into a full-fledged union, becoming one city.
- **1442**: Margrave Frederick II dissolves the merger of the two towns in order to establish his authority, occupies the city hall, disbands the assembly of patrician town councillors, forbids Berlin and Cölln to enter into alliances, forces them to withdraw from the Hanseatic League, assumes all their trade, coin-minting, and judicial privileges, confiscates substantial plots of land in Cölln, and starts construction of a palace there.
- **1470**: The Cölln Palace becomes the permanent residence of Brandenburg's ruler and elector, and the town becomes the official capital.

The Reformation

The 16th century was a time of social unrest and religious upheaval throughout Germany. Martin Luther, destined to become the father of the Reformation, opened a battle against the excesses and abuses of the Catholic church that had far-reaching implications. Luther's belief in personal Christian freedom based on inner inspiration inspired the German peasants to demand a return of their ancient rights and led to their eventual (unsuccessful) revolt. (Luther himself denounced the peasants' demands.) As the Reformation spread under the efforts of Calvin and other Protestants, the Catholic Church launched the Counter-Reformation, which culminated, nearly a century later, in the bloody Thirty Years' War, pitting northern Protestants against the Catholic south and affecting the whole of Europe.

- **1483**: Martin Luther is born in Eisleben.
- **1517–1522**: Luther posts his 95 theses on a door of the castle church at Wittenberg, burns the Papal

Bull (the fundamental law of the empire), and translates the Bible into German.

- **1520:** Emperor Charles V is crowned at Aachen.
- **1525:** The Peasants' War breaks out as Luther's battle against authority sows the seeds of social revolution.
- **1539:** Elector Joachim II converts to Protestantism and introduces the Reformation to Brandenburg and Berlin.
- **1545–1563:** The Council of Trent, which established the basic doctrines of the Counter-Reformation, moves to reform church abuses.
- **1570:** Joachim II's passion for ostentatious construction bankrupts his creditors (that is, nearly all Berlin-Cölln merchants), and triggers a Europe-wide recession.
- **1576–1611:** Berlin and Cölln are repeatedly hit by epidemics of the plague that take the lives of thousands. The population in 1600 is around 10,000.
- **1618:** The Thirty Years' War breaks out in Bohemia and continues until the Peace of Westphalia in 1648. Results: the realignment of much of Europe, the laying waste and carving up of Germany, and an equal-rights guarantee to German Catholics and Protestants. During the war Berlin-Cölln is thrice under siege, and thousands more die of the plague. The population declines to 6,000.
- **1640–1688:** Under Frederick William, the Great Elector, Brandenburg-Prussia begins its ascent to power. He sets about reconstructing and redesigning the war-ravaged city, fortifies it, connects the Elbe and Oder rivers with a canal, establishes trading companies, and incorporates two suburbs into the walled defensive system of Berlin-Cölln. In 1685 he invites persecuted French Huguenots to settle in Berlin-Cölln and Brandenburg; by the 1690s they account for one-third the city's population.

Prussia Ascendant

The ongoing competition for power in Germany resulted in the rise of two absolutist ruling dynasties: the Hapsburgs, who had recovered Austria as their stronghold at the end of the Thirty Years' War, and the Hohenzollerns, who were building a powerful state in Brandenburg-Prussia. Under Frederick the Great (1740–1786), Prussia forcibly acquired the Austrian province of Silesia and gained the status of a great European power, although it remained a component of the Holy Roman Empire ruled by the Hapsburgs. Berlin became a major European capital during this period, and German culture rose in prominence as the works of German artists, writers, composers, and philosophers helped usher in the "Age of Enlightenment."

- **1701**: Frederick, son of the Great Elector, crowns himself king of Prussia.
- **1709**: Berlin, Cölln, and the suburbs of Friedrichswerder, Dorotheenstadt, and Friedrichstadt are united to form one municipality, population 56,000.
- **1740**: Frederick II (the Great) ascends the Prussian throne and makes Berlin into a major European capital. The "Linden" (today's Unter den Linden) is expanded into a grand boulevard in 1770 and the palace of Sanssouci in Potsdam is built as his summer residence.
- **1756–1763**: During the Seven Years' War Prussia, in cooperation with England, fends off the allied armies of France, Austria, and Russia. Russian and Austrian troops occupy Berlin briefly in 1760.
- **1767**: Karl Wilhelm von Humboldt, the Prussian statesman and educator, is born in Potsdam. His brother Alexander, the naturalist and geographer, is born in Berlin in 1769.
- **1781**: Immanuel Kant, born in Königsberg, East Prussia, and the founder of critical philosophy, in which he sought to determine the limits of man's knowledge, publishes *The Critique of Pure Reason*. Karl Friedrich Schinkel, Prussia's preeminent architect, is born in Neuruppin.
- **1786–1797**: During the reign of King Frederick William II of Prussia, Berlin becomes the "City of the Enlightenment." The Brandenburg Gate is completed in 1791 and becomes a symbol of the city.

Napoléon and the Collapse of the Holy Roman Empire

To counteract governmental anxiety about the ongoing threat of French power following the French Revolution,

Prussia, Austria, Russia, and England formed a coalition against Napoléon. After a brief period of peace in the early 1800s, Napoléon defeated the Austrian and Prussian armies and occupied several German cities. With the abolition of the Holy Roman Empire in 1806, Prussia became more independent and after 1815 began the process of political and economic modernization, challenging Austria for dominance in the German-speaking countries.

- **1795**: After their unsuccessful attempts to intervene in the post-Revolutionary affairs of France, Prussia and Austria are forced by Napoléon to sign the Peace of Basel. Prussia promises neutrality and the left bank of the Rhine becomes French.
- **1800**: Napoléon's troops occupy Trier.
- **1806**: The Holy Roman Empire officially ends with the abdication of Hapsburg Kaiser Franz II as Holy Roman Emperor. The Confederation of the Rhine is formed when German states bordering on France unite under Napoléon. After the collapse of the Prussian military forces in the Battle of Jena and Auerstadt, Napoléon marches into Berlin and a two-year French occupation of the city begins.
- **1810**: The University of Berlin (which is to become Humboldt University during the GDR years) is founded by Wilhelm von Humboldt.
- **1812**: Napoléon's forces again occupy Berlin.
- **1813**: Napoléon's armies forced to retreat across the Rhine back into France. Richard Wagner is born in Leipzig.
- **1815**: The initial defeat of the French in the Battle of Nations in Leipzig is followed by the decisive Battle of Waterloo. Berlin's population is around 190,000.

Revolution and German Unity

The defeat of Napoléon awakened in many Germans a strong sense of national pride and unity. The country's aristocratic and conservative military and political rulers, however, were determined to defeat liberalism (based as that was on Republican ideals) and return to their old system of absolute monarchy. The rapidly industrializing German Confederation experienced several decades of relatively quiet political activity, during which rapid advances were made in the fields of transportation and communication. But the underlying social demands for basic German rights and the question of independence and national unity finally came to a head in the 1848 revolution. When the revolution failed, the Austrian monarchy reimposed its sovereignty over the German Confederation and Prussia.

- **1815**: The Holy Alliance between Prussia, Austria, and Russia is signed on September 26, helping to preserve absolute monarchy. Under the conservative leadership of Prince Metternich, the Congress of Vienna carves up Europe anew and promotes the German Confederation, a Hapsburg-dominated confederation of 35 princely states and four free cities.

- **1816**: Karl Friedrich Schinkel, the sculptor Christian Daniel Rauch, and the landscape architect Peter Joseph Lenné begin to redesign Berlin along Neoclassical lines, creating Unter den Linden and the Tiergarten as they appear today.

- **1819**: Theodor Fontane, the Prussian novelist, poet, essayist, and journalist, is born in Neuruppin.

- **1834**: The German Customs Union (*Zollverein*) economically unites the German states and free cities by creating a free-trade area under Prussian leadership. Austria is excluded.

- **1838**: The first Prussian passenger railway opens for service between Berlin and Potsdam.

- **1848**: Revolution breaks out in Italy and spreads to all of Central Europe, threatening conservative monarchies. Frederick William IV of Prussia pledges his support for the unification of Germany, and a short-lived German National Assembly is convened in Frankfurt. But he crushes democracy and parliamentary rule in Berlin and Prussia. However, he allows laws concerning the basic rights of the German people to be passed, and a year later Frederick William IV declines the imperial crown offered him by the Frankfurt parliament.

- **1850**: The Frankfurt parliament is dissolved. A reactionary "imposed constitution" of the Prussian government takes effect on January 31 and remains in force until November 1918. Berlin's population, swelled by an influx of industrial workers, is 400,000.

Bismarck and the German Reich

As Germany continued to industrialize, it became an economic rival to England, and also a center of great social conflict through the growth of the revolutionary Social Democratic movement, which the autocratic Bismarck declared illegal for 12 years. With the emergence of political thinkers like Karl Marx and artists like the working-class Käthe Kollwitz, the writers Thomas and Heinrich Mann, and others associated with the Berlin Secession movement, the city's cultural and intellectual life in this period began to transcend the conservatism and authoritarianism that characterized so much of Germany.

- **1861**: The towns of Moabit, Schöneberg, Tempelhof, and Wedding are incorporated into Berlin.
- **1862**: Otto von Bismarck is appointed prime minister of Prussia. Ferdinand Lassalle, one of the 1848 revolutionaries and founder of the Universal German Workingmen's Association, a forerunner of the Social Democratic Party, publishes his labor program in connection with a lecture in Berlin. The copies are immediately confiscated.
- **1864**: War breaks out between Denmark and Prussia, which annexes Schleswig and, in 1866, Holstein.
- **1866**: Prussia defeats Austria, resulting in the foundation of the North German Confederation (which replaces the old German Confederation) and the dual monarchy of Austria-Hungary.
- **1867**: Käthe Kollwitz, graphic artist and sculptor, and ardent Socialist and pacifist, is born near Königsberg, East Prussia. She studies and marries in Berlin and becomes widely known for her powerful woodcuts and lithographs depicting the misery and hunger of society's dispossessed.
- **1867**: Karl Marx publishes the first volume of *Das Kapital*. (Friedrich Engels will complete the work in 1885 and 1894).
- **1869**: The Social Democratic Party is founded with leadership provided by August Bebel. In 1872 Bebel, a member of the Reichstag in Berlin, along with Karl Liebknecht, is sentenced for plotting treason.
- **1870–1871**: The Franco-Prussian War results in the collapse of the French and, ultimately, in Bis-

marck's success in having Prussia's King Wilhelm I proclaimed German kaiser at Versailles—completing the groundwork for the unification of Germany. Berlin becomes the capital of Germany.

- **1888**: Rapid industrialization and the demand for cheaper labor has again more than doubled the city's population, to more than 800,000. Kaiser Wilhelm I dies. His son, Frederick III, a socially conscious liberal who envisioned Germany as an open, democratic society, reigns only 99 days, dying of cancer. The imperial crown goes to his conservative, authoritarian son, Wilhelm II.

- **1889**: Adolf Hitler is born in Braunau, Austria.

- **1890**: Kaiser Wilhelm II dismisses Bismarck, who has challenged his authority, as Reich chancellor and Prussian prime minister.

- **1898–1909**: The German navy steadily grows in power until it equals the strength of the British navy.

- **1900**: Berlin's population reaches 1,900,000. The first subway line opens in 1902.

World War I

For many observers, the Great War represented a German attempt to dominate Europe. The military conflict on the eastern front resulted in the defeat of Russia, while fighting on the western front ultimately led to German defeat. Although the war was not fought on German soil, it resulted in severe food shortages throughout the country and intensified political unrest.

- **1914**: The heir apparent to the Austrian throne is assassinated in Sarajevo on June 28, precipitating World War I. Germany declares war on Russia on August 1, and on France two days later. On August 4, Great Britain declares war on Germany. Japan declares war on Germany on August 23.

- **1914–1918**: Fully mobilized, Germany fights the war on the eastern and western fronts. Berlin, the German capital, remains outside the front lines of fighting but it is increasingly difficult to keep the city stocked with food, and rationing goes into effect in cities throughout Germany.

- **1917**: The United States declares war on Germany, bringing the number of nations opposing Germany to 28. Hunger and war-weariness, compounded by political grievances, culminate in mass strikes in 1917 and 1918.

- **1918**: At war's end, Kaiser Wilhelm II is forced to abdicate. The November Revolution ends Hohenzollern rule in Germany (the second Reich), and Friedrich Ebert, the head of the Social Democratic Party, is named chancellor of the provisional government in Berlin. Philipp Scheidemann, also a Social Democrat, proclaims the "German Republic" from the Reichstag, whereas Karl Leibknecht, leader of the separatist Spartacus League, precursor of the German Communist party, proclaims a soviet—that is, a workers' council—republic from a gate of the imperial palace.

The Weimar Republic

In its attempt to establish a democratic and republican government, the so-called Weimar government represented a break in the dominant traditions of Germany's history. Residual issues from the war and the hostility of conservative groups conflicted with the reformist and radical impulses of the left and the cultural avant-garde. During the "Golden Twenties," Berlin—the capital of the republic—blossomed into the economic and cultural center of Germany as well.

- **1919**: Germany signs the Treaty of Versailles, which limits the army to 100,000 officers and men, although a "free corps" of soldiers remains. The Allies determine the total reparations bill in 1920. Rosa Luxemburg and Karl Liebknecht, the Communist leaders of the Spartacus League, are assassinated in Berlin. Walter Gropius founds the Bauhaus school in Dessau, south of Berlin.
- **1920**: Worker uprisings in the industrial Ruhr basin help to spread a wave of lawlessness and disorder. A police operation against leftist radicals in Berlin ends with 42 dead. The government flees Berlin in March in the face of an attempted right-wing takeover, the Kapp Putsch. A dozen independent cities, including Spandau, Köpenick, and Charlottenburg, plus 59 smaller towns and villages, are incorporated to make Berlin the vast city it is today. The incorporation doubles Berlin's

population to more than four million and increases its surface area thirteen-fold.

- **1921–1923**: Large-scale strikes disrupt and paralyze Berlin. Political violence escalates and culminates in the assassination of Foreign Minister Walter Rathenau in 1922. The number of unemployed soars, and inflation, which reaches ludicrous proportions, is stabilized in 1923 when one new banknote (Rentenmark) is issued to replace 1,000 billion denomination old paper marks.
- **1924–1925**: The Social Democrat Friedrich Ebert dies and Paul von Hindenburg is elected *Reichspräsident*.
- **1926**: Germany is admitted to the League of Nations.
- **1928**: The Brecht/Weill *Threepenny Opera* premieres in Berlin.
- **1929**: The Great Depression creates greater political and social tensions within Germany. There are 600,000 unemployed in Berlin.

The Rise of Nazism and World War II

The economic crisis in Germany was a major factor in the rise of the Nazi movement, but the old authoritarian, nationalistic, and imperialistic attitudes of the country also provided a ripe environment for the National Socialist party to take control. As the brutal anti-Semitic political agenda of Adolf Hitler became apparent, thousands of German Jews—including many prominent artists, scientists, and politicians—fled the country to escape persecution. Millions of Jews and other "undesirable" minorities throughout Germany and the rest of Nazi-occupied Europe were systematically exterminated in one of the most horrifying chapters in world history. By the end of the war, Berlin and Germany's other major cities lay in smoldering ruins and Germany ceased to exist as an independent state.

- **1933**: On January 30 Hitler is appointed Reich chancellor and his brownshirt storm troopers (SA) march triumphantly down Unter den Linden and through the Brandenburg Gate in a torchlight parade. On February 27 the Reichstag building is set afire, possibly by the SA itself, providing a pretext for President Paul von Hindenburg to give Hitler dictatorial powers. The Nazis embark upon the "Third (or 1,000-year) Reich," a concept patterned after the Holy Roman Empire of the German Nation, the first Reich. On April 1 there is the first public boycott of Jewish-owned stores in Berlin. On May 10 Joseph Goebbels, the propaganda minister, stages the first book burning in front of the opera house on Unter den Linden. On October 14 Germany withdraws from the League of Nations.

- **1934**: Hitler organizes the "Blood Purge" to rid the party of all opponents. On the death of President Hindenburg, Hitler is appointed führer (leader).

- **1935**: Universal conscription is established. The Nürnberg Laws deprive German Jews of citizenship, deny them all civil rights, prohibit them from marrying Aryans, and bar them from the liberal professions.

- **1936**: The Olympic Games open in Berlin's new stadium. Hitler storms out of the stadium when a black American named Jesse Owens wins four gold medals.

- **1938**: On November 9, synagogues and Jewish businesses throughout Germany, including Berlin, are savagely attacked and destroyed in the officially organized Crystal Night. The Munich Pact marks the culmination of British and French attempts at appeasement, on the assumption that Hitler's aims are limited.

- **1939**: Germany invades Czechoslovakia and Poland. On September 3, Great Britain and France declare war on Germany.

- **1941**: Hitler invades the Soviet Union in June. In December, Hitler declares war on the United States following the bombing of Pearl Harbor.

- **1942**: At a conference in a mansion on the western shore of the Wannsee, subsequently known as the "Wannsee Conference," top Nazi government and SS officials, including Adolf Eichmann, adopt the program of organized genocide that is called "the final solution to the Jewish question." The destruction of German cities through Allied aerial bombardment begins.

- **1943**: After Germany's large-scale defeat at Stalingrad, Joseph Goebbels stages a mass rally February 18 in the Sports Palace, at which he declares "total war." The first major air raid on Berlin takes place on March 1, and in November the Allied forces begin the steady bombardment of Berlin.

- **1944**: Allied troops land at Normandy and air attacks on Germany and Berlin are intensified. On July 20 Wehrmacht Colonel Claus Schenk von Stauffenberg, leader of a long simmering opposition to and resistance against the Nazis, attempts to assassinate Hitler by placing a bomb in the führer's military headquarters on the eastern front, then, believing Hitler dead, flies back to army headquarters on Bendler Strasse (now Stauffenbergstrasse) to organize the coup, which fails within hours. He and co-conspirators are executed in the courtyard of the building, and a mass prosecution of anti-Nazi officers, diplomats, and government officials begins, with hundreds executed at Berlin's Plötzensee concentration camp.

- **1945**: Churchill, Stalin, and Roosevelt meet at the Yalta Conference in February to determine the course of Allied occupation policy. Germany is invaded on two fronts, and major cities are virtually destroyed by Allied bombing. Soviet troops reach Berlin on April 21. On April 30, after marrying his long-time mistress, Eva Braun, Hitler and she commit suicide in the bunker beneath the Reich Chancellory on Wilhelmstrasse. The Soviet conquest of Berlin is completed on May 2. On May 8, World War II ends with the Allied occupation of Germany. Berlin is partitioned into East (Soviet) and West (American, British, and French) sectors governed by the Allied Control Council. The Potsdam Agreement between the United States, Great Britain, and the Soviet Union divides the rest of Germany into occupation zones in August. The Nürnberg trials begin in November.

Two Germanies and Two Berlins

Having at first intended to govern conquered Germany as one unit, the victors divided it into two states as disagreements over reparations and the Cold War intensified. The two separate states, the Federal Republic of Germany and the German Democratic Republic, developed with highly differing political, economic, and social systems.

- **1946**: The Iron Curtain (Churchill coins the term) rings down. From this time, the separate eastern and western zones develop separately, in accordance with the desires of the Western states or the Soviet Union.
- **1947**: On February 25 Prussia is formally abolished and liquidated by a law of the Allied Control Council.
- **1948**: West German reindustrialization and recovery, the fabulous *Wirtschaftswunder* (Economic Miracle) gets under way, with U.S. assistance in the form of the Marshall Plan, or European Recovery Program. In June the establishment of the West German Deutsche mark (DM) as replacement for the old Reichsmark, and Anglo-American determination to introduce it to Four-Power Berlin, sparks a Soviet protest and a land blockade of the city's western sectors. The American and British governments respond with the Berlin airlift, which lasts until May 12, 1949.
- **1949**: On May 23, the Basic Law for the Federal Republic of Germany is instituted and Bonn becomes the capital of West Germany. The German Democratic Republic (GDR) is established in the Soviet-occupied zone, with Berlin as its capital, NATO is founded.
- **1953**: A strike on June 17 by construction workers building East Berlin's Stalin-Allee (now Karl-Marx-Allee) turns into a popular uprising throughout the eastern part of the city and the GDR, and is quashed by Soviet tanks.
- **1958**: Worsening economic conditions and stepped-up collectivization of agriculture in the GDR prompt a heightened exodus of East Germans and East Berliners to the West. As the GDR's borders are already virtually impassable, the escape route is via East to West Berlin, where sector borders remain open and the subway and S-Bahn systems still operate as one. This triggers the long-simmering "Berlin Crisis," during which Soviet leader Nikita Khrushchev calls for "internationalization" of the city.
- **1961**: On August 13 construction of the Berlin Wall begins, effectively sealing off East from West Berlin and cutting West Berlin off from its Brandenburg

hinterland. American and Soviet tanks take positions at Checkpoint Charlie between the two sectors, and for a while it looks as if World War III is about to begin. The Allied show of strength is meant to secure access for American, British, and French military personnel to East Berlin, and does. But West Berliners remain barred and East Berliners are virtually locked up.

- **1963:** President John F. Kennedy visits West Berlin on June 26. In a famous speech from the balcony of Schöneberg Rathaus he emphasizes American and Allied solidarity with West Berliners and declares, "Ich bin ein Berliner."

- **1970:** West German Chancellor Willy Brandt meets with East German Prime Minister Willi Stoph to discuss relations between the two countries. The meeting, held in Erfurt, starts the process that leads to an improvement of ties.

- **1971:** The Four Powers Pact on Berlin, September 3, confirms the legal and political ties between West Berlin and the East German Federal Republic. In December the GDR and the Federal Republic sign the intra-German agreement on transit traffic to and from West Berlin. West Berliners can again enter East Berlin and the GDR; transit formalities are simplified.

- **1972:** West and East Germany sign a treaty on basic relations between the two countries.

- **1973:** Both Germanys join the United Nations.

- **1974:** The two Germanys recognize each other as independent sovereign states de facto by exchanging quasi-diplomatic missions.

- **1983:** East German leader Erich Honecker and West Berlin's Governing Mayor Richard von Weizsäcker meet in East Berlin.

- **1987:** Erich Honecker visits West Germany and is received in Bonn by Chancellor Helmut Kohl with all honors formally accorded a head of state.

Germany Reunited

The opening of the Berlin Wall in 1989 marked for East Germany the culmination of a wave of previously suppressed revolutionary sentiment across Central and Eastern Europe. The reforms of Mikhail Gorbachev and the underground, grass-roots communication between citizens in East Germany lead to massive demonstrations against the repressive, Stalinist government of the GDR. Freedom of travel and an end to the East German secret police (*Stasi*) were among the demands. The events surrounding the opening of the East German border are all the more remarkable for being entirely unexpected. The initial euphoria has inevitably become subdued as the very real problems of reunification make themselves known, and the hard work of social, economic, and political restructuring begins.

- **1989**: In May, East German "vacationers" crowd into Hungary and continue across the newly opened border into Austria and West Germany. Gorbachev visits East Berlin in October for the 40th anniversary celebrations of the GDR. In November Erich Honecker is replaced by Egon Krenz as general secretary of the Communist Party. Mass demonstrations are held in Berlin and Leipzig. The East German Politburo resigns and the Central Committee of the Communist Party recommends that a new government be formed. By November 9, East Germans are allowed to travel to West Germany without special visas. Hundreds of thousands of them pour into West Berlin, and the two sides celebrate the opening of the Wall that had separated them for 28 years. Calls for full reunification with West Germany continue. Erich Honecker and other top party members are placed under house arrest as details of official corruption and abuse of power are made public. Entry visas and compulsory exchange are abolished for visitors to the GDR and East Berlin. On New Year's Eve half a million people ring in a new decade for Germany at the officially opened Brandenburg Gate.
- **1990**: The dismantling of the Wall continues as the Allied side of Checkpoint Charlie, one of the two crossing points into East Berlin, is removed in June. East and West Germany adopt a single monetary system on July 1, the same day that all border controls in and around Berlin are suspended. The four wartime Allies sign a document on September 12 relinquishing their occupation rights in Berlin. On October 3 the two Germanys are officially reunified as a single political entity, and the

GDR ceases to exist. In December, Helmut Kohl becomes chancellor of a united Germany in the first free nationwide elections since Adolf Hitler was named chancellor of the Reich in 1933.

- **1991**: Berlin is made the new capital of Germany, although the move is not expected actually to take place before 2000. Evidence of environmental destruction under the government of the GDR is made public. Hundreds of thousands of East Germans lose their jobs as eastern Germany privatizes industry. The former East German price constraints on basic necessities such as food and housing are eliminated. Neo-Nazi demonstrations take place in Berlin, Leipzig, and other German cities.

- **1992**: Former East German citizens are allowed access to the secret files kept on them by the Stasi, the GDR's secret police. Reunited Berlin's combined population is now 3.5 million.

Issues resulting from reunification continue to dominate German politics. Erich Honecker, former head of East Germany, returns to Berlin after 16 months as a fugitive in Moscow. Honecker and his former security chief, Erich Mielke, are charged with corruption and manslaughter involving shoot-to-kill orders against people attempting to flee across the former East German border; Honecker and Mielke go on trial in Berlin in November. Several groups of former East German border guards are convicted of similar charges, but most receive suspended sentences. Investigators uncover evidence that at least 350 people died trying to escape, twice the previously documented number.

The number of refugees, most of them from Eastern Europe and seeking asylum in Germany, is expected to reach 500,000 by the end of 1992, twice the 1991 number. Neo-Nazis demanding the expulsion of refugees stage riots and firebomb refugee housing in Rostock and several other eastern German cities. In September, the German government signs agreements with Romania and Poland that pave the way for Germany to deport tens of thousands of Poles, Gypsies, and other Romanians; similar agreements with Czechoslovakia and Bulgaria are planned. Former West German chancellor Willy Brandt, a Nobel Prize laureate for his work to overcome the postwar division of Europe, dies in October.

In November 300,000 Berliners demonstrate in and around the Lustgarten against racism, xenophobia, and neo-Nazism. Late in the year the government bans the Nationalist Front and the Deutsche Alternativ, two neo-Nazi parties, and begins a wave of house searches and arrests.

—Donald S. Olson and John Dornberg

INDEX

Here's what others say...

"As a longtime reader of *Passport*, I trust it as a source of intelligence and ideas on independent travel."

Alan Deutschman
Associate Editor
Fortune Magazine

"The best little newsletter in America."
Crain's Chicago Business

"*Passport* has been appearing for more than 20 years with a brisk, colorful roundup of travel information. Substance prevails over style."
National Geographic Traveler

"In *Passport*, I consistently find the kind of information I want from a travel newsletter—sophisticated, concise and straightforward, without a lot of ego to get in the way."
Travel Editor
Town and Country Magazine

"The first and unquestionably the best luxury travel newsletter."

Alan Tucker, General Editor
Berlitz Travellers Guides

Since 1965, *Passport*, the monthly letter for discriminating travelers, has revealed hard-to-find information about the world's best destinations. Return this card for a free issue or call 800-542-6670. Available worldwide!

Please send a free issue of *Passport* to:

Name

Address

City   State   Zip

"*This* is the granddaddy of travel letters... *Passport* emphasizes culture, comfort, and quality...it can glow with praise, or bite with disapproval."

Condé Nast Traveler